RENAISSANCE

GEORGE HOLMES

RENAIS

ST. MARTIN'S PRESS
NEW YORK

SANCE

GEORGE HOLMES

RENAISSANCE

Copyright © 1996 George Holmes

Printed in Italy. No part of this book may be used or reproduced in any manner whatsoever without written permission except in the case of brief quotations embodied in critical articles or reviews. For information, address St. Martin's Press, 175 Fifth Avenue, New York, N.Y. 10010.

ISBN 0–312–15318–X

First published in Great Britain by Weidenfeld and Nicolson Ltd.

First U.S. edition
10 9 8 7 6 5 4 3 2 1

CONTENTS

PREFACE

R ENAISSANCE IS AN ELASTIC TERM which has been used with a dozen different meanings. The reader will want to know what meaning is attached to it in this book.

First of all Renaissance means 'rebirth', the revival of Latin and Greek and the culture of the ancient world. That sense is central. But, secondly, it has normally been used to imply the more general renewal and expansion of cultural life in the fifteenth and sixteenth centuries which established the modern European outlook.

I take that to mean the expression of new attitudes to humanity by painters, sculptors and writers. I shall not be much concerned here with the natural sciences or exploration, which, of course, also changed the character of Europe very substantially. This book is about the picture of men and women presented by artists.

This main subject matter has to be set in the framework of a view of society in which the changes took place. My aim is to place the Renaissance in the context of the expanding and prosperous life of the European cities. I see the commercial city as the heart of modern European life, in contrast to the medieval, Byzantine and Muslim worlds. This is not a particularly original view and I owe much, for instance, to the opinions of Fernand Braudel, expressed in his *Civilization and Capitalism*, *15th to 18th Centuries*. Braudel's book is about economics and is long. This book is a very brief attempt to place ideas in the context that he outlined.

I take the view that there are certain large and central changes in attitude, developed by the artists, which then entered into the general European consciousness. My aim is to identify these and to describe them by looking fairly closely at a few of the artists' creations. The reader will find that I have something to say about the Sistine ceiling and *Hamlet,* but do not say much about Columbus' discovery of America or Galileo's idea of the solar system, not because I do not think them important but because they do not come within my brief. The reader may find also that there are certain approaches to the history of this period which have become fairly prominent but which are not reflected here. I am writing about high culture and its revolutions, not about everyday life, except as a background. I have little to say about cultural interactions with America or Asia, or about 'receptionism', the way in which society reacted to ideas. Of course these are all important aspects of the history of the period. If they are ignored here, it is in order to present simply a series of important changes in the European mind in relation to the main development in European economics and society. That is a limited purpose, but I hope that it will usefully highlight some essential features of this extraordinarily innovative period.

Two people have helped me a great deal in the final stages by trying to make the book readable: Anne Holmes, my wife, and Rebecca Wilson, my editor.

CHAPTER ONE

THE CITY AS AN AGENT OF CULTURAL INNOVATION

FROM THE AGE OF DANTE when modern European culture was conceived to the age of Proust when it died, the moments of intense perception and originality in European history were inseparable from the life of the city and the expansion of opportunities caused by commercial imperialism. Those aspects of the European spirit that appear the most magnificent and the most deplorable were linked. This is a reason for studying history as a whole rather than, as has become common, following separately threads such as art, literature, gender or religion. This book will be mostly concerned with art and literature but will try to show them in their economic and social setting. When one finds, for example, that Benedetto Marchionne of Florence, a contemporary of Leonardo da Vinci, was already famously involved in the import of African slaves to Portugal and the Mediterranean at the end of the fifteenth century, one realises that the fundamental motive power of European progress, effective into the nineteenth century, was already in existence. The most delicate and the most cruel aspects of society were connected and could not exist without each other. Brutality and exploitation make possible wealth and the prosperity of the city, where refinement encourages an original creativity.

The commercial city was the creative focus of Europe. It is difficult to be precise about the mechanism of this social phenomenon. Wealthy cities were not always creative. In the Renaissance period Genoa has often been described as the 'city without culture', though it was creative in other respects and Columbus was one of its offspring. The creativity of a city requires a link with an intellectual or aesthetic impulse, such as the expertise in Latin at Florence or the theatrical tradition at London. The city is important for its accumulation of wealth, spread among a number of free citizens rather than centralised, and for its cultivation of intense competitive intercourse between highly intelligent individuals. The court and the cathedral, which had been centres of limited intellectual creation in early Europe, could not provide these essential circumstances. As one surveys the history of art and thought in early modern Europe, the places that matter are Florence, Venice, London, Amsterdam, Paris and Vienna, in which the great city atmosphere provided stimulus. The reason the Renaissance began to flourish in the fifteenth century was that European cities then had much greater significance than they had had earlier. This was the result of a peculiar and temporary circumstance of considerable importance for the whole of European history: the fall in population following the Black Death of 1348. The Black Death was a sudden shock of massive proportions which eliminated a third or more of the population in most parts of Europe. The

Marriage at Cana,
Veronese, 1562-3 (Louvre, Paris)

Town plan of Bruges,
1562 (Bibliothèque Nationale, Paris)

decline of population also continued long after that date. In 1450 Europe's population was probably somewhere in the region of a half of what it had been in the early fourteenth century, when agriculture had been extended in many areas to lands which produced poor crops in order to feed large numbers of country-dwellers crowded into an over-populated countryside. The period of low and often falling population from 1350 to 1450 was unique in the history of Europe, which has usually been propelled by slow or fast *increases* in population. The most obvious effect of this demographic slump was to make land more abundant and labour scarcer. The landlord therefore became weaker and poorer, the tenant and labourer stronger and richer.

The effects of the fall in population extended into vast social and political changes because the decline in the cost of basic foodstuffs led to a greater demand for manufacture. Industry and commerce became relatively more important and in consequence wealth and power shifted from the sectors of society dependent on land and rent to those dependent on industrial production and trade. This was a fundamental change in the direction of European expansion and the first major movement that set Europe advancing in the direction of industrial and commercial enterprise.

The political and cultural results of population decline depended on the fact that it became more difficult to extract money by taxation from agrarian communities and

View of Flemish town from Madonna of Chancellor Rolin,
Van Eyck, c.1435 (Louvre, Paris)

easier to extract it from traders and manufacturers. This general phenomenon lay behind the increased political independence and security of the great cities. Venice, the wealthiest of the great commercial cities, could raise more money by taxation than the king of England. The costs of the land war waged by Venice at the time that the Wars of the Roses began in England in the 1450s, not counting the expense of maritime warfare in the Adriatic and the Eastern Mediterranean, were about 550,000 ducats per annum, roughly the equivalent of £100,000 sterling. A decade later in the 1460s the total amount of money available to Venice from taxation, as a result of taxing the city and its landed possessions, was about 900,000 ducats, or £180,000

sterling. In contrast the unavoidable annual expenditure of Henry VI of England was calculated at £56,000 in 1433 and later King Henry had great difficulty in raising £100,000. These figures indicate the shift of wealth and power from kingdoms and nobles to cities.

There was also a more accidental political reason for the independence of the many European cities in the first half of the fifteenth century. This was the relative weakness of monarchies in France, Germany and Spain which reduced the threat of invasion or external control in those parts of Italy and the Low Countries that were most important for city life. The period between 1401 and 1494 saw Italy relatively free from the danger of monarchical invasion, a

Bird's-eye View of Venice, *woodcut,*
Jacopo de' Barbari, 1500 (Museo Navale, Venice)

very marked difference from the situation in the fourteenth century or later in the sixteenth. The effects of the madness and political ineptitude of Charles VI of France (1381–1421) and the occupation of parts of the kingdom by Henry V of England needed a long recovery so that the danger from France was remote until late in the century. The kings of Germany from the houses of Luxembourg and Habsburg before the time of Maximilian I (1493–1519) were in practice the rulers of relatively poor territories in the East – Austria, Hungary, Bohemia – which did not qualify them as serious dangers to the Italian cities, enjoying a century-long golden age of undisturbed isolation.

The most aggressive powers of the early fifteenth century were both princely families based in cities: the Visconti and the Sforza families who were dukes of Milan and a branch of the Valois family, the dukes of Burgundy,

most of whose income was drawn from the cities of the Low Countries that they controlled. Until the 1460s the dukes of Burgundy were cautious and halting in their dealings with the great urban centres of their empire, Bruges, Ghent, Brussels and Antwerp. Then came Duke Charles the Bold (1467–77), arguably the strongest ruler of his age and the first to revive the medieval assumption that a city was to be obedient to its lord, as he showed in his destruction of Liège in 1468. The house of Burgundy was extinguished by Charles's death in 1477. The monarchical powers that threatened the cities from 1494 onwards were those of the French Valois, the Austrian Habsburg and the Spanish house of Aragon.

In the fifteenth century Europe was developing industrial processes that put it well ahead of the Asiatic and oriental worlds. In 1444 Bessarion, a visitor to Italy from

12

Constantinople, who had been much involved in the attempt to reunite the Greek Orthodox Church with the Catholic Church and later became a Roman cardinal, leaving his collection of Greek manuscripts to found the Marciana Library at Venice, wrote back to an acquaintance in Greece. He gave a picture of the industrial methods that he had seen in Italy which he thought the Greeks ought to copy. 'Mechanical engineering facilitates the drawing of heavy objects, the demolition of ruins, the grinding of what needs grinding: boards are sawn automatically; mills turn as rapidly and exactly as possible; in metallurgy bellows are inflated and deflated without the touch of human hands, separating the metal from the base material in the flux.'[1] That was the comment of a man from the Near East who could see the advantages of western technology, perhaps the first comment of this kind of which we have record. Visitors to Italian cities from other parts of western Europe were also impressed. In 1494 the Arsenal at Venice, the biggest shipyard in the world, where the cargo vessels bearing Venetian trade were built, was described by Pietro Casola, a pilgrim on his way to the Holy Land from Milan, who expressed wonder at the scale and complexity of the industrial organisation:

'In one part of the Arsenal there was a great crowd of masters and workmen who do nothing but build galleys or other ships of every kind. There are also masters continually occupied in making cross bows, bows and large and small arrows ... In one great covered place there are twelve masters each one with his own workmen and his forge apart; and they labour continually making anchors and every other kind of iron-work necessary for the galleys and other ships. There seems to be there all the iron that could be dug out of all the mountains of the world. Then there is a large and spacious room where there are many women who do nothing but make sails.

Within the walls of the Arsenal, above the water which enters, there is a most beautiful contrivance for lifting any large galley or other ship out of the water with little fatigue. Outside the Arsenal ... there is a place where they make all the ropes used at sea on the galleys and all the other ships... It is a place all covered below, and so long that I could hardly see from one end to the other. The number of masters and workmen who are constantly employed there is amazing.'[2]

Among the innovations of the fifteenth century with the most cultural effect was Gutenberg's invention of the printing press. This industrial process was intellectually significant because it eventually led to the production of large numbers of relatively cheap books. The Bible, classics of the ancient world and the latest thoughts of a modern poet or political agitator could be widely distributed in a manner inconceivable in the previous age of manuscript. Gutenberg lived in Mainz and Strasbourg in the 1440s and 1450s. His technical expertise, which made possible the creation of metal typefaces, was probably derived from his experience in the trade of polishing precious stones and making small metal objects. The development of the printing press also involved investment far ahead of repayment to make possible the lengthy process of building the type and press, printing the books and selling them, which, like the physical process, could only be provided by a city. The printing of the forty-two-line Bible, a major breakthrough, was probably made possible by a loan of 800 gulden which Gutenberg raised in 1450 at Mainz. Once begun, the custom of printing books spread fairly rapidly throughout Western Europe in the next fifty years. The next big change in the process was carried out by Aldus Manutius at Venice around 1500 when he began the production of small, handy editions of the classics, as opposed to the unwieldy folios which had existed before. This innovation had an effect like the introduction of the Penguin paperback, and marked the birth of the modern book. The work of Gutenberg and Aldus was dependent on the city which provided technology, ready money for investment, contacts with a world-wide market. Printing is the most obvious case of the city producing cultural change.

The activity and wealth of the commercial cities in the fifteenth century were based on particular economic relationships and channels that made industry and trade possible. The first factor was the advanced industrial development of some parts of Europe. Cheap woollen cloth was made in large quantities in the Low Countries (modern Belgium, Holland and northern France) and in England, with its greatest concentration in Flanders and Brabant. The vestiges of this industry survive in the tapestries of Arras and Brussels in modern museums. There was also textile manufacture in North Italian cities, where Florence and Lucca, for example, were important in silk weaving. Textiles were the most basic, large-scale industrial products exchanged by trade in great quantities, but glass, ceramics, metal knives and armour were also exported.

The industrial progression of Europe was accompanied by the backwardness of the Near East. In the regions governed by the Ottoman sultans of Constantinople, finally conquered in 1453, and the Mamluks of Cairo, industry was primitive and these countries offered a market for European manufacturers. In return they could provide various non-industrial goods that Europeans wanted such as raw silk, sugar and pepper. There was therefore a natural commercial link between industrial northwest Europe and the non-industrial East. As the fifteenth century progressed there was also increasing interest in non-industrial Africa and its adjacent islands: Madeira for its sugar and Guinea for its slaves. Use of imported slaves, though not on a very large scale, was normal in Mediterranean Europe. A Medici Archpriest of Prato was probably the son of a Circassian slave-woman owned by Cosimo de' Medici.

The commercial intercourse necessary to exploit these industrial advantages was made possible by ships and letter-writing. The Mediterranean, the eastern Atlantic and the North Sea were alive with trading vessels of Italy, Spain and the Netherlands, and also with the numerous pirates who preyed on them. The cities of Venice and Genoa had many ships engaged in long-distance trade. Venice, where shipping was centralised in the state's hands, dispatched regular fleets to Constantinople and Alessandria in one direction and to London and Bruges in the other. The Genoese, whose shipping was more privately managed, operated in a still more enterprising manner and it was probably for this reason that it was a Genoese who first crossed the Atlantic. In northern Europe, beyond the reach of the Italians, much trade was carried in ships from Flanders and Holland.

The letter was essential because commerce required the frequent exchange of information and instructions between merchants operating in widely separated places. Commerce also needed a system for the transfer of payments over long distances without the impossibly dangerous carrying of coin. This was provided by the bill of exchange, which promised payment in a foreign city, at a date in the future, at a certain rate of exchange. As the seas were alive with shipping, the roads were alive with the carriers of innumerable letters between commercial centres: from Florence to Lyon and London, from Venice to Bruges and Constantinople flowed an endless interchange of pieces of paper, like the telephone system in the modern world. The Italians were the masters of international commerce and of the international monetary exchange system. Therefore they were the most literate people in the world. No merchant could survive without writing many letters.

In the fifteenth century Europe's southern and western coasts were lined by ports linked by shipping and commerce. These were also the places where the main developments of the early Renaissance took place. The main cities which concern us here were of quite different types. Venice, the richest city of the fifteenth century, was different from all other European cities in that it was built on an island, totally dependent on the sea. It was governed

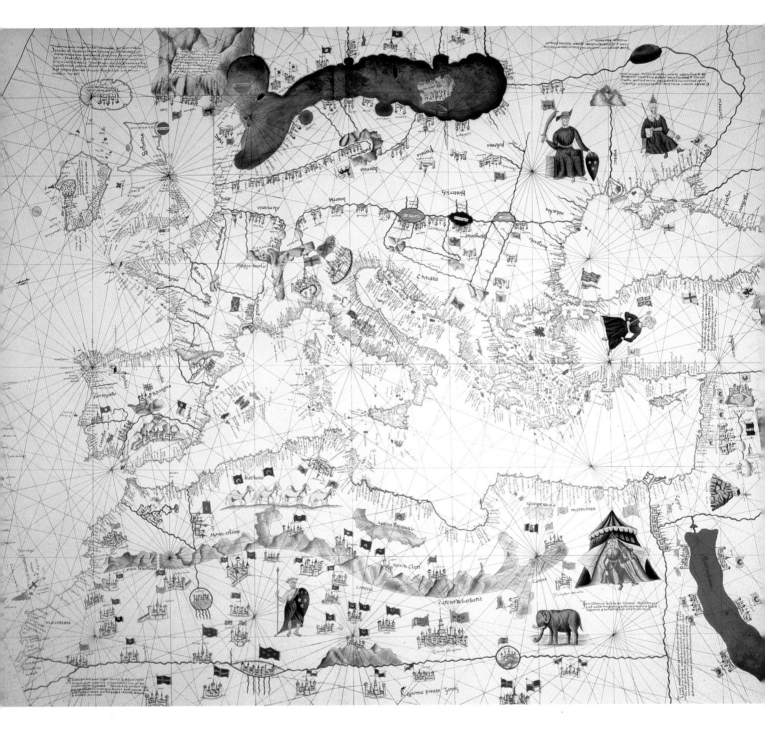

Carta nautica, *a portolan map of the Mediterranean,*
Battista Beccario, 1435

A Florentine merchant from De Sphaera,
fourteenth century (Bibliothèque de l'Arsenal, Paris)

rather peacefully by a class of rich patricians and possessed an extensive commercial empire in the eastern Mediterranean. It was not peculiar, however, in its land empire in eastern Lombardy and the Veneto, controlled, without representation, from Venice. Florence was another republic controlling subject cities, but it was dependent on Pisa for its access to the sea. In contrast, the most notable Flemish cities, Bruges and Ghent, were not entirely free of princely intervention from the Duke of Burgundy. Bruges, the most important entrepôt of northern Europe, was a meeting place for the cloth producers of Flanders, Italian merchants and Hanseatic merchants from Germany. Ghent, essentially an industrial inland city, was the heart of the Flemish textile industry. These four – Venice, Florence, Bruges and Ghent – were not the only places that mattered in the early Renaissance, but they were outstanding in importance and their character gives some idea of the range of city types.

These cities were all in different ways republican, although their origins were diverse and were reflected in the varying political systems. The Flemish cities had originated as privileged trading centres without much external influence. The Italian cities had begun as places where families lived close to each other for protection and had acquired substantial landed empires outside. 'Republic' is a misleading term in some respects because it implies a connection with the commonwealths of ancient Greece and Italy and modern nation-states. 'Commune' might be a more suitable word. We shall, however, use 'republic' and 'republican' because they convey the important negative characteristics of these cities. They were not princely or ecclesiastical communities. They were not dominated by the court of a duke or by a cathedral or university. They were communal or republican in the sense that they were ruled by laymen with a fair degree of equality in social and political power.

Europe between the thirteenth and the nineteenth centuries was broken up into a very large number of political units with different characteristics. Some were kingdoms, dukedoms or principalities ruled by one monarch and his advisers. Some were dominated by ecclesiastical powers, such as the Pope at Rome or the Archbishop at Trier. Some were republics. But in most cases the three types of structure – princely, ecclesiastical and republican – were not completely separated. Every city had a cathedral, many had universities. The intermingling of contrasting kinds of authority could be either in the form of an external power – as with the dukes of Burgundy who had some authority in Bruges – or it could be internal – as with the Medici family in Florence which in the fifteenth century was developing towards the princely rule it achieved in the next century.

The fact that these types of society and government overlapped did not destroy the importance of the distinctions between them. Ecclesiastical society demanded acceptance of dogma. Princely society demanded acceptance of sovereignty of the court of a ruler. Republican society was attached to republicanism but it offered a wide range of options in the development of ideas because it contained roughly equal citizens whose ideas might interact. It may be objected that the distinction we are making is really not between republics or principalities but between cities and courts. There is some truth in this. The social fact of the multifarious intercourse of the city was vital. But its intellectual development could be crushed by a ruler as was the case in seventeenth-century Rome – magnificent architecture but no ideas of any value – or Habsburg Milan. Republicanism, as we have said, was not a total explanation of originality but it was a necessary condition, and it might be fulfilled in cities living under the authority of a prince if his government was sufficiently distant or sufficiently tolerant. Elizabethan London, for example, was far from being totally free of princely authority and interference but it had enough independence to offer a fairly free interchange of ideas.

An example of the interaction of different social systems, which was so prominent throughout the Renaissance, occurred in the 1480s when Lorenzo de' Medici allowed Giovanni Pico della Mirandola to take refuge in Florence. Pico was an ambitious philosopher-theologian whose opinions about the relationship between Christianity and other religions had been condemned at Rome by the Pope. Lorenzo gave Pico refuge because he respected his ideas and because Lorenzo had enough influence in his city, which was still a republic, to make his wishes effective in certain respects. He would not have protected Pico in this way if he had not been influenced by the free development of the study of the classics in republican Florence which had a considerable impact on the philosophers and artists in the circle that Lorenzo patronised. In this episode Lorenzo used his seigniorial patronage and influence within a primarily republican society.

In the sixteenth century principalities and kingdoms played a larger role in the Renaissance story for two reasons. One was that the power of princes had recovered from the population decline of 1350 to 1450 and they had recovered a greater prominence on the European stage. The other was that the enormous prestige of forms and ideas, which originated in republican cities, had made them irresistible in the princely world outside to kings such as Francis I of France and Philip II of Spain who had to employ artists and writers from the cities. But this should not blind us to the continued importance of the city. As we move to the period around 1600 we have to take note of the contributions of Antwerp, London and Amsterdam, none of them as independent as Florence and Venice had been, but all cities free enough to maintain a life of their own.

The word Renaissance, meaning rebirth, usually refers to the recovery, after the death of culture during the Middle Ages, of good Latin, Greek, a knowledge of classical art, literature, history and philosophy, in part a balance against the Christian tradition derived from the revelations embodied in the Bible. This was certainly an important part of the history of the period between 1400 and 1600, but the word can also be used in other ways. In this book it is taken in a more general sense to mean the evolution of a new and distinctively modern European conception of man and the universe, involving individual identity, space rationally observed, society and history as the work of cooperating and conflicting individuals, and artistic excellence as a high value. Though these may seem to be a miscellaneous collection of items they were all in fact connected with the revival of antique culture, which provided not only models of individual personalities and of social and historical analysis but also, for instance with the recovery of Ptolemy's *Geography*, inspiration for the reinterpretation of space. They were all essential parts of the new *Weltanschauung* that became the general European spirit in the seventeenth century. The aspects of classical antiquity that the Renaissance revived in the fifteenth century provided a better basis for the European spirit than the scholastic philosophy and gothic architecture of the thirteenth century, from which Europe turned away. But this evolution would not have been possible without the essential framework of the city, which provided men, as it

ABOVE *Posthumous medal with portrait of Cosimo de' Medici*
RIGHT Portrait of a Young Man holding a
medallion of Cosimo de' Medici,
Botticelli, c.1475 (Uffizi, Florence)

Port of Genoa,
Cristoforo Grassi, 1485 (Museo Civico Navale di Pegli, Genoa)

RIGHT *Ships in the harbour at Venice from the* Legend of St Ursula, *Carpaccio, c.1490-95 (Accademia, Venice)*

had done in ancient Greece, with the best environment for exploration and originality.

The sixteenth century has understandably been seen as the age of the Renaissance and Reformation, two different, sometimes conflicting, sometimes cooperating movements. The relationship is a problem that will have to be faced when we come, for example, to Erasmus and Calvin. Religious life was affected by Renaissance ideas, by the Greek New Testament and the moral philosophy of Cicero. But revelation and religious enthusiasm were not new in the sixteenth century. The power of churches, both Catholic and Protestant, was very largely dependent on landed property which had been in ecclesiastical hands since the early Middle Ages. Religious inspiration and religious conflict were obviously very important aspects of European history, but it was not these aspects which were tending irresistibly to create a new world view. Churchmen, popes included, were often patrons of Renaissance art and thought, but these were being created in the secular city.

The religious enthusiasm that was so prominent in, for example, Luther's Germany or Teresa of Avila's Spain, was a continuation of tendencies inherent in the human mind and not a novel contribution to the world view produced by the Renaissance. It is justifiable to separate Renaissance and Reformation as intellectual structures of quite different kinds.

The power of religious ideas in the sixteenth century, on both the Catholic and Protestant sides, was dependent on the possession of land. The beliefs associated with Canterbury Cathedral or St Peter's in Rome could not be ignored because these churches were landowners whose rents provided livings for a large number of priests. The decline in the power of religion in Europe since the sixteenth century, which had already begun in the Renaissance period, was largely the result of the shift of wealth from landownership to industry and trade, which deprived religious communities of their power. That power had been based on estates which had often been in ecclesiastical hands since the eleventh century or earlier, when Europe was sparsely populated and land was cheap. In the sixteenth century the European mind was divided between ecclesiastical establishments, largely funded in this way, and industrial and commercial sectors that provided laymen with increasingly large incomes. The relationship between the two was extremely complicated. Religious practice may involve withdrawal from the world but religious beliefs can easily be attached to political forces and become rallying cries in war. Conversely Luther and Calvin may have had a powerful influence on action in this world but they were concerned principally, as religious teachers, with man's relationship with God. The complex relationship between Reformation and Renaissance ideas does not alter the fact that they were separate. When we speak of the Renaissance we refer to ideas in art and philosophy about man in this world.

This book begins with the explosion of humanism and the reception of ancient civilisation which occurred in Florence at the beginning of the fifteenth century. This is a convenient starting point because from that time the movement of ideas and art became broad and continuous, although there were earlier, more hesitant and intermittent, developments. Florentine and Sienese art a century earlier, the paintings of Giotto and the sculpture of Giovanni Pisano, were influential predecessors. In the mid-fourteenth century the Sienese painter Ambrogio Lorenzetti had shown a highly developed perspective in painting the interior of a church, which foreshadowed Florentine and Flemish painting a century later, though it had none of the mathematical precision of Brunelleschi's perspective. The poet Petrarch (1304–74), the most notable precursor of the fifteenth-century humanists, was the first man to attempt to revive antique culture as an independent system distinct from and superior to medieval Europe. He was a cultural innovator in various literary fields but his school evolved only gradually and it was not until a generation after his death that the humanist flood burst forth. At that point this book starts.

The first half of the book presents a fairly concentrated account of the evolution of the Renaissance in Italy and Flanders down to the early sixteenth century. During this period the evolution of ideas can be regarded as a continuous story limited to certain places. After that the character of the narrative will change. We shall be concerned with the spread of Renaissance ideas, emanating from Italy and Flanders, in Europe. The account will inevitably become much more selective, in order to illustrate the diffusion of ideas in a continent. Eventually, of course, the Renaissance becomes absorbed into the general picture, like a dye coming from one source being diffused through a lake.

Finally, this book is concerned with events and ideas I judge to have changed the perceptions of the European mind. It is about a revolution in the European

22

Miracle of the Holy Cross,
Gentile Bellini, c.1494-1505 (Accademia, Venice)

consciousness, made up of many innovations over a period of 200 years. It is not intended as a total account of art and thought during that period. Many artists whom others may regard as important are left out in order to allow space for concentration on central figures whose leaps in imagination were more influential. Attention is given to Leonardo da Vinci, Michelangelo and Erasmus, but not to the artists of Mannerism, a movement that included many delightful painters and sculptors. This is based on the belief, right or wrong, that Pontormo and Bronzino, Correggio and Cellini were less significant, that they were exploiting developments in perception already made and, to that extent, were not inventors of the first rank. Such choices are based on personal views that are inevitably subjective.

But it is important to state the purpose which lies behind them. The book concentrates on innovations in European attitudes and new ideas that made the European consciousness different from what it had been before. It therefore presents only the major inventors of these new ideas, selected from the mass of reflection and creation spread over 200 years. Its aim is to show, in broad outline, how the distinctively European mind was formed between 1400 and 1600.

23

THE HUMANIST REVOLUTION

THE FIRST MAJOR EXPANSION of people's knowledge of the classical world, which provided a basis for all future developments in the Renaissance, took place principally at Florence in the first half of the fifteenth century. This stage in the Renaissance encouraged a close acquaintance with all aspects of classical civilisation, including Latin and Greek, literature, history, philosophy and art. It also brought about a close association between the classical humanist and the artist which established for the first time a conception of the artist as a respected creator.

The group of humanist enthusiasts in Florence was originally inspired and led by the Chancellor of the city, Coluccio Salutati. He persuaded the Florentines to pay the Byzantine scholar Manuel Chrysoloras to teach Greek between 1397 and 1400. Chrysoloras excited his listeners with an interest not only in the Greek language but also in ancient philosophy and art, and it may well have been his instruction that provided the essential spark to fire an intense enthusiasm for the ancient world and everything connected with it: Latin script for writing manuscripts; Roman and Greek history and the ancient forms of city state, so easily regarded as akin to modern Italian republics; ancient philosophy including Plato, who had been neglected in favour of Aristotle by the medieval universities; Latin literature with Petrarch's idol Cicero at its head; classical buildings with round arches in contrast to the gothic style that had become normal in fourteenth-century Italy; ancient sculpture with its lifelike representation of the human figure. The Florentine intelligentsia, predominantly lay people including notaries and lawyers rather than priests, was captivated by the dream of recreating the classical world as a superior civilisation.

One of the most interesting factors in the background to this humanist movement was the relationship between Florence and the papacy. Between 1305 and 1377 the popes had been based in France and the personnel of the papal court heavily gallicised. For thirty years after this there were two rival popes, one at Rome and one at Avignon, dividing Western Europe. After the Great Schism the Church was finally reunited in 1417 under a single pope, the Roman nobleman Martin V. He returned to Rome but during the pontificate of his successor, Eugenius IV, in the 1430s, the Church was again divided by the pretensions of the widely supported Council of Basel, and Eugenius was for a time a refugee living in Florence. As a result a thoroughly Italian papacy was established, which was intimately involved in important sections of the Italian Renaissance story in the late fifteenth and sixteenth centuries. In the early fifteenth century, however, there was a Roman papacy that was sometimes in a political condition of precarious weakness. It was deserted by parts of the

RIGHT *Exterior of lantern or cupola of Florence Cathedral, Brunelleschi, after 1436*

Loggia of Ospedale degli Innocenti, Florence,
Brunelleschi, 1419

Catholic world, assailed by enemy armies near Rome and was sometimes dependent for survival on close alliance with Florence as one of the powerful neighbouring states. But even in its weakened state the papacy was never destitute of money and always had a great court. It employed the best financial experts to transfer its money from other parts of Europe and the best letter-writers to carry on its extensive correspondence. There was no better source of money-changers than the Florentine merchant class and there were no better letter-writers than the Florentine humanists. Florence, therefore, enjoyed for much of this period a close political, financial and intellectual association with the papal court. Papal money was handled by Florentine merchants and the papal chancery staffed by Florentine rhetoricians or men sympathetic to Florentine attitudes.

The papal court became a humanist sanctuary, offering good salaries to experts in the classics, and a place where humanist tastes could be discussed and developed. Curiously, the lay intellectual movement centred on Florence acquired accepted prestige in the capital of the Church. This gave a sense of intellectual freedom that encouraged the humanists in the pursuit of their ideals. However much these men were linked with admiration for classical paganism they could not be viewed as disreputable if they were accepted by the papacy.

26

Salutati was Chancellor of Florence from 1375 until his death in 1406 and he fostered the old tradition of humanism established by Petrarch. A crucial patron was Cosimo de' Medici, the first famous member of the family that is inseparably linked with Renaissance history at Florence. Cosimo's father built up a successful bank which acted as the chief financial agent of the papacy after its reunification and resettlement at Rome. Cosimo was thus possibly the richest man in Florence, and also a man with great influence at the papal court, especially during the pontificate of Eugenius IV (1431–47). The fact that the Pope was in exile for several years in Florence was one of the reasons that Cosimo was able to acquire a position of political predominance in Florence after he himself had been exiled in 1433–4. Cosimo was also an enthusiastic and apparently knowledgeable lover both of classical scholarship and of art that used classical models. He distributed funds without which the searchers for Latin manuscripts, the translators from Greek, the architects reviving classical forms and the sculptors imitating ancient figure-sculpture would have been distinctly less able to follow these pursuits.

As well as having highly developed industries, Florence had an upper class that absorbed the wealth of Tuscany. In some ways it was rather like one of the great imperial capitals of the nineteenth century, London or Paris, in which the wealth of the nation was concentrated in the hands of an upper class rather than a monarch. The Renaissance depended on luxury production and luxury consumption: churches, palaces, paintings, carvings, books. The Florentine upper and middle classes were exceptionally capable of demanding and supplying luxury. Leonardo Bruni, who was with the papal court in the country at Viterbo in 1405, wrote to a friend, 'There flowed before my eyes the delights and conveniences of the city of Florence: the wealth of doctors, the exquisite and delicate foods created to suit the tastes of invalids by the most expert cooks, the abundance of the smoothest wines.' The

same could no doubt have been said about other Italian cities that became prominent in the Renaissance.

LEONARDO BRUNI AND HUMANISM

Salutati had among his pupils and admirers several practising humanists. The most important of them in terms of the ideas which he developed was Leonardo Bruni, a secretary at the papal court until 1415. He then returned to Florence, where he became Chancellor as Salutati had been, and lived there until his death in 1444. Bruni's intense devotion to things classical, his immense output as a translator from Greek into Latin and a writer in Latin, combined with his position as a respected senior civil servant in Florence, made him the effective continuator of Salutati's tradition. He was able to establish the humanist point of view firmly at the centre of the Florentine patrician imagination. Those devoted to Latin and to Rome separated themselves quite self-consciously from the scholars of the many European universities, whose classes were, of course, conducted entirely in Latin. Bruni translated Aristotle's *Ethics* from Greek into Latin, although there was already a translation widely used in universities, 'because they had been so translated that they seemed to have been made barbarian rather than Latin'. Contempt for linguistic skills at the universities was coupled with a dislike of scholastic philosophy and a wish to substitute a *belle-lettrist*, Ciceronian, non-technical philosophy. Other notable proponents of the humanist education helped to establish it more widely in the Italian cities. But Bruni and his acquaintances in Florence and Rome made the most significant developments in humanism as a system of ideas.

Bruni's contributions were closely connected with the Florentine city state as a political organism. He was the first great forerunner of Machiavelli and the inventor of the Renaissance method of writing history. His great and original monument was his *History of the Florentine People*. In the first place it was based on historical research. The

Interior of Old Sacristy, San Lorenzo, Florence,
Brunelleschi, 1421-30

Florentines knew that the foundation of their city took place in the Roman republican period and they ascribed it to Caesar. Long before Bruni there had been a tradition of writing about this with enthusiastic emphasis on the connections between Florence and the Roman Empire. Bruni himself overturned this tradition, using references to classical writers to show that Florence was a republican foundation. When he came to the medieval history of the city he did not accept unquestioningly the accounts that he found in earlier chroniclers, but looked up the records of the city councils, and often used them to improve his narrative. The method which Petrarch had used to improve the text of Cicero was applied to large-scale history.

The other novel aspect of this work was Bruni's successful attempt to make republicanism the political virtue most admired. The contemporary situation in Florence was easily related to the republican origins of the city, since the Florentines were conscious of the need to defend the republican city against despotic enemies, especially the Visconti of Milan who were the most

Interior of Pazzi Chapel, Florence,
Brunelleschi, 1433-61

powerful Italian rulers at the time. But the political argument also had wider implications. 'I judge,' said Bruni, 'that the beginning of the decline of the Roman Empire is to be put at about that time when, having lost its liberty, Rome began to serve the emperors.' The conflict between republicanism and monarchy became a conflict between republican virtue and tyrannical vice. This was the beginning of the vision of history as the history of civilisation and of social qualities, which could include the arts and literature as well as the art of political management, rather than history as a string of political events or as an account of the interventions of God in human affairs.

It was natural for Italians to take up the political theory of the city state to be found in the writings of Plato and Aristotle and apply it to their own cities, which appeared to have something in common with Athens and Sparta. During the first forty years of the fifteenth century Bruni produced several essays in which he considered the city as a completely self-contained political system, not requiring

29

theological justification and not placed within the context of church–state relations. Foreshadowing Machiavelli, he argued that the citizen's duty was to defend the state in war rather than to allow it to be dependent on buying the unreliable services of mercenary *condottieri*. Bruni was, however, an unsophisticated political theorist who paid little attention to the difficult philosophical problems raised by any system of government. He was the first to revive the idea of the city-state as a self-sufficient political system, justified simply by its own secular purpose of providing for the good life. A considerable body of writing about the self-sufficient state was produced in fifteenth-century Italy and the idea eventually spread to the great monarchies.

The origins of the connection between humanism and the visual arts are more obscure than those of the connection between humanism and politics. There are a few humanist letters that praise classical buildings and sculpture, but not much more. Apart from Chrysoloras, the Greek imported into Florence, one of the most prominent figures among the Florentine humanists of the early fifteenth century was Niccolò Niccoli who may have been another of Salutati's disciples. Although he left no significant writings, he was credited by others with a fastidious and eccentric fascination not only with Roman script but also with ancient art and coins. It is clear that the influence of humanism on the artists resulted from the fact that the humanists wanted to revive the whole of ancient civilisation, even its handwriting, which they confused with early medieval hands, and its buildings and sculptural styles, for the imitation of which they were, of course, completely dependent on craftsmen. As it happened there were brilliant craftsmen in Florence who were willing to meet their wishes.

Most of the important architecture, sculpture and painting of the Florentine Renaissance was paid for either by guilds, which were associations of businessmen, or by well-to-do patricians, who were often also, in our sense of the term, businessmen. The building and decoration of the cathedral and the Baptistery were controlled by the guilds of cloth merchants and wool manufacturers. The greatest individual patron in this period was Cosimo de' Medici who was an international financier. When the *Gates of Paradise* were being designed for the Baptistery, to be sculpted in bronze by Ghiberti, the preliminary design was by a committee that included humanists like Leonardo Bruni. There were, of course, other commissions in which clergymen played a large part but most of the Florentine art of this period was paid for and presided over by laymen, often highly educated, living in a city which was self-consciously aware of being a bulwark of republicanism surrounded by a partially hostile external world.

BRUNELLESCHI AND PERSPECTIVE

The most remarkable innovator of early fifteenth-century Florence was perhaps Filippo Brunelleschi who invented both Renaissance architecture and perspective drawing, both of which had a decisive influence on sculptors and painters. Brunelleschi was most famous among his fellow citizens for building the dome of Florence cathedral. This was an achievement of technical ingenuity, which borrowed from the methods of Byzantine architecture, of which he had seen imported examples at Venice and Padua. This revival of a Mediterranean tradition was prominent in the Renaissance and inspired, amongst other works, the design for the new St Peter's at Rome. Brunelleschi's dome was less important stylistically than for its establishment of a new system of architecture that used the rounded arch and the centralised church.

During the thirteenth and fourteenth centuries gothic architecture, invented in France, had taken root in Italy. This involved pointed arches, an emphasis on height, and a church design characterised by long naves crossed by short transepts. The return to a Roman style was suggested by humanist enthusiasm at the beginning of the fifteenth century. Neither the humanists nor the artists, however, were able to distinguish at this stage between the genuine Roman architecture of the ancient world and the Romanesque architecture with its round arches that had been prevalent in Italy up to the thirteenth century. Florence did not offer models of genuine Roman architecture and Brunelleschi's early work was most influenced by Romanesque buildings in Florence, notably the Baptistery and San Miniato. His taste made excellent use of them in a remarkably fresh way.

His first classical building was the loggia outside the orphanage, the Ospedale degli Innocenti, built in 1419–24. This is an arcade of round arches springing from Corinthian capitals, joined to the wall by similar arches with small cupolas in between. Many loggias of this kind were built in imitation in succeeding centuries. Brunelleschi's new plan had produced an architectural style entirely different from the gothic, creating an impression of exquisite lightness while emphasising square and round forms. In the 1420s Brunelleschi was given the bigger challenge of rebuilding the church of San Lorenzo. This commission was more difficult because it was not easy to depart from the traditional church layout. What he produced was a compromise of a long church with transepts balanced by classical arches within the main structure. The nave consists of two arcades of Corinthian columns with a clerestory of round-topped windows above. The aisles on each side of the nave are rows of cupolas with pilasters on the walls between round arches matching the columns. It is an elegant design, which has the Romanesque basilica as its origin.

Brunelleschi's plans for two other buildings show him beginning to move in the direction of the centralised church, which became a Renaissance ideal. The first was for the Old Sacristy, attached to San Lorenzo, which contains the sarcophagus of Cosimo de' Medici's father. Here the main room is a cube topped by a dome that rounds off the upper corners. Off the main room is a chancel that is entered through an arch, framed by an arched entablature, which was a new idea. The building is in part an example of a cooperation between Brunelleschi and the sculptor Donatello who made roundels of low relief placed on the upper walls, though Brunelleschi is said to have objected to the bronze doors designed by Donatello. The Old Sacristy was actually built in the 1420s. In the next decade Brunelleschi went on to design the Pazzi Chapel, attached to Santa Croce, which was not completed until long after his death but is clearly related in conception to the Old Sacristy. This is a free-standing building, highly finished on the outside as well as on the inside, and certainly one of the most attractive structures in Florence. The main room is rectangular, instead of square as in the Old Sacristy, and barrel-vaulted spaces were added on each side of the main cupola. More light comes into the building from the lantern above the cupola. Donatello's dark roundels of low relief have been replaced by brightly coloured ceramic reliefs, designed by Brunelleschi. The result is a building of quite extraordinary lightness and peace, dependent on both the genius of the designer and his use of Roman and Romanesque forms.

It seems likely that at some time in the early 1430s Brunelleschi visited Rome and fell under the influence of genuine Roman architecture. By the 1430s Florentine humanism at the papal court was beginning to arouse much more humanist interest in the buildings, archaeology and history of Rome itself which were to have a central position in thought throughout the Renaissance period. The view of classical architecture which a man might discover at Rome was quite different from that which he would experience by looking at the relics of the Romanesque at Florence. In the later 1430s Brunelleschi displayed an interest in concentric design that was at the farthest remove from the plans of gothic church architecture. His most important work in this style, the church of the monastery of Santa Maria degli Angeli, was never finished and can be observed only in an incomplete way. This was a sixteen-sided polygon, almost circular, whose roof was supported by eight pillars, the spaces between them forming chapels. About the same time he was crowning the cupola of Florence's main cathedral with a large concentric classical lantern, much less gothic than the dome itself, and adding semi-circular classical apses to the base of the cupola.

These experiments in concentricity received their fullest expression in another building begun by Brunelleschi. The rebuilding of the church of Santo Spirito at Florence offered him freer play of his imagination than San Lorenzo. This time, if indeed the existing church, finished long after his death, does follow his plans in these respects, he produced a design in which the east end is in fact a completely symmetrical concentric church. That is,

the two transepts and the choir are identical and the nave would form the fourth identical leg of the cross if it were cut off instead of being extended to the west to correspond with the traditional plan of the medieval church. Brunelleschi also introduced details into the interior design that emphasised its concentricity. The columns of the arcades are matched along the walls by half-columns, instead of pilasters as at San Lorenzo, and between them are semi-circular chapels that give the walls an appearance of undulation. The result is that standing in one of the transepts you have the sensation of being in a heavily columnated building without the impression of length and height which predominates in a gothic church.

It was very likely in connection with his architectural plans that Brunelleschi made the experiments that

Cantoria,
Donatello, 1433-9 (Museo dell' Opera del Duomo, Florence)

constituted his invention of perspective drawing. This accurate picture of what buildings looked like, or what they would look like if constructed, has obvious value to an architect. Earlier artists had been interested in space but had not given the picture of space mathematical exactitude. This was what was done in the early fifteenth century. As a result it became possible, by using plans before drawing a picture, to give the space an absolutely clear accuracy, to make it a picture of what we actually think we see. This is true, it should be added, only on the assumptions that light travels in straight lines and that the two eyes of the observer provide a single viewing point. Even though it could be argued that Renaissance perspective is in a sense over-simplified, it does provide the artist or observer with a remarkably clear and coherent view of the space before him. It is most easily used for the representation of space around square or round buildings. But with some elaboration it can be adapted to the representation of hills, human bodies and animals. In the years after Brunelleschi invented his system it was used most ambitiously by the painters Masaccio, Uccello and Piero della Francesca. They created a physical world of coherent space which we have largely accepted ever since as 'the world as it really is'. Departures made from it, for example by post-impressionists and cubists, have been deliberate attempts to present reality in a way that does not conform to our natural impression of it.

The success of the perspective experiments of the early fifteenth century was the result of a very strong tendency towards a simplified realism. It was antipathetic to the atmosphere of symbolism and mystery characteristic of much medieval art, which later artists reintroduced by using perspective to create spatial illusion, as for instance in the ceilings of late Renaissance buildings where heaven appears to rise above the space of the room. But artists could do this only by making heaven part of the common-sense visual space around them. To that extent their visions merely submitted to the everyday realism that had taken control of the physical world.

In about 1415 or 1420 Brunelleschi made a panel with a painting on it of the Baptistery seen from the door of the cathedral and a hole at the point on the Baptistery opposite the observer's viewpoint. If the back of the panel was held to the observer's face and a mirror held before him at arm's length, he would see through the hole a perspective view of the Baptistery. It has been suggested that mathematical calculation determined the view chosen because the distance from the cathedral to the Baptistery, the width and the height of the Baptistery are all about sixty times an arm's length. Twenty years later in his book *On Painting* Alberti provided the first precise statement that has survived of a method for establishing the vanishing-point in a drawn space, and relating the size of the figures in the space to their positions on the orthogonal lines leading from the foreground to the vanishing-point. Even earlier than this first written statement, Masaccio in the 1420s used a carefully worked out spatial perspective in his fresco of the *Trinity* that must have been based on the teaching of Brunelleschi, to whom we owe the inauguration of the spatial field worked out on rational principles.

DONATELLO, GHIBERTI AND SCULPTURE

Brunelleschi's closest artistic association was with the sculptor Donatello, who died at the age of eighty in 1466 after sixty years of astonishingly creative work. He was a genius with a supreme capacity for conveying emotional power in stone and bronze. A good indication of his originality is available to anyone who compares the two *cantorie*, singers' galleries, that were sculpted by him and Luca della Robbia for the cathedral at Florence and now stand opposite each other in the cathedral museum. Luca's *cantoria* has a relief of singing boys of very remarkable grace and charm that would be an achievement for any sculptor. Donatello has a line of dancing *putti*, children inspired by

Interior of Santo Spirito, Florence,
Brunelleschi, after 1446

Judith and Holofernes,
Donatello, 1456 (Palazzo Vecchio, Florence)

classical models, whose movements and faces are animated by a mad and slightly sinister exuberance. Their mysterious power makes Luca's figures seem bland in comparison with this artistic force.

Donatello was also distinguished by exceptional technical inventiveness. His skill in the casting of complicated free-standing figures in bronze, shown in his *St Louis of Toulouse* and in his *Judith and Holofernes*, raised bronze figure-sculpture to a level of sophistication that had not been known in the medieval world. His development of very low relief looks like an attempt to produce a sculptural equivalent to painting with figures and landscape cut out of the stone, like a profile on a coin, instead of standing out from it. He was also very much influenced by classical models which he absorbed and transformed into his distinctive style. Humanist letter-writers in 1428 and 1430 tell us of pieces of ancient sculpture that Donatello had seen and approved. By this time the association of humanists and artists, soon to be shown most fully in Alberti's *On Painting*, which mentions Donatello, had been established at Florence. Some of Donatello's pieces, for example the *putti* on the *cantoria* just mentioned or the low reliefs on the pedestal of *Judith and Holofernes*, are clearly imitations of classical models. The stances of his clothed figures, the male nude of the bronze *David* and the lifelike individuality that he gave to the human face, were also the result of observing classical works. Donatello, however, had too strong a personality to be an imitator; nor did he indulge in the kind of artistic antiquarianism of many of his contemporaries, including his partner Michelozzo.

If we look at Donatello's work over sixty years we can see two main strands running through it: an interest in the free-standing human figure and in story-telling in relief. He

St Louis of Toulouse,
Donatello, 1422-5 (Museo di Santa Croce, Florence)

the adolescent innocence of the young David is captured in the facial expression. *Zuccone* is clad in a toga but the right shoulder is bare and the structure of the body is visible behind the clothing. The gaunt face is a remarkable presentation of powerful old age. *St Mark*, also toga-clad, has his face largely hidden by his beard, but again the relationship between the body, this time invisible, and the clothing is carefully worked out, as is the distribution of the weight. *St George*, like *David*, is a picture of youthful innocent strength, dressed in modern armour, but the stance and face convey a more powerful presentation of forthrightness. Donatello's first and very remarkable experiment in bronze casting is *St Louis*. This is a young man clad in the dress appropriate to his rank as a bishop so that, although the body is invisible, we are aware of its existence beneath the voluminous clothing. In these statues Donatello was working broadly within the tradition of ecclesiastical figure-sculpture but he made substantial advances, no doubt under classical influence, in both the realism of the separate figure and the individuality of the personality expressed in the faces.

One of Donatello's most delightful creations was the *Annunciation* in limestone which is situated on the wall of the nave of Santa Croce in Florence. This sculptured Annunciation, in which the figures of the Virgin and the angel are placed within a limited space, was an original conception, but it gains its power chiefly from the combination of innocence and youthful seriousness infused into the attitude and radiant face of the Virgin. The gentleness of this Annunciation, however, is unusual in Donatello's art and does not point in the direction which his figure-sculpture was to take. During his later years he produced several very powerful statues all of which betray a strange or harsh quality.

Two of them, the bronzes *David* and *Judith and Holofernes*, once stood in the Medici palace. But it is not known whether they were the result of Medici patronage,

made his first free-standing figures before 1430 for two major enterprises that were being patronised in Florence, the decoration of the cathedral and campanile, and the filling of the niches around Or San Michele, both controlled and paid for by guilds. For the cathedral he sculpted the marble *David* and the so-called *Zuccone* (the statue to which, we are told, he kept saying, 'Speak, speak!' as he sculpted it), and, for Or San Michele, *St Mark*, *St George* and *St Louis*. The body of the marble *David* is tilted somewhat awkwardly to fit the position for which it was designed. The statue has, however, a realistic distribution of weight on the legs, while

Annunciation,
Donatello, c.1433 (Santa Croce, Florence)

or whether they were intended as a pair, each portraying youth triumphing over wickedness. *David* is one of the most revolutionary and puzzling works of the Renaissance. The statue represents a nude boy, both self-satisfied and slightly sullen, adorned with a fancy hat and boots, with the feather of Goliath's helmet clinging to the inside of his thigh. The face and figure are remarkably sensual. We have no idea what persuaded Donatello to transform the Old Testament hero into this young god who inspires admiration of his somewhat feminine physical beauty rather than his fortitude. *Judith and Holofernes* on the other hand is a

complicated piece of sculpture carrying further the success that Donatello had had with the clothing of *St Louis*. Holofernes is seated, his head half hacked off, his hands falling to his sides. Judith stands above him, trampling on his groin and his right hand, voluminously clothed, sword raised, a hard and triumphant woman's face showing satisfaction in her victory. Whatever the intentions that led to the creation of these two works, Donatello undoubtedly raised the emotional power of figure-sculpture and its capacity to portray strong and complex feeling.

Donatello produced a great deal of low relief sculpture

Feast of Herod,
Donatello, c.1425 (Baptistery, Siena)

for a number of different buildings. Most of it is marked by an interest in the opportunities for portrayal of space, using complicated architectural settings, which had been made possible by Brunelleschi's experiments. A fairly early example is the bronze plaque of the *Feast of Herod* which he made for the Baptistery font of Siena in the 1420s. This has in the foreground the feast itself with, on the one side, Herod's amazement as the head of John the Baptist is presented to him on a platter and, on the other, a group of figures including the dancing Salomé in swirling robes, who is clearly inspired by a classical dancer. The plaque seems to be designed, however, to show off his command of perspective space. The feast takes place before a low wall. Behind that is a space backed by an arcade, behind that a further space in which there are musicians, and a wall with windows through which a yet further space can be seen. What Donatello has presented is a sophisticated visual field, not in paint but in low relief. About twenty years later he did both figure and sculpture reliefs for the church of the Santo at Padua. The reliefs embody an extreme extension of, and enthusiasm for, perspective design which the sculptor shared with the painters Uccello and Piero della Francesca. The bronze relief of the *Healing of the Irascible Son* is perhaps the best example. The actual story is largely

LEFT David,
Donatello, c.1440 (Museo Nazionale, Florence)

39

Healing of the Irascible Son,
Donatello, c.1446-50 (Sant' Antonio, Padua)

Mary Magdalen,
Donatello, 1454-5 (Baptistery, Florence)

depicted by the group of figures in the foreground. Behind the foreground building a vast arena stretches into the distance with long steps rising on either side above ground level, and figures, diminishing towards the back, leaning on the railings. This setting therefore presented a splendid opportunity for exhibiting space in depth.

Donatello appears in the narrative sources of his life as a temperamental individual. There may have been people before him who had the artist's devotion to the inventive powers of his craft combined with a disregard for accepted standards of behaviour which patrons had to accept if they wished to employ this genius. If so we do not know of them. He is the first person to be celebrated as an artist and perhaps this is a result not merely of the improvement of biographical sources but also of the freedom that some artists gained from the new dignity of their connection with the humanists. Donatello continued to be inventive throughout his life. About 1450 he made the equestrian statue of the mercenary soldier Gattamelata which stands near the Santo at Padua, showing a further extension of the technique of bronze casting. This revival of the bronze equestrian statue was to be followed by an immense line of imitators in the Renaissance period. As he grew old he developed an interest in the aged, the old Mary Magdalen and the old St John the Baptist. One of his last and greatest creations was the series of scenes of low relief bronze plaques that he made for pulpits at San Lorenzo. By this time he had lost interest in the slightly meretricious capacity for complex perspective drawing and also in the difficulties of very low relief. What absorbed him, as it had in his earliest days, was revealing humanity in the figure and the face. The Christ in the *Resurrection* at San Lorenzo is a highly original conception. This Christ is not youthful or commanding. He steps out of the tomb old and weary, exhausted by his trials, but displaying in his stance and expression a sense of deep human suffering and knowledge.

One of the best-known and most delightful creations of

Resurrection,
Donatello, 1460-70 (San Lorenzo, Florence)

Jacob and Esau from the Gates of Paradise,
Ghiberti, c.1435 (Museo del Opera del Duomo, Florence)

the early fifteenth century was the *Gates of Paradise* made for the Baptistery at Florence by Donatello's contemporary, the sculptor Ghiberti, between 1429 and 1437. Ghiberti was trained as a goldsmith and his work exhibits the utmost technical skill and capacity for delicacy for which the Florentines were famous. The *Gates of Paradise* have ten plaques of scenes from the Old Testament placed on two large doors. We happen to know, because of an exceptional survival of documents, that trouble was taken in choosing and designing the stories. The panels of gilded bronze combine low relief, probably imitating Donatello's technique, and high relief. The grace and realism of the figures standing out from the plaques show the crafts of both the goldsmith and the sculptor.

Ghiberti was also, however, thoroughly aware of the intellectual and artistic movements of his time. He had defeated Brunelleschi in the competition devised to choose an artist for the north doors of the Baptistery in 1403. On the *Gates of Paradise* he introduced perspective designs which show that he was interested in profiting from the

innovations of Brunelleschi and Donatello. In both the Isaac and the Joseph panels the background is occupied by large and complicated buildings with round arches and classical capitals in which the rules of perspective were largely observed, conveying a sense of spatial depth. In the later years of his long life, although he was not at all a learned man, Ghiberti turned to literature and produced the *Commentaries*, which are actually the first statement of artistic ideals by a Renaissance artist. The *Commentaries* contain an account of artists since Cimabue, sometimes preserving useful biographical information while in a sense foreshadowing the work of Vasari, published more than a century later. But they also report, rather laboriously, views about sculpture and ancient art copied from Vitruvius and Pliny, and medieval philosophers' theories of light. Ghiberti said that his aim as an artist was 'to imitate nature' and he emphasised the importance of perspective. This highly successful sculptor, who was still essentially a craftsman, was aware of the intellectuals' views about art and wanted to show that he too understood and practised their precepts. Ghiberti's writings show better than anything else how completely art and humanism had been wedded.

MASACCIO AND THE NEW PAINTING

The most remarkable painter of the early fifteenth century was Masaccio, who died in 1428 at the age of twenty-seven. In his brief life he succeeded as a painter in using the lessons of Donatello and Brunelleschi, and created works of monumental grandeur. Little is known of Masaccio's life but it is clear that he knew Brunelleschi and Donatello personally. His most striking innovations are contained in two works, the fresco of the *Trinity* on the wall of the nave of Santa Maria Novella and the frescoes in the Brancacci Chapel in Santa Maria del Carmine. The *Trinity* fresco was painted for the Lenzi family and the donor and his wife can be seen kneeling at the front of it. Behind them is a chapel; within the chapel are the Trinity – a crucified Christ, the

Trinity,
Masaccio, 1428 (Santa Maria Novella, Florence)

Tribute Money,
Masaccio, 1425-8 (S. Maria del Carmine, Florence)

dove of the Holy Spirit and God the Father – and standing figures of the Virgin and St John the Evangelist. Described in this way the fresco may seem traditional but everything about it is actually revolutionary or mysterious. The design of the chapel, with its columns, pilasters, capitals, rounded and coffered barrel-vault, is entirely classical. In 1425 this was a novelty in painting and shows the influence of Brunelleschi. The space of the chapel is drawn with such a consistent use of perspective that the ground plan can be reconstructed from the painting. This picture is, as it were, Brunelleschi's panels in reverse, an imaginary building drawn geometrically on the basis of a ground plan. The two kneeling donors are outside the chapel but they are in the same realistic space which extends beyond it. The figures are drawn with a rounded realism that makes this physical position and form clear. They may owe something to Donatello's improvement of the relation between body and

clothing in his early figure-sculptures. The mural as a whole foreshadows much later developments in illusionism because the observer appears to be seeing a real chapel set in the wall of the church.

The culmination of Masaccio's painting, and indeed of Florentine painting in this period, was the great series of frescoes in the Brancacci chapel in Santa Maria del Carmine which he painted in the late 1420s. The most prominent of the paintings is the *Tribute Money* that illustrates the passage in St Matthew's Gospel in which we are told that the apostles were asked for tribute money by the Roman tax-gatherer at Capernaum. St Peter was told by Christ to find the money in the mouth of a fish in the lake. He did so and brought back the money for the tribute-collector. The story probably had contemporary significance because in 1427 the commune of Florence, hard pressed by war with Milan, was thinking of new ways to tax its subjects, and the painting,

44

Deluge,
Uccello, c.1445-6 (Chiostro di Santa Maria Novella, Florence)

with its implication of the duty of all, laity and clergy alike, to support the state, may refer to demands for money from the local church.

In Masaccio's fresco we are presented with a serial narrative of three successive scenes: Christ and the apostles in the middle receiving the demand from the tax-collector; on the left Peter extracting the money from the fish; on the right Peter handing over the money to the collector. The landscape in the background, of both buildings and countryside, is common to all three scenes. Our attention is concentrated, however, on the large central group of Christ, apostles and tax-gatherer. They are seen from a low viewpoint so that their figures, decorously arranged in a circle, tower imposingly. Visual depth is given to the fresco by the diminution of the figures in the rear. Their bodies have a substantiality that is defined by the light falling from one direction, while in the foreground the outstretched

arms of the figures nearest to us create a visual rhythm.

In the decades following the death of Masaccio in 1428 the new grasp of space and figure representation was exploited by a number of important painters: Fra Angelico, Domenico Veneziano, Paolo Uccello, Piero della Francesca, Filippo Lippi and Andrea Castagno, to mention only the outstanding masters. Among these Paolo Uccello (1397–1475) illustrates best the excitement aroused by the new grasp of space. Uccello was obsessed by the possibility of applying mathematical principles to the correct portrayal of complicated objects, like a chalice, of which he left a detailed geometrical drawing, or a foreshortened body lying on the ground, of which there are examples in the various panels that he made depicting the *Battle of San Romano* about 1445. His most elaborate essay in spatial principles was the fresco of the *Deluge* that he painted, also in the 1440s, on the wall of a cloister at Santa Maria Novella. On either side of the painting are perspective visions of the wooden ark, one looking across the end of it, the other straight down the side. This creates a long perspective funnel down the middle of the scene between the two wooden walls, an extreme example of the visual pyramid extending towards a distant vanishing-point. In this visual field the figures are arranged in dramatic postures, clinging to the side of the ark, floundering in the waves, climbing out of a barrel. One of the figures has an elaborate wickerwork circlet around his neck which displays Uccello's detailed perspective expertise. The scene is meant to be a dramatic presentation of both the terrors of the flood – lightning strikes near the vanishing-point – and thankfulness for its ending. Uccello's purpose was clear: to demonstrate how perspective could intensify drama, an aim which was to have a long history in succeeding centuries.

Self-Portrait,
Alberti, mid-fifteenth century (Samuel H. Kress Collection, National Gallery of Art, Washington)

Uccello's interest in space also made him a landscape painter. Among other Florentine painters, he was influenced by his northern European contemporaries whose great interest in nature gave them a different vision of the world from that induced by the Florentine concentration on figures seen in relation to buildings. Perhaps the most attractive result of the influence was Uccello's painting of the *Hunt*. The scene is a forest and the action takes place among widely scattered, slender trees. Between them are huntsmen on horses, spearmen and prancing dogs. The trees create a visual framework which simplifies the scenic problem of applying perspective to a natural scene that is focused, as clearly as if there were walls, towards a vanishing-point in the distance. This painting was probably done in the 1430s, and in it Uccello combines his two interests in mathematical space and nature.

ALBERTI AND VALLA

The artists working in Florence were observed by a member of an exiled Florentine family, Leon Battista Alberti, who wrote the first Renaissance book about art, inaugurating the Renaissance tradition of artistic theory which continued through the next two centuries. Alberti was a member of an international banking family rather like the Medici, and an expert humanist. He attached himself to the papal court as a secretary, but the movements of the popes brought him to Florence, and his acquaintance with the artists there partly determined the character of his book *On Painting* which was published in 1435. This gave a learned man's approval to contemporary art.

'Since I returned from the long exile in which we Alberti have grown old to our supremely beautiful city I recognised first in you Filippo [Brunelleschi] and our very good friend Donatello and in those others Nencio [Ghiberti], Luca [della Robbia] and Masaccio a genius for every laudable enterprise in no way inferior to any of the ancients who gained fame in these arts.'

Ideal City,
anon., c.1475 (Galleria Nazionale delle Marche, Palazzo Ducale, Urbino)

In the book, Alberti took up the idea of perspective drawing, developed by Brunelleschi, who had not, so far as we know, written about it. Alberti expounded it with the mathematics and optical theory available only to a scholar. This kind of mathematical writing about art was to be continued in later years by Piero della Francesca and Leonardo but the scholarship begins with Alberti. He also expressed other ideas about the way painting should be done, turning away completely from traditional notions of symbolism, allegory or mere decoration to a wholehearted presentation of art as realistic portrayal of nature and humanity. The use of gold should be avoided. Even black and white should be used sparingly. Colours should represent what the painter saw. Human figures should be based on a study of anatomy, starting with the bones and adding the flesh and the clothes. Movements should be appropriate to the characters in the painting: graceful and simple for young maidens, powerful and vigorous for men, slow and weary for the aged. The weight of a figure should appear to rest where it really would rest. The painting as a whole should portray the interplay of emotions between the

figures. 'I like to see someone who tells the spectators what is happening there; or beckons with his hand; or menaces with an angry face and with flashing eyes so that no one should come near; or points to some danger or marvellous thing there or invites us to weep or laugh together with them.'

Alberti presented painting as a liberal art like poetry, suitable for educated men, and not an activity for unlettered artisans. Painters should 'take pleasure in poets and orators, for these have many ornaments in common with the painter', and should remember their kinship with Phidias and Apelles in classical antiquity. Alberti's book is one of the most revolutionary in the history of aesthetics, and it established almost overnight the image of the artist as a man of culture portraying nature.

Fifteen years later Alberti produced another book, *On Architecture*, which again gave a new view of the subject. For Alberti the object of architecture was to create a city designed to accommodate the various classes of the population in harmonious concord and elegance. Alberti had a sense of the city as a social organism with houses

47

Façade of Palazzo Rucellai, Florence
Alberti, 1446-51

arranged around state buildings, temples and senatorial palaces. This combination of utility and grandeur, set in a society analysed according to the functions of political and religious wisdom, business and wealth, marked the beginning of the idea of the Utopian city discussed by a hundred writers in succeeding centuries and of course very different from the unplanned proliferation of buildings characteristic of the medieval town. It began to affect Rome in the grandiose plans initiated by Popes Nicholas V and Julius II and others in the Renaissance period. Alberti was the founder of the idea of the rationally planned city.

He was also keenly interested in the architectural design of individual buildings. His book contains an account of this subject, based partly on his reading of the book on architecture by Vitruvius, written in the first century AD, partly on Alberti's own careful examination of ancient buildings, such as the Pantheon and the Basilica of Constantine, still standing in Rome. On the basis of these studies Alberti became a practising architect. After Brunelleschi, he was the second founder of the new classical style that gained popularity in Italy. This second stage, however, was in some ways very different since Alberti moved away from the light elegance of Brunelleschi, inspired by Florentine Romanesque, to a heavier and more monumental style that owes its inspiration to genuinely classical buildings at Rome.

Two of Alberti's new creations were designed about 1450, at the same time as he was writing his book on architecture. At Rimini there is the exterior of the so-called Tempio Malatestiano, the 'temple for the Malatesta' who were lords of Rimini. The motifs that go around the outside wall are heavy round-topped arches and half-columns standing out from the wall. Although this is actually a church, any observer approaching it would be much more likely to think he was entering an ancient temple. About the same time Alberti designed the façade of the palace of the wealthy Rucellai family in Florence, known as the Palazzo

Tempio Malatestiano, San Francesco, Rimini,
Alberti, c.1450

Rucellai. The family palaces that were commonly built in Italian cities during the Renaissance period were typically solid rectangular buildings with a courtyard inside but externally looked rather bare and forbidding. Alberti's façade is a confection of classical motifs, round arches and pillars let into the wall, set against a background of large rectangular blocks of stone. This style enormously influenced later palace building.

The most delightful of Alberti's designs was the façade, also paid for by the Rucellai family, for the gothic church of the convent of Santa Maria Novella in Florence. This is not a whole building, but a façade added to an existing structure. It rises wonderfully above the square before it, partly because of its design and partly because of the colourful combination of white and grey-green marble of which it is made. The shapes again are mostly classical – round arches, straight columns, a classical pediment, circles – but it is not really a classical construction. By fitting his pattern into an elaborate system of overlapping squares and circles, Alberti created a novel patchwork of classical shapes which matched the form of the gothic church externally, but resembled a fretwork of coloured stone rather than a building. It showed the possibility of creating something original out of essentially Roman parts.

Alberti was a polymath, interested in a variety of pursuits, whose career has given rise perhaps more than anyone else's to the legend of the 'Renaissance Man', standing at the centre of knowledge and science and uniting in his mind the whole world of the spirit. He was a classical scholar, a mathematician, a connoisseur of art, an architect and also a writer. Although so much of his inspiration was classical and he was devoted to ancient writers of Latin and

Greek, he did more than any other fifteenth-century humanist, with the exception perhaps of Poliziano, whom we shall consider in a later chapter, to apply humanist forms to writing in Italian. Nearly all the writings of his humanist contemporaries were in Latin and they tended to despise their native tongue, with disastrous effects for Italian literature. Alberti, however, composed one major dialogue – a literary form based essentially on imitation of Latin and Greek authors – in Italian. This was his *Della Famiglia* (*On the Family*). Here we move into another sphere in which he was profoundly original: the literary perception of social and political life.

Della Famiglia is an imaginary discussion between real members of Alberti's family who, although exiled from Florence, had been important in the international financial world in the early fifteenth century. From one point of view the main object of the dialogue is the presentation of two attitudes, that of the plain businessman and that of the businessman who is an enthusiastic humanist. The humanist view is a satire of the Stoic philosophy that tended to be the viewpoint of humanists in the age of Bruni. The world is a theatre in which the individual must make the best of his life by constant ambition and competitive enterprise; like a Venetian boat-race, we are told, in which only the winners can regard themselves as successful. Internal capacities produce the external goods of life. The plain businessman on the other hand believes that only careful management of his money can make him successful. Aristocrats are to be regarded with suspicion; they are better at borrowing money than paying it back. The plain businessman is snobbish, enjoying his acquaintance with nobility, but conscious that only diligent husbanding of his resources will

RIGHT *Façade of Santa Maria Novella, Florence*
Alberti, 1456-70

improve his position in the world.

Alberti is no doubt giving his view of the well-to-do in the Italian city. The book is a social portrait. But there is also a more abstract discussion of the things that mattered to this commercial society: the family and the household, marriage, the bringing up of children, the extent to which it was sensible for a merchant to give his time to city politics which were important – 'it is on the public squares that glory is won' – but wasteful of time and effort. *Della Famiglia* also presents a view of ideas that are prominent in the Renaissance philosophical view of society, particularly the interaction between Fortune and Virtue. The Alberti were acutely aware of the uncontrollable impact of external events – Fortune – on their expulsion from their native city and their dispersal throughout the world. Virtue – an important concept to be met with later and frequently in Machiavelli's writings – is the armour of the individual or society with which external events are confronted. The Virtue of the individual man, meaning his moral health, is easy enough to grasp. Renaissance writers also paid attention to the Virtue of the state, which is a rather more difficult concept. It embraces, in Alberti's words, 'just laws, virtuous princes, strong and constant deeds, love of one's country, faith, diligence and the chaste and praiseworthy observances of the citizens'. Macedonia had been a 'virtuous' state until the death of Alexander the Great, as Rome had been until it fell under the domination of the emperors. Virtue was destroyed by faction and tyranny. This may seem to be an impressionistic and perhaps unclear definition of a state of society. However, one can understand its attractiveness in Renaissance Italy, composed of a multitude of small political units, constantly in conflict with each other, and conscious of the differences made to political fortune by the rise and fall of good leaders, the fair and unfair management of internal politics, the zeal and good faith of some and the disastrous effects of corruption and vendetta. *Della Famiglia* is a picture of a society and of its conception of itself.

The most remarkable thinker among Alberti's contemporaries was Lorenzo Valla, a Roman and, like Alberti, much more connected with the papal court than with any of the republican cities but, again like Alberti, a humanist whose framework of ideas would have been unthinkable without the inspiration of the classical expertise created by the Florentines. In 1431 when he was a lecturer in rhetoric at Pavia, Valla produced his book *On Pleasure*, which, with Alberti's *On the Family*, is the most remarkable of the fifteenth-century dialogues. *On Pleasure* was written in Latin, since Valla's devotion to the classics never allowed him to write in any other language. The book, which is a satirical exposé of the humanist world written from within, consists of a dialogue between three main speakers. Two of them are Florentine humanists, Leonardo Bruni speaking for Stoic virtue and Niccoli for Christian faith, and the third was a humanist known for his obscene poetry, Panormita, who represented Epicurean pleasure. Bruni is a grave and pretentious censor of human failing, defending an abstract attachment to absolute virtue in a wicked world. Panormita defends sensual pleasure in all its physical manifestations, which allows him to indulge in long passages of celebration of sexual lust. He recommends the more frequent public exhibition of the nude female body and argues that fornication and adultery should be encouraged. The institution of female chastity owes its origins to old men who are too thin-blooded to appreciate the deprivation they are causing and too mean to pay dowries for their daughters.

Though it is amusingly written and intended to entertain, the aim of *On Pleasure* was to demolish the Stoic idea that the pursuit of virtue is an absolute end in itself. Panormita puts forward the contrasting view that virtues are not ends in themselves but only means towards the superior end of obtaining pleasure, which can be identified with utility. When these opinions have been presented,

Niccoli, the Christian exponent, caps them by arguing that the only true good end is the felicity of the Christian heaven. This view he defends with an absurdly satirical description of the sensual joys of heaven that was no doubt intended to ridicule devotional literature. The real philosophical point that Valla was making was not the Christian one but the Epicurean destruction of the high-minded stoicism that had become a common conviction of the Florentine humanists.

On Pleasure contains linguistic arguments used to back up the moral position. The late Roman philosopher Boethius, a powerful authority throughout the Middle Ages, was criticised by one of the speakers for using the word 'good' in a way that confused two quite separate things: the good action and the ultimate good towards which men aim. Valla was critical of his humanist contemporaries, critical of the translators of Aristotle, so influential in medieval universities, and of Aristotle himself. The writers he admired, in true humanist fashion, were the Roman writers Cicero and Quintilian, and the Christian fathers, like Augustine, who presented Christianity in a truer light than their successors, the university schoolmen. This attitude was based partly on common sense, and partly on Valla's profound philological sense of the meaning of Latin and Greek, which was the basis of his scholarly reputation. The book for which he has been best remembered in modern times is the *Donation of Constantine*. That document, purporting to be the Emperor Constantine's grant of land and jurisdiction to the pope in the fourth century, was one of the common authorities on which modern popes founded their claims to temporal power. The document was in fact an early medieval forgery and Valla proved that it was a forgery by historical and philological arguments.

In later years Valla turned towards arguments of serious theological and philosophical import in which he used his linguistic expertise to criticise Latin and Greek writings. He collected notes on the Latin translation of the Greek New Testament which he never published but which were discovered many years later by Erasmus, with important consequences, because Erasmus' text of the Greek New Testament was based on them. He also wrote, though again he did not publish it, the *Dialectical Disputations* in which he set out to demonstrate the invalidity of the terminology of Aristotelian philosophy as used by scholastic philosophers in universities, in effect to discredit the whole apparatus and method of contemporary scholasticism and to show that Aristotle, so revered, was an emperor without any clothes. The argument is again linguistic and philosophical. Valla argued that the scholastics had not understood the Greek of Aristotle when they translated it into Latin and that many of Aristotle's ideas, such as the idea that a good quality is a mean between two evils, were absurd.

Valla aimed at a highly paid position at the papal court which he eventually obtained. For that reason he did not publish many of the theological and philosophical arguments that might have brought him discredit. His writings demonstrate the philosophical half-heartedness of the new humanism of the early fifteenth century, which revolutionised attitudes based on a scholarly understanding of the ancient world but carefully avoided a collision with ecclesiastical authority by not carrying the ideas to their logical conclusion. The humanist revolution was a one-sided affair that did not dare to present a whole new vision of the world. Valla was right to criticise Bruni but he offered nothing better himself. In spite of this limitation, by the middle of the fifteenth century the Florentine school with its Roman adjunct had created a new art, history and political thought, and shown the possibilities of a critical approach to scripture. This constituted in effect a new culture, widely divergent from Europe's medieval background, which set the European mind moving in a new direction.

CHAPTER THREE

FLEMISH PAINTING

IN THE FIRST HALF OF THE fifteenth century, two revolutions in painting were taking place simultaneously but independently from one another. One was in Tuscany, the other in the Netherlands. Both movements were concerned with developing the realistic depiction of space and of the human figure. But the kinds of naturalism that they adopted differed considerably, as did the casts of mind which lay behind the two schools. During the period of the artistic revolution in the North, from 1420 to 1480, Tuscans and Flemings learned something from one another, but the movements were essentially separate. Early Netherlandish painting displays unmistakably the faces and bodies of Northerners, the awkwardness of postures derived from earlier medieval art, a relative indifference to the idea of a unified space, a great interest in landscape, an acute religious intensity, and a close attention to physical detail derived from the practice of the illuminators of manuscripts, characteristics that give it a different impact from the work of contemporary Italians. By the sixteenth century, however, the two movements were combined to some extent in the painting schools of both Italy and the Netherlands.

The amalgamation of Northern thought and art with Italian ideas did not really happen before the days of Dürer and Erasmus at the end of the fifteenth century. The humanist pope Pius II, Aeneas Sylvius, who spent some time in Germany in the mid-fifteenth century, thought it was because Northern princes 'pay more attention to

horses and dogs than to poets, and thus neglecting the arts they die unremembered like their own beasts'. Whether or not they liked poetry, there was certainly plenty of patronage of painting by the Burgundian dukes. Its most important effects are visible in portraits and in the painting of landscape. Netherlandish landscape was a new view of the countryside, inspired partly by the love of nature, animals and the seasons which had not affected so deeply the Italian imagination. It flourished in towns, where painters who worked for confraternities and merchants observed the world romantically with a city dweller's eye, and as a result of an interest in hunting, agriculture and the forest. Eventually the movement influenced the Italians and was to some extent incorporated into Italian painting.

For the background to Flemish art we have to look at illuminated manuscripts. These are, of course, in almost every way a different kind of art from painting on large panels or frescoes on walls. They are small in scale – even the grandest illuminations were restricted to the size of a page in a book – and tend to encourage a concentration on minute detail rather than on sweeping structures. They are also more exclusive, as a book can be read by only one person at a time and the reader who could pay a first-class illuminator would have to have been a wealthy man interested in giving pleasure to himself and a small circle. The best illumination, therefore, tends towards extreme refinement and an appeal to the tastes of an artistocratic audience. Hence the fairy castles and the exquisitely dressed

Purification of the Virgin,
from Très Riches Heures, *Limbourg brothers, 1413-16*
(Musée Condé, Chantilly)

Plate for September *from* Très Riches Heures,
Limbourg Brothers, 1413-16 (Musée Condé, Chantilly)

ladies of the Limbourg miniatures. This was not the same audience that the Netherlandish panel painters had to satisfy. They did sometimes paint for the Duke of Burgundy or other noblemen, and the chapels they painted belonged to the well-to-do. But they were town-dwellers, involved in the life of the cities and quite considerably influenced by the common scenes of city and country life in Flanders, Brabant and surrounding districts.

The aristocratic art of illumination reached its high point in the work of those who produced books for French noblemen in the reign of King Charles VI (1380–1422). The collapse of French court culture with the invasion by Henry V of England in 1415 ended this period rather suddenly, but for a while the French nobility patronised an artistic movement that might be regarded as the culmination of the medieval art of illumination. The two most remarkable artists, both working in the early fifteenth century, were, firstly, the anonymous Master of the

Boucicaut Hours, the book owned by Jean Boucicaut, Marshal of France, and secondly the Limbourg brothers who produced the *Très Riches Heures* for the Duke of Berri, uncle of the king.

An important historical fact about the extravagantly romantic paintings of the *Très Riches Heures* is that they took over the command of space and figure that had been acquired by the Sienese and Florentine artists of the fourteenth century. The most famous example of this borrowing from the Italians is the painting of the *Purification of the Virgin*. This shows the Virgin, carrying her Child, approaching a flight of steps leading up to a rather elaborate temple in which the priests are waiting. It has distinct resemblances to the fresco of the *Presentation of the Virgin* painted by a successor of Giotto, Taddeo Gaddi, in Santa Croce at Florence in the 1330s, which is dominated by a complex perspective drawing of an elaborate temple at the top of a flight of steps. It is difficult to resist the conclusion that one of the Limbourg brothers had seen and been impressed by Gaddi's fresco and adapted its scheme. Throughout the *Très Riches Heures* there is evidence that the artists had adopted Italian practices. One of the most interesting paintings in the book, which contrasts with the brightly lit scenes of meadows and castles, is the full-page illustration of *Christ in Gethsemane* after he has uttered the words, 'I am he.' This is a night scene and the impression of a landscape lit by the stars and moon is conveyed realistically. The bodies of the stunned soldiers who have fallen to the ground are shown with foreshortened torsos and limbs such as are found also in contemporary Italian painting. Though this scene contains no buildings or elaborate landscape, the use of light and the figure-painting constitute an advanced exercise in realism.

The *Très Riches Heures* exhibits other characteristics that show less the influence of Italy. Distinctions of social class are emphasised. The ladies and gentlemen parading in their long robes in the pages set aside for the months of April and May clearly belong to the top class, while the peasants are pulling up their skirts to warm themselves before the fire in February and the tattered labourers are ploughing and preparing the fields in March. Buildings, which are often identifiable – St Michael fights the dragon, for example, above the monastery of Mont Saint Michel – have nevertheless an air of fairy distance and delicacy that belongs to the Northern tradition of chivalric romance in which knights ride forth to seek castles hidden in the forest. Perhaps most Northern of all and most important for the future is the elaborate landscape in the pictures. It contains a large element of fantasy, but it is displayed with a rich and varied attention to detail unlike any earlier treatment of landscape.

BURGUNDY

The Netherlandish panel painting of the fifteenth century, which succeeded the work of the great illuminators, was a product of the peculiar social and political circumstances of modern Belgium and Holland. Like Tuscany, the Netherlands was a world of cities. Ghent, Bruges, Antwerp and other towns, clustered around the mouth of the Rhine and in the flatland to the north of Paris, had an industrial and commercial culture that was probably wealthier than that of the cities of northern Italy or any other part of Europe. These cities had long been the centres of Europe's major cloth industry which, though it was in decline in the fifteenth century, gave way to a more complex industrial network, manufacturing many things from tapestries to clocks. The portrait of a city in Flanders or Brabant is painted in the background of many Netherlandish paintings and, as a result, has become our standard image of a medieval town. It is a complex setting which opens onto countryside but also contains intricate representations of churches, houses and harbours. Netherlandish culture's physical form and its products in metal and cloth mark it as the ancestor of modern industrial society in a more direct

Mérode Altarpiece,
Campin, c.1425-30
(Cloisters Collection 1956, Metropolitan Museum of Art, New York)

sense than the tightly concentric communities of Italy that were descended from the cities of the ancient world.

For most of the fifteenth century Flanders and Brabant were ruled by dukes of Burgundy who also governed Burgundy itself and the northern provinces of the Netherlands, Holland and Zeeland. Between 1419, when they quarrelled severely with their relatives the kings of France, and 1477, when the line of dukes was extinguished by the death of Duke Charles the Bold, Burgundy was a separate state and was for some of that time the most powerful state in Europe. After 1477 the French dukes were succeeded by the German Habsburg Maximilian who became Holy Roman Emperor and attached the Netherlands to his possessions in and around Austria. Whilst Florence, Siena and Venice were totally independent states, the Netherlandish cities were enmeshed in feudal

principalities. The Duke of Burgundy was also Count of Flanders and Duke of Brabant and, though Bruges and Antwerp had a good deal of independence, they were also subject to the Duke's court.

Netherlandish high culture, in spite of the fact that it stemmed from a rich industrial society, was not so completely the creation of the city as was the culture of contemporary Florence and Venice. The Netherlandish cities had their religious movements like the Brethren of the Common Life, but produced no great urban humanism. In northern Europe the intellectual monopoly of the Church was stronger. Unlike most Florentine painters the Netherlanders were very affected simultaneously by town patronage and the patronage of the duke or another nobleman. Unlike the Florentines they were not, during the fifteenth century at least, obsessed by the framework of the city with its classical buildings. But it was also the case that Netherlandish painters were sometimes patronised by Italian merchants, who were prominent in Bruges and provided a link between Netherlandish and Italian painting.

CAMPIN AND VAN EYCK

The great movement of Flemish painting was initiated by two contemporaries, Robert Campin and Jan Van Eyck, who painted under rather different patronage conditions. Campin, who died in 1444, worked in the town of Tournai, on the southern border of Flanders. He played an active part in the city politics and was condemned for leading a dissolute life with a mistress. Although his punishment was mitigated by the intervention of Countess Jacqueline of Hainault, the indications are that he worked mainly for the well-to-do of Tournai and Flanders rather than the nobility. Apart from its high quality, the most striking feature of his painting is the direct representation of the interiors of middle-class houses. Campin is the propagator of the long tradition of Netherlandish *genre* painting.

Two paintings of the late 1420s indicate his style. The *Mérode Altarpiece* is a triptych whose three panels show, on the left, the donor and his wife, in the middle the Annunciation, and on the right St Joseph. It contains obscure and complex traditional symbolism. St Joseph, portrayed as a carpenter, makes mousetraps, an evocation of the idea, derived from St Augustine, that the Passion of Christ is a snare baited with his blood to catch Satan. The flat piece of wood in which he is boring holes with a brace and bit might be the bottom of a press for grapes suggesting that Christ is squeezed and his blood becomes the wine of the Eucharist. The room in which the Annunciation takes place is lit by seven of the sun's rays entering on the left wall, with a miniature crucified Christ carried on one of them to indicate that the whole life and Passion of Christ enters the Virgin's body with his conception. The lily, the candle, the cushion on the bench are all connected

Salting Madonna,
Campin, c.1435 (National Gallery, London)

symbolically with the Annunciation. The mysterious figure by the door in the wall of the left wing who bears a badge with the arms of the town of Malines has been rather improbably thought to be the prophet Isaiah.

Nevertheless it is also clear that Campin is presenting us with a faithful picture of the Flemish urban world. The Annunciation does not take place in princely circumstances. The room is solid but modest and, apart from the gothic and ornamental details necessary for the conception of Christ, an ordinary interior. The settee which the Virgin leans against is of a type common in the Netherlands. Joseph appears to be in a carpenter's shop, tools on the

59

Portraits of a Man and Woman,
Campin, c.1430 (National Gallery, London)

bench, mousetrap exposed for sale, a view of a city square through the windows. The donors, who are of equal size with the biblical figures, kneel before a door that appears to lead into the main room. Campin has intended to present us with realistic, ordinary scenes made extraordinary by the presence of the angel and by the work's symbolism.

The *Salting Madonna* is a simpler single panel. A Madonna sits facing us, the Child on her knees, preparing to suckle the infant. Again it is not difficult to find symbolical elements in the painting: the chalice at the Virgin's elbow, the gothic carving on the chest on which her arm rests, the lions at the corners of her settee indicating that it is her throne, the plaited firescreen behind her head that provides a halo. But this is also a domestic scene. The Madonna has an admirable physical solidity; she looks like a well-fed mother. The room with its tiled floor is for the most part simply representative. So is the view of the city through the window. This painting and the *Mérode Altarpiece* both contain an abundance of theologically significant detail, and give a rather plain picture of the Flemish world.

Campin's capacity to paint the world as he saw it, however, is perhaps most strikingly displayed in his portraits. The two portraits, a man and a woman, probably man and wife, in London's National Gallery show his skill in capturing the personalities of his sitters. Both are dressed fairly simply: the man has a turban thrown around his head, the woman a white wimple. The faces are the centres of attention. The man is middle-aged with an expression of intelligent, sensitive indecision. The woman is still more remarkable. Her younger, plumper face has an immediately recognisable combination of bossy decision with slightly anxious uncertainty. There are no such delicate and complete portrayals of character from an earlier time. These faces may not have the complexity of Rembrandt's portraits but they strike one as authentic people whose forms of expression and behaviour we can imagine.

Campin's contemporary Jan Van Eyck had a very different kind of career and had much more intellectual weight. He worked for Philip the Good, Duke of Burgundy from 1425 until his death in 1441, a period that covers all his known works. Philip was godfather to his son and a dispute about his salary provoked a letter from the Duke saying that 'we could find no other artist to our liking who is so accomplished in his art and science'. Van Eyck was several times sent on missions abroad for the Duke. In one case the purpose of his journey was to paint a portrait of a Portuguese princess whom the Duke was thinking of marrying. He may also have been sent to produce maps or perhaps drawings of the Holy Land in connection with Philip's unrealised interest in a crusade.

Van Eyck travelled to Portugal with the nobleman Baudoin de Lannoy, the subject of a notable portrait. The repetition in inscriptions in his paintings of a quotation from the *Book of Wisdom*, 'she is more beautiful than the sun...' in Latin, applied to the Virgin, suggests that he was an educated painter. It has often been thought that the *Man in a Red Turban*, with an intelligent stubbled face, is actually a self-portrait and another portrait is certainly his wife. Van Eyck comes to us as a more substantial, individualised personality than his predecessors; with him the Northern artist begins to emerge out of the mists of the past as did his contemporary Donatello in Florence.

But we know nothing about him which helps in the interpretation of his works. The obvious characteristics of Van Eyck's painting are that it portrays in a highly realistic way both figure and space, building up its realism out of minute detail. Though there are no manuscripts that can confidently be assigned to him, his painting looks as though it had grown out of manuscript illustration. But the minute

Baudoin de Lannoy,
Van Eyck, 1435 (Gemäldegalerie, Staatliche Museen, Berlin)

61

Arnolfini Marriage,
detail, Van Eyck, 1434 (National Gallery, London)

detail is not there for its own sake; it is often used to convey a complex message that may be symbolic or may remain baffling. For instance the *Arnolfini Marriage* presents us with a man and woman, who may or may not be a Lucchese merchant called Giovanni Arnolfini and his wife, facing us hand in hand, the woman apparently pregnant. Behind them on the wall is a mirror, above it the inscription '*Johannes de Eyck fuit hic 1434*', 'Jan Van Eyck was here 1434'. The painting of the convex mirror on the wall behind the pair is a remarkable piece of miniaturist technical brilliance, surrounded by ten small circles each containing a tiny scene from the Passion. The mirror itself shows the backs of the man and woman and beyond them two more people. Are they witnesses to a marriage or were they put there as extra decoration without significance? We can easily imagine the domestic and religious symbolism intended by the bed, the rosary, the brush, and the statuette of St Margaret, patroness of pregnant women, and we can enjoy the

Madonna of Chancellor Rolin,
Van Eyck, c.1435 (Louvre, Paris)

exquisite treatment of the chandelier, the window and the clothes, but, quite apart from the names of the chief characters, which perhaps do not matter much, the central intention of the painting remains obscure.

A similar case of obscurity, this time in the treatment of a clearly religious subject for a very wealthy patron, is provided by the *Madonna of Chancellor Rolin*. Rolin was a notable administrator, the chief servant of the Duke. Here he kneels at a prie-dieu looking across to the space on the other side of the picture in which the Virgin sits with her Child on her knee and an angel holding a crown above her head. They are in a space surrounded by Romanesque arcading. Through the arcade at the back we look down on an extensive, minutely painted landscape. It is not surprising or unprecedented to find a donor in the same space as the Virgin and Child to whom he prays, but most of the further implications of this design are unclear. What is Rolin looking at? Not the Virgin or the Child. Is there an altar in the space outside the painting? Above Rolin's head are capitals at the tops of pillars around the room on which are carved episodes from Genesis, the expulsion from Eden, Cain and Abel, Noah and his sons. Presumably these are intended to characterise him as a victim, like other members of the human race, of the development of original sin. The scene on the capital above Mary's hand is partly obscured by the crown and impossible to identify. Is it an Old Testament scene prefiguring the Passion of Christ? The hem of the Virgin's robes bears embroidered lettering which can be partly read and seems to consist of passages from the Psalms and the Book of Ecclesiastes taken from the service of matins. Their significance in the painting is not clear, nor is the placing of the crown on the Virgin's head. The space has three sides formed by triple Romanesque arches, very likely triple because of the Trinity and perhaps Romanesque because of Van Eyck's interest in earlier styles of church architecture. We look out apparently to a garden with peacocks, though it seems to be high above ground level. This may be the Enclosed Garden sometimes associated with the Virgin, but we have difficulty in explaining the two figures with their backs to us looking out of it over the wall. The landscape beyond is divided by a river. One side looks like a village set in green fields, the other a great city with tall buildings. Does this, as some have thought, constitute a reference to the Heavenly and Earthly Cities? The whole of this masterpiece is painted with exquisite, pleasure-giving precision. But its meaning may have been as obscure to contemporaries as it is to modern scholars.

A different kind of puzzlement is produced by Van Eyck's pictures of the Virgin in a church. The most famous are the *Annunciation* (Washington) and the *Virgin and Child in a Church* (Berlin). In both cases the aim is evidently to establish a complex relationship between the Virgin and the building. In the case of the *Virgin and Child,* both the figures and the church are painted with considerable realism but the Virgin is a gigantic figure taller than the arches of the nave. Van Eyck presumably intended to imply that in a figurative sense, with which medieval theologians would have sympathised, the Virgin is the Church and therefore it is proper for her form mystically to fill what appears to be a cathedral. In the work of painters before the fifteenth century this would not seem strange because we would expect symbolism rather than realism. In the painting of Van Eyck, who is so laboriously convincing in dealing with both figures and space, it becomes a convention more difficult to accept. Scholars have pointed out that in the *Virgin and Child* the light of the sun seems to enter the church from the north, a deliberate reversal of physical reality to symbolise the supernatural illumination of the Virgin and her Church. Van Eyck appears to have been fascinated by the complexity and grandeur of late medieval church-building and the church is painted with exact attention to the detail of gothic architecture. But the source of the light is a large and deliberate irrationality, matching the other irrationality of the size of the Virgin.

In the *Annunciation*, where the size of the figures is more normal, we have a curious, presumably deliberate, architectural absurdity. The upper parts of the building are Romanesque, the lower gothic, a reversal of the real history of architecture. The aim is probably to stress that the Virgin's conception descends from heaven. A different kind of complication appears on the floor, another exhibition by Van Eyck of detailed miniature painting with an intricate message. The floor of the nave has paving of inscribed slabs displaying line-drawings, not uncommon in late-medieval churches, partly covered by the robes of the Madonna and the Archangel. Those drawings which can be seen clearly enough are apparently episodes from the lives of David and Samson; in other words they present the pre-Christian world and also the human strife that Mary stands upon, subduing it.

It is impossible to understand fully this imagination

Virgin and Child in a Church,
Van Eyck, 1437-8 (Gemäldegalerie, Staatliche Museen, Berlin)

which appears to be made up of two such contradictory aspects. Van Eyck's portraits, on the other hand, are masterpieces of reportage. The *Man in a Red Turban* and *Margaret Van Eyck* are both characters recorded without concessions to imaginary beauty or amiability. Van Eyck captures vividly individual personality, displaying an empiricism that is more obvious here than in his interiors or landscapes. But the visual precision was combined in the other pictures, which are not portraits, with passages of elaborate code language, that can be interpreted according to preference as survival of traditional modes of thought or as spiritualism.

The most elaborate painting with which Van Eyck was associated, and one of the most grandiose pieces of medieval panel painting, was the *Ghent Altarpiece of the Adoration of the Lamb*, produced jointly by Jan and his less well-known brother Hubert. It is a large altarpiece with hinged doors painted on both sides, making up twenty-four different panels. When it is closed we see the kneeling donors with an Annunciation above them. When opened it reveals a broad panorama of the Adoration of the Lamb in the lower half, in the upper God in Majesty with the Virgin and John the Baptist, Adam and Eve. Because of its size and

Annunciation,
Van Eyck, 1435-7
(Andrew W. Mellon Collection, National Gallery of Art, Washington)

66

Man in a Red Turban,
Van Eyck, 1433 (National Gallery, London)

complexity the *Ghent Altarpiece* is an extreme demonstration of the virtues and limitations of Flemish painting. Many of its details are wonderful. Adam and Eve are beautiful nudes even if Eve, with her large belly and hips, fits firmly into the non-Mediterranean type. The paradisal landscape, the setting of the Adoration of the Lamb, is filled not only with many figures, some of them portraits, but with a mass of precisely painted vegetation. The broad room in which the Annunciation takes place, quite apart from its complex symbolism, is a clearly devised piece of internal spatial perspective. But the total design of the altarpiece is a collection of particulars which, although its theological purpose is fairly clear, does not add up to an aesthetically satisfactory whole. It differs in this respect, for example, from Michelangelo's Sistine ceiling, a total design that has artistic as well as theological symmetry. Some may feel that

Margaret Van Eyck,
Van Eyck, 1434 (Groeningemuseum, Bruges)

Ghent Altarpiece,
Van Eyck, completed 1432 (St Bavo Cathedral, Ghent)

in the *Ghent Altarpiece* the artist has not been successful in investing his subject with either grandeur or beauty, however effective the crowds of worshippers in the landscape around it may appear. The tendency towards creating a theologically significant visual machine out of a collection of meaningful particulars, in contrast to the pattern-forming instinct of Mediterranean art, was a constant aesthetic feature of Northern art, until it allowed itself to be taken over by Italian ideas.

BOSCH AND GRÜNEWALD

Though the comparison may at first sight seem odd, it is worth looking at Van Eyck's painting beside that of a very different artist of a later generation, Hieronymus Bosch

(d. 1516). Van Eyck's pictures have a kind of religious inwardness and are often a collection of related panels that are not easily seen as an artistic whole, as in the *Ghent Altarpiece*. Both the mysteriousness and the awkward complication of design are to some extent features of the Northern art world. Bosch may not have been such a technically perfect painter as Van Eyck – there is nothing in his work to compare with, say, the *Arnolfini Marriage* and some of his work seems closer to cartoon art – but like Van Eyck, he was a man of intense religious seriousness and orthodoxy who used his painting for the individual expression of that attitude. Also, to a much greater extent, he was an exponent of the generous untidiness of the Northern imagination. The combination of this

Ecce Homo,
Bosch, c.1480 (Stadtlisches Kunstinstitut, Frankfurt)

characteristic with moral austerity and a tendency to refer to an underworld of symbols and popular moral lore makes one inclined to regard Bosch, in spite of his peculiarity, as a prime example of an artist even more rooted in Netherlandish life than artists more affected by the traditional piety appropriate to ecclesiastical commissions.

As far as we know, Bosch lived in 's Hertogenbosch, a small town in northern Brabant, now Holland. The life of that area, together with the Netherlandish asceticism expressed in Thomas à Kempis' *Imitation of Christ* and the ideals of the Brethren of the Common Life, must have influenced the work of both Bosch and Van Eyck.

Bosch's art is savagely pessimistic, disabused and critical of human failings. An example of this attitude that requires no elaborate explanation is his painting *Ecce Homo*. The Christ brought before the crowd is a harmless-looking man, almost naked, bent, smeared with blood from his tortures. He is surrounded by smug, self-satisfied, prosperous, hard-faced, ugly, jeering humanity, enjoying the spectacle.

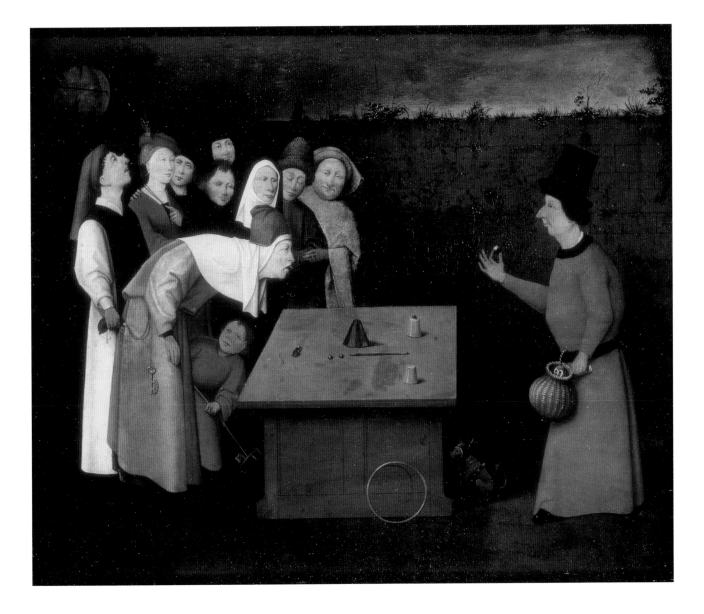

Bosch's faces are disfigured by cruel wickedness which sometimes makes his paintings appear as unreasonable, even pessimistic, comments on the human race. But he also painted comic scenes. In *The Conjuror*, which may be a copy, a frog is being made to come out of the victim's mouth while the conjuror's assistant removes his purse. The expression of combined sanctimoniousness and crookedness on the conjuror's face is memorable.

In addition to these readily understandable features, Bosch also presents difficulties. Some of his paintings are infested with weird hybrid organisms made up of combinations of men, animals, plants and utensils. They may have been inspired originally by simpler hybrids that are sometimes found in decorations to manuscripts, but in Bosch they are both comically pervasive and carried to bizarre extremes. His paintings also contain strange structures made up of globes and huge plants, fruits or shellfish. It is possible that these fantasies were inspired by knowledge of texts of alchemy or astrology, both widespread and generally respectable sciences in his day. But in spite of substantial scholarly effort, their meaning remains unclear and large parts of Bosch's painting have not been properly explained. This does not necessarily mean, however, that the essential message is obscure. In most cases Bosch was warning against the hellish disasters that will face men as a result of their natural inclination to folly and lust.

The grandest of Bosch's designs is the *Garden of Earthly Delights*. Like many other religious works this is a triptych with closing doors, but its contents are highly original. When the triptych is closed it shows a globe, with God looking down on it, containing a section of idyllic landscape with no man visible and an angry sky above. Perhaps the globe signifies the earth in the early days of creation when the waters of the Deluge were receding. The implication is that the subject of the painting is early humanity. When the triptych is opened a fantastic riot of colours and shapes is revealed. On the left panel is a delightful landscape with a large number of birds and animals. In the foreground a nude man and woman are being blessed by a robed clerical or divine figure. In the central panel, which is the largest, crowds of nude men and women are apparently exploiting nature and giving way enthusiastically to their baser instincts. In the centre young women are bathing in a pool and looking out at a procession of males circling around on a variety of animals. In the lower part of the panel men and women mingle, playing and making love. Adam and Eve look on gloomily from the lower right-hand corner. The third, right-hand panel is a scene of catastrophe, destruction and punishment. It is night. Buildings are burning; soldiers march across the bridge; crowds flee. In the foreground individual figures are subjected to bizarre tortures.

Many of the details in these panels are obscure, but the message that Bosch wished to convey is plain enough: man's enjoyment of the physical world that was granted to him is vitiated by lust which will be punished by demons in the most stringent manner.

The prevalence of religious elements in many of Bosch's paintings shows that his comment on human conduct is theological, not merely psychological. Some of his other pictures are much closer to normality than the *Garden of Earthly Delights*. For example, *St John on Patmos*, which shows the saint absorbed in a vision while the world is destroyed about him, contains a few strong touches typical of Bosch but is not fundamentally different from Memling's painting of the same scene which would be regarded by many as a rather tame work. In other works fantasy and comedy abound in a manner far removed from the usual atmosphere of ecclesiastical art. But the teaching is essentially the same as that offered in Last Judgments, and Bosch's manner only serves to reveal more of the underlying fears which elsewhere are smoothed over by the conventionalism of religious images. Bosch was an expert painter who had no difficulty in conforming with the normal standards when he wanted to do so. The sexual and moral frankness and the folk element in his work enable it to express more strongly than that of other artists the elements of cruelty and distortion in the Northern artists' view of human nature in contrast with the calmer aestheticism of the Italians.

A long way to the south of 's Hertogenbosch one of the most powerful of all altarpieces was designed in about 1515 by Mathias Grünewald for the Antonine monks who ran a hospital at Isenheim in Alsace. The *Isenheim Altarpiece* is one of the masterpieces of Northern art but, as in the case of Bosch's works, it is strange to think that it was produced

RIGHT Garden of Earthly Delights,
Bosch, c.1510-15 (Prado, Madrid)

72

Crucifixion, Isenheim Altarpiece,
Grünewald, c.1515 (Musée d'Unterlinden, Colmar)

during the period when Dürer's importation of Italian methods was well under way. It belongs entirely to the world of Teutonic pietism. Like Van Eyck's *Ghent Altarpiece*, it is a complicated structure of large panels, which can be opened to reveal three quite different sets of scenes: one which centres on the Crucifixion, one whose central painting is of the Nativity, and finally one in which the centre is a sculpture of the enthroned St Anthony (appropriate for the order running the hospital) with paintings on either side of the *Temptation of St Anthony* and *St Anthony's meeting with St Paul*.

The *Crucifixion*, which descends from many other gruesome crucifixions depicted in the later Middle Ages, is a terrifying portrait of a tortured and disfigured body nailed to the cross in the agony before death, its discoloured skin marked by the wounds inflicted by the thorns. The *Nativity* on the other hand is a scene of radiant joy, with a delightful landscape stretching back behind the Enclosed Garden associated with the Virgin, and to its right is a panel of the *Resurrection* in which the head of the Saviour is shaded into the light which surrounds it, not a halo but a heavenly brilliance. In the third set of panels the *Temptation of St Anthony* shows the saint prostrate, tormented by a host of hybrid monsters reminiscent of the creations of Bosch.

Nativity, Isenheim Altarpiece,
Grünewald, c.1515 (Musée d'Unterlinden, Colmar)

Grünewald was schooled in the techniques of figure-composition and perspective. The kinds of naturalism which these methods implied, however, had little interest for him: the sizes of his figures vary in an irrational fashion and natural scenes merge into mystical visions. Many of the detailed components of his scenes remain mysterious. The area of which this is most obviously true is the portion on the left side of the *Nativity* panel, where a heavenly orchestra plays beneath a structure resembling a tabernacle, with a group of beings, perhaps Lucifer and the fallen angels, behind them. The relationship between these figures of the *Nativity* is unclear. Grünewald's aim was to represent

the cruelty of temporal suffering, to which the patients in the hospital were condemned, and the joy of spiritual salvation to which they might aspire as a result of the Crucifixion. This message required an untidy complex of images drawn from the religious experience of his world. The decaying wasteland in which St Anthony meets St Paul and the awkwardly rendered ecstasy of the Virgin are both remote from the ordered beauty of Italian painting. Though these projections of Northern life and thought were combined with the Italian vision in the fifteenth and early sixteenth century, they stand apart from it in the inelegance of their spiritual intensity. The point of this temporary

75

Entombment,
Van der Weyden, c.1450 (Uffizi, Florence)

diversion from early Flemish painting to Bosch and Grünewald, half a century later, is to emphasise the great difference between the Italian and Northern worlds, which were eventually amalgamated to some extent when the Italian Renaissance was adopted in the North without a loss of the Northern sense of pitiful common humanity.

VAN DER WEYDEN AND VAN DER GOES

Most people would agree that Netherlandish painting reached its height in the work of Rogier van der Weyden (d. 1464), a younger contemporary of Van Eyck and probably the pupil of Campin, and Hugo van der Goes

(d. 1482). This was the generation immediately following Van Eyck. Like other Netherlandish painters, Rogier was patronised both by noblemen – though not as much as Van Eyck – and by townsmen. He was successful and well-to-do and had relations with Italian customers too, encouraged in part by his journey to Rome for the jubilee of 1450. The *Entombment*, which may have been painted for the Medici, is an obvious adaptation of the design of a painting by Fra Angelico. His style is, however, wholly Netherlandish. He has all the precise miniaturism, the relative indifference to spatial perspective and symmetrical design, the complex liveliness of other Netherlanders. He also has distinct peculiarities that are quite different from those of Van Eyck. One of his pictures, *St Luke Painting the Virgin*, might almost be taken as a parody of Van Eyck's *Madonna of Chancellor Rolin*. It has the same trio of a mortal kneeling before the Virgin and Child in a space with a triple window looking out on an enclosed garden and below it an urban scene divided by a river. Rogier might be saying, 'Van Eyck baffled us with Rolin looking away from the Virgin. Here is someone plainly looking at the Virgin because he is painting her.' His extraordinary *Altarpiece of the Seven Sacraments*, in which all of them – baptism, confirmation, penance, Eucharist, holy orders, marriage and extreme

unction – are taking place simultaneously in the church with a bed provided for the recipient of unction in a side-chapel, has some similarity with Van Eyck's *Virgin and Child in a Church*. It also contains a Calvary with figures twice as large as the mortals involved in the sacraments. But there is no mystery in Rogier's work. The subject is a 'mystery' but its presentation is straightforward.

The first major characteristic of Rogier's painting is the intense depiction of character and emotion in the faces. Though Campin and Van Eyck were considerable portraitists, the faces in their religious paintings do not equal Rogier's in this respect. He provides a stronger

St Luke Painting the Virgin,
Van der Weyden, c.1432-6 (Museum of Fine Arts, Boston)

Descent from the Cross,
Van der Weyden, c.1436-7 (Prado, Madrid)

expression of the individual emotion that forms the content of religious subjects. The second important feature is the capacity for pattern-making. Rogier's paintings are more complete and independent. In the *Descent from the Cross*, for example, a scene is packed into a frame that only just contains it laterally. It also offers only a shallow space in front of a wall that has depth for nothing more than the necessary figures. Christ has been brought down from the cross almost to the ground. His body is supported by Joseph of Arimathea. The Virgin swoons, held by St John and by one of the other Marys. What strikes us first is the interlocking pattern of the figures – the almost horizontal form of Christ's body repeated in that of his mother below him, the bent body of John at one end of the panel, balanced by the desperate, twisted figure of the Magdalen with clenched hands at the other end. No one had a greater capacity than Rogier for the depiction of tear-washed, taut faces, the plain, unvarnished, non-exhibitionist desolation

78

Columba Triptych,
Van der Weyden, c.1460 (Alte Pinakothek, Munich)

Philip the Good,
Van der Weyden, c.1460-61 (Koninklijk Museum, Antwerp)

picture of noble, regally generous, veneration of the baby Christ. This time the figures are placed before the Holy Family's shed in a much more elaborate and typically Flemish setting with a distant landscape stretching away to the rear and sufficient space in the foreground. The faces of the Magi are fine and serious, appropriate to their rank. The three figures descend before the Child in their varied poses creating a pattern: the back figure upright, the middle one genuflecting, the one in front kneeling to touch the babe. The Magus at the back is a particularly resplendent, erect nobleman displaying grandiloquent gestures, whose face is thought to bear the strong Gallic features, no doubt idealised, of the Duke of Burgundy's son Charles, who later became Charles the Bold, the last and most ambitious of the dukes.

Rogier's powerful faces appear both in religious scenes and portraits. *Philip the Good* is a great Flemish and mature face; evidently that of a likable man. The *Young Woman* in Berlin carries further the success of Campin in his female portrait in the National Gallery. Again we have the plump, eager face of a fairly young matron, but this time with a little more impenetrable subtlety in her expression. The Mary Magdalen in the *Braque Triptych* looks as if it has been painted from life and the face has been given a questioning, uncertain anxiety that lingers in the observer's mind. The art of portraiture in northern Europe does not make much advance on the quality of these highly individualised faces during the remainder of the Renaissance period.

Rogier made other advances in the spatial design of painting, notably in his elaboration of the scene framed by an ecclesiastical arch. This reached a new level in the three panels of the *St John Altarpiece* – the birth of John, the baptism of Christ, the beheading of John – in which the main figures are clustered in the archway or slightly in front of it in a very free use of space, while scenes stretch far back behind the arches to include landscape, complex interiors and other figures. He also pioneered the type of triptych in

of extreme sadness. There is little joy in his art whose subject is the seriousness of life. We see it here in all the faces, most movingly in St John and the Mary who is captured with her hand held to her face. The painting repays minute examination of the faces, which are rendered with striking realism and truth. The whole completely artificial arrangement of forms within a limited space is simultaneously a faithful depiction of humanity's suffering.

In a similar way the central panel of the *Columba Triptych*, which is an Adoration of the Magi, presents a

St John Altarpiece,
Van der Weyden, c.1440-45
(Gemäldegalerie, Staatliche Museen, Berlin)

which a single landscape, spanning all three panels, gives unity to the design of the whole. These spatial innovations were important for the design of future Netherlandish paintings but Rogier's particular significance in aesthetic history was his combination of emotional seriousness with psychological realism, so that the religious story became not so much an obscure mystery as a lived experience.

Hugo van der Goes' *Portinari Altarpiece* was painted in the mid-1470s for a member of Lorenzo de' Medici's commercial branch in Bruges, Tommaso Portinari, and

Portinari Altarpiece,
Van der Goes, c.1475-6 (Uffizi, Florence)

Portrait of a Young Woman,
Van der Weyden, c.1460 (Gemäldegalerie, Staatliche Museen, Berlin)

soon after brought back to Florence. It is one of the most ambitious Flemish paintings of the fifteenth century, and it was historically important that it was available to Florentine artists of the generations of Ghirlandaio and Leonardo da Vinci. It now stands in the same room in the Uffizi in Florence as its rough contemporary, the *Birth of Venus* by Botticelli, offering a demonstration of the contrasts between the two schools of Flanders and Tuscany. The outer panels contain the kneeling donors and their children with Saints Thomas, Anthony Abbot, Margaret and Mary Magdalen. The main central panel is a very elaborate Adoration of the Shepherds. The child lies on the ground,

the Virgin kneeling behind him, to the left the ox and the ass and St Joseph, to the right the shepherds. Hugo is more interested in presenting a wide range of significant detail than in painting a realistic scene. Miniature figures of angels abound; the position and pose of the Virgin are not very clear. But he is extremely concerned with lifelike painting of details that constitute a long catalogue of significant elements and episodes, ultimately providing an atmosphere rather than a theme. The shepherds are enthusiastic and crude labourers, prominent examples of the kind of class-consciousness that has a stronger place in Northern than in Italian painting. The backgrounds are complicated. For example, the top of the left-hand panel has two charming countryside scenes: the side of a country house set among trees, and a moving moment from the journey to Bethlehem of Joseph and the pregnant Mary, when she dismounts from the mule anxiously attended by her husband. Apart from the cheerfulness of the shepherds this is not a joyful picture. Mary's face is sad as she looks down at the fragile, naked child on the ground. The faces of the female saints and the children are strikingly beautiful, as is the distant landscape in all three panels. But sadness, apprehension and a resultant spirituality are dominant. From an aesthetic point of view, perhaps we should give most prominence to the extreme complexity of the whole painting which contains people in different stances, a wide variety of landscape, a subtle balance of figures but little attempt to provide symmetrical unity. There could not be a clearer attempt to place a vision of the events connected with the birth of Christ in a Northern setting.

Hugo not only became a monk a few years before he died in 1482 but also suffered from acute depression. The sombre atmosphere of the *Portinari Altarpiece* presumably reflected this. In spite of his melancholy nature, he had unprecedented success in designing dramatic crowd scenes, as in this altarpiece, which were not merely patterns of figures but represented complicated psychological tensions and emotions. Another remarkable painting, quite different in character, is the *Death of the Virgin*. The Virgin lies on a solid, square bed with a convincingly foreshortened face. The perspective of the room is imperfect, but the sense of interior space is nevertheless conveyed. In a half-circle of light above the Virgin hovers a mystical vision of flying angels and the Christ figure. The twelve elderly apostles who cluster around the bed are drawn as a remarkably varied group in different postures of prayer and regret. They are well-rounded forms set in a clearly modern spatial arrangement. It would be difficult to find a more convincing and satisfactory group of figures in paint before Leonardo's *Adoration of the Magi*.

Flemish artists had thus created, by the late fifteenth century, a style of painting which reached great heights in the depiction of individual character and religious emotion. As in Italian painting, the result was produced by a combination of ecclesiastical prescription with the artists' interest in naturalism and psychology. But the two schools were also made up of very different tendencies. It was the linking of the Italian and Northern approaches to life which was to produce some of the most important work in the later stages of the Renaissance, in the painting of Rubens and Rembrandt, and in the plays of Shakespeare. But, before that, there were to be some further considerable upheavals in the Italian scene.

LEFT Death of the Virgin,
Van der Goes, c.1481-2 (Groeningemuseum, Bruges)

CHAPTER FOUR

LAURENTIAN FLORENCE

THE REVOLUTIONARY MOVEMENT of the early Renaissance took place in republican Florence. The culmination of this movement in the 1430s in the writings of Bruni and Alberti, the sculpture of Donatello and the architecture of Brunelleschi coincided with the beginnings of Medici predominance in the city. Though the Medici were excluded from the city from 1494 to 1512, when there was an attempt to return to republicanism, their influence was never totally destroyed after Cosimo became powerful in 1434, and they were eventually to become dukes of Tuscany. From 1434 to 1494 Medici influence was continuously strong and, though Florence was certainly not a despotism like Milan and many other Italian cities, it was no longer a republic in quite the way that it had been before. It was now a quasi-republic in which one supremely powerful family commanded the majority of political support and was regarded externally as governing a sort of principality.

Medici power was based on wealth gained in commerce of a particularly sophisticated kind, the trade in money. In the early fifteenth century the Medici bank established a monopoly, which lasted for several decades, in the management of papal money. Since the papacy drew payments of various kinds from all over Europe, requiring the expertise of international money-changers like the Medici, this gave the firm a commanding position in ecclesiastical finance and to some extent in other movements of money as well. By the 1430s Cosimo de' Medici was one of the richest men in the city, the inheritor of a commercial power that gave him considerable political

influence. In 1433 he was expelled by his republican enemies who believed him to be a danger to the free regime. In 1434 he came back, carried irresistibly into power by his numerous dependents in the city and helped by his friendship with Pope Eugenius IV, who happened at that time to be himself an exile in Florence. Until his death in 1464 Cosimo remained a power behind the republican government. He was succeeded in that position by his short-lived son Piero de' Medici, until 1469, and then by his grandson, Lorenzo the Magnificent, who lived until 1492 and whose regime was at the centre of the movements described in this chapter.

During this period, 1434–94, the Medici held no princely office. In official terms they were ordinary private citizens. They survived in the republican state, which remained fully in existence, because their dominance was preferred by a substantial section of city families. They also adapted the republican regime to make their control easier, chiefly by increasing the importance of choice rather than lot in the selection of republican officials. This largely informal system of government was by no means secure. The Medici were always in danger of being ousted by their enemies and several times faced serious threats, the best-known being the Pazzi Conspiracy of 1478 which was produced by a combination of enemies in Florence and at the papal court. But until 1494 they were not overturned.

This was partly because both Cosimo and Lorenzo were men with considerable intelligence and political dexterity, and partly because their wealth gave power over other men. The circumstances of Italian politics also made it attractive to their fellow citizens to have the leadership of someone they could trust. Florence was still a relatively small state in a chaotic and dangerous peninsula, whose dangers were not easily overcome by a cumbrous republican system of government. Guidance gave greater security and comfort, relieving the Florentines of the expense of war and the fear of occupation by a foreign power. Cosimo was able to turn Florence around from its duel with Milan, which had lasted for decades, into alliance with that city. From 1454 to 1494 Florence enjoyed a long period of international peace without serious warfare within Italy and without invasion by the great powers beyond the Alps. In that last age of quiet isolation, before Italy was torn apart by the French and Spanish invasions that started in 1494, the Florentine Renaissance flourished.

Cosimo and Lorenzo were not only able politicians, they were also discerning patrons. This description is particularly appropriate for Cosimo who combined great wealth with a genuine interest in both classical literature and the arts. Cosimo fell under the spell of a belief in the spiritual value of truths to be gained from ancient literature, which could be revealed only with the help of a command of Greek. He was encouraged in this by his meetings with Greek churchmen and scholars who in 1439 attended the Council of Florence, which set up a fragile and quickly destroyed union of the Catholic and Greek Orthodox Churches. It was as a result of his romantic enthusiasm that, at the end of his life, Cosimo patronised the work of a young scholar, Marsilio Ficino, who in 1463 began his monumental task of translating the whole of Plato's works into Latin.

After the 1450s the Medici bank declined. Though Lorenzo built villas outside Florence, he never undertook expenditure comparable with that required by Cosimo's great building schemes within the city at San Lorenzo and San Marco. But he was a poet and a man with literary taste. In the contacts between the Medici and Brunelleschi,

Marsilio Ficino, bust,
Andrea Ferrucci da Fiesole, late fifteenth century
(Florence Cathedral)

Donatello, Ficino, Poliziano and Botticelli, in the Medici collection of ancient and modern art and manuscripts, Florence had, from 1434 to 1494, the embryo of a system of court patronage embedded informally within a republican society. It is difficult to think of a parallel case of a cultivated city governed for a long period by connoisseurs.

One of the few letters of artists surviving from such an early period was written by Domenico Veneziano to Piero de' Medici in 1438, asking for support in obtaining a commission from Piero's father Cosimo. Later in the fifteenth century Michelangelo was supposedly allowed to work as a youth among the ancient sculptures assembled in the Medici garden. Medici patronage, the significance of which was in part a legend developed in the sixteenth century, was genuinely important in supporting the aspirations of writers and artists. It is perhaps right to see some difference between the art of 1434 to 1494 and art produced in the more republican periods before and after. The poetry of Poliziano and some of the paintings of Botticelli suited the taste of the immensely rich Medici family in being both heavily classical and imbued with a superior elegance and frivolity.

Florence was also a rich and cultivated society. In the second half of the fifteenth century recovery from the demographic decline of the century following the Black Death was under way. Population and opportunities for trade were growing. Florence governed and taxed most of Tuscany and the wealth of the province flowed into the city. Upper-class Florentines were still unparalleled in their command of humanist culture. We have to take this general Florentine situation into account as well as the patronage of the Medici as we observe the wealth of new and avant-garde art that flooded the churches and palaces of the city in the later part of the century.

Lorenzo de' Medici was a leading politician, with an unrivalled influence in the city, a patron of poets, classicists and painters, and above all, the centre of a group of literary friends of great originality, who created a new intellectual movement, identified in particular with Ficino's Neoplatonism. The group has traditionally been known as the Platonic Academy, a phrase that should not be taken too seriously because it was not an academy in the modern sense of a formal institution. Nevertheless it was a group of friends who met frequently at the Medici palace in the city or at Medici villas in the country like the one at Careggi.

Apart from Ficino, the group included Cristoforo Landino, a literary critic who wrote new interpretations of Dante and Virgil, and Angelo Poliziano, the classical scholar and poet. They had in common a love of literature, of the classics in general and of Plato in particular, and they constituted something like a school.

Poliziano's most famous poem, the *Stanze*, was loosely connected with a joust held in Florence in 1475 and won, no doubt easily, by Lorenzo's brother Giuliano. In the poem Giuliano appears as Iulio. Hunting in the forest, he was entranced by a meeting with a beautiful nymph called Simonetta. The real Giuliano was supposed to be in love with Simonetta the wife of Marco Vespucci. Iulio's love is favoured and promoted by Venus. He sees her in a dream but, after he has justified his quest by victory in battle, he finds her transformed into Fortune. The death of the real Simonetta a year after the joust and a second disaster, Giuliano's death in the Pazzi Conspiracy, no doubt accounted for Poliziano's abandonment of the poem.

The theme of the poem was partly related to the old courtly-love tradition of the pursuit of the woman by the man, but also enriched by Poliziano's borrowing from Roman poets, and to some extent affected by the contemporary Neoplatonic faith in the value of love as an uplifting power. The divine power of the goddess and her beauty can be seen in this description of Venus as sculpted by Vulcan in the garden of Venus:

You could swear that the goddess had emerged from the waves, pressing her hair with her right hand covering with the other her sweet mound of flesh; and where the space was imprinted by her sacred and divine step, it had clothed itself in flowers and grass; then with happy, more than mortal appearance, she was received in the bosom of the three nymphs and cloaked in a starry garment.

With both hands one nymph holds above the damp tresses a garland, burning with gold and oriental gems, another adjusts pearls in her ears; the third, intent upon her beautiful breast and white shoulders, appears to strew round them the rich necklaces with which the three girded their own necks when they used to dance in a ring in heaven.

Thence they seem to be raised towards the heavenly spheres, seated upon a silver cloud: in the hard stone you would seem to see the air trembling and all of heaven contented; every god takes pleasure in her beauty and desires her happy bed: each face seems to marvel with raised eyebrows and wrinkled forehead.

The passage is reminiscent of Botticelli's *Birth of Venus* where Venus resembles the goddess in the poem. Botticelli was an artist, not elevated enough to be a member of the Laurentian circle. Poliziano's poetry springs from the adoration of poetic classicism which Lorenzo's friends shared.

In some ways the most remarkable figure in Lorenzo's circle was Ficino. Between the 1460s and the 1480s Ficino carried out a long programme of translation. The works of Plato, the Neoplatonists, Plotinus, and the hermetic writings now became available in Latin which westerners could read. The horizon of western perception of the ancient world was extended. Ficino also wrote a number of original works in which he expressed his own view of philosophy, and its relation with theology, and of astrology and magic.

The effect of Ficino's work was to establish a tradition of thought that had marked differences from the scholastic tradition originating in thirteenth-century universities and still prevalent in most of Europe in his own time. He believed in the existence of a perennial philosophy which had been known to spiritual writers before Plato, and he thought, quite mistakenly, that the 'hermetic' (the word comes from the name of the mythical Hermes Trismegistus) writings dating from the Roman Empire were much earlier

texts.

The mixture of a modern sense of the historical evolution of thought with the gross historical error is curious. However, he belived that Christianity was one, and the best, of a long series of varied accounts of the spiritual world, written since early times. Because of the continuity of the tradition, Plato was a valid authority for the Christians. 'If I did not fear that someone would misinterpret what I say, I would demonstrate that Socrates was not the figure of Christ, like Job and St John the Baptist, but a sketch of him.' The Neoplatonic idea that the universe is a scale of spiritual levels, up which men can rise by their own efforts, and the related idea that events on earth are powerfully influenced by spiritual forces residing in the heavenly circles – of Mercury, Venus, the Sun, Jupiter and Saturn – between heaven and earth, had an interesting attractiveness for the Italian Renaissance mind for aesthetic reasons. It received expression in a new and much more substantial structure of ideas from Ficino.

Plato was followed because he believed that 'bodily things … are not real things but images or shadows of real things.' Aristotle, in contrast, was mistaken in his more scientific emphasis on the natural world and was essentially pagan. In contrast Plato's philosophy was compatible with the idea that man's soul contained an inner light, attracted by the light of God. Creation was the work of love and human love was a desire for beauty which was ultimately a desire for God. Ficino was not a very original or precise technical philosopher, and he would no doubt have received damaging treatment from logical analysts of his own or any other time, but he was capable of setting up a system of thought that was attractive to sympathetic classicists, spiritualists, and artists.

He was also attracted himself by astrology. The ancient gods had a place in medieval ideas because the stories about them were useful if they were treated as allegories. Ficino gave them a new importance because he accepted the idea

Flagellation of Christ,
Piero della Francesca, 1455 (Palazzo Ducale, Urbino)

that the gods were equivalent to the astrological forces operating from the heavenly circles: the circle of the planet Venus, for example, was connected with the classical idea of the goddess Venus. So it was not nonsense to say that lovers were influenced by Venus. Ficino was also susceptible to ideas about the efficacy of magic. He believed that good, natural magic, as opposed to bad magic, could be beneficial and advised people who wanted to attract the influence of the life-giving Jupiter or Venus, rather than the melancholy Saturn, to seek contact with the roses and crocuses connected symbolically with Venus, or to use a talisman

inscribed with her image. Many serious ecclesiastical authorities were suspicious of the ideas of astrology and magic. Ficino, who was a priest, and thought that he was expanding, rather than contradicting, Christian consciousness, had to protect himself against ecclesiastical censure by protestations of his orthodoxy. It is doubtful whether he would have survived if he had not been comfortably ensconced in independent Florence, surrounded by friends, including the powerful Lorenzo, who was sympathetic to his views. This pro-classical tolerance is one main reason for the importance of

Laurentian Florence in the history of thought.

Within his secluded and brilliant world Ficino was able to develop and publish his system of thought, which was later to have a wide circulation in many parts of Europe until the seventeenth century, when historical research destroyed the belief that hermetic thought was pre-Platonic, and scientific thought destroyed the belief that the earth was the centre of the universe. In the intervening period the conception of a unitary universe, centred on the earth, within which spiritual and magical powers were effective, had a wide currency and greatly affected the attitudes of artists. Shakespeare's Lorenzo, for example, in *The Merchant of Venice*, reflects the widely diffused and diluted Neoplatonism that remained part of the culture of his age with his words:

> look, how the floor of heaven
> Is thick inlaid with patines of bright gold:
> There's not the smallest orb which thou behold'st
> But in his motion like an angel sings,
> Still quiring to the young-eyed cherubins;
> Such harmony is in immortal souls.

In the world of Laurentian Florence, the most interesting significance of Ficino and his friends was the probable effect that they had on visual artists. I say 'probable' because it is difficult to find a direct connection between philosophers and writers, on the one hand, and painters and sculptors on the other. We do know, however, that the gods and their stories became for the first time an accepted subject matter for high art. Condivi tells us in his life of Michelangelo that, when the artist was a young and unimportant man working in the Medici garden, near the end of Lorenzo's life, he was instructed about classical stories by Ficino's friend, the poet Poliziano. 'He himself loved Michelangelo greatly, knowing him for the exalted spirit he was, and, though not needing to, he constantly

spurred him on to study, always expounding to him and giving him things to do. For instance, one day he suggested to him the rape of Deianira and the battle of the centaurs, and he expounded the whole story to him stage by stage.' The probability is that the expansion of high art into classical subjects, which took place in Lorenzo's Florence, was inspired by the circle of Ficino and Poliziano providing programmes for artists.

PIERO DELLA FRANCESCA

The most classical in manner of the painters of the mid-fifteenth century appears to have worked little if at all in Florence and almost none of his paintings can be found in the great Florentine collections. Piero della Francesca is first heard of in Florence in 1439 but does not appear there again. Those of his works which have not been moved remain in his homes, Borgo San Sepolcro, Arezzo, Urbino and Rimini. Piero stemmed from the tradition of Masaccio, though it is not clear how he acquired knowledge of it. The distance between him and the Florentines protected him from the light and elegant nervousness of slim figures which became a feature of Florentine art in the age of Lorenzo the Magnificent. His figures have more in common with the full, smooth, static and almost heavy forms that are sometimes found in ancient sculpture. They provide reassurance, rather than excitement. That is not to say that Piero was an outsider incapable of appreciating metropolitan refinements. On the contrary, he had clearly grasped the significance of the Florentine advances during his early visit to the city. In addition to being a painter he was also a mathematician, the author of three treatises on that subject and, apart from Brunelleschi and Leonardo, probably the artist of the fifteenth century closest to the ideas of Alberti and most affected by the tyranny of numbers and theorems.

In the ducal castle at Urbino there is a small panel painted by Piero with one of his best-known paintings, the

Flagellation of Christ. It is divided into two sections, with a group of three men in the right-hand half of the picture, outside the room where the flagellation is taking place but apparently in the same space, who appear to be holding a private conversation. The intention and subject matter of this picture have never received an explanation that has won total acceptance. There are several reasons for the perplexity it causes. One is that we do not know who these three figures are: they may be the likenesses of contemporaries but, if so, it is not clear which contemporaries or why they were thought to be appropriate to the flagellation. Their curious detachment from it has no apparent meaning either. Another reason is that Piero has used an elaborate system of perspective and lighting to give depth to the flagellation half of the painting. The interior stretches far back and the interior light comes from a different source from the light outside the building. This aspect of the painting is a striking case of Piero's application of his mathematical expertise. What exactly did he intend to convey? The third reason is that Pilate is watching the flagellation dressed like the Emperor of Constantinople. Byzantine references are to be found in other paintings by Piero, the *Baptism of Christ* and the *Legend of the Holy Cross*, but we do not know how they are related to the historical events of the Byzantine attendance at the Council of Florence in 1439, the conquest of Constantinople by the Turks in 1453 and the flight of Greek scholars to Europe. Piero or his patrons may have been taken up with the Greek question and the Turkish threat to Italy. It has been suggested that the subject may not be Christ's flagellation at all but the flagellation which St Jerome reported he had experienced in a dream.

Even if the meaning of the *Flagellation of Christ* is not clear, it nevertheless presents us with aesthetic features of Piero's art that are indisputable. Space is precisely defined. The grave, square tranquillity of the scene is promoted by the careful use of classical architecture of the type developed by Alberti. The figures stand with a firm and calm solidity. The colours are pale and give the painting a delightful open freshness, characteristic of Piero. Throughout his work he presents us with this vision of a light and stable universe which is entirely his own and instantly recognisable in the full, cool faces of his figures.

Piero's *Baptism of Christ* in London's National Gallery, set in the landscape of the upper Tiber valley in which Piero was born, is in contrast without architecture. The baptism by John the Baptist takes place in the centre of the painting with Christ and the dove above him given absolute centrality. Farther up the stream on the right is the nearly naked figure of another man undressing for baptism. To the left are three angels in solemn immobility, who remind us of the three men in the *Flagellation of Christ*. This is the most developed of Piero's landscape scenes. Even more than the architectural setting of the *Flagellation of Christ,* it conveys, by the manner in which Piero depicts physical objects and persons, a mood of quiet, pale, light-filled serenity.

The largest surviving work by Piero is the *Legend of the Holy Cross* painted in fresco in a number of scenes, in the chancel of San Francesco at Arezzo. The scenes were taken from the *Legenda Aurea*, a popular late medieval collection of religious stories. After Adam's death a branch from the tree, whose apple he ate, sprouted again in his mouth to grow into another tree which King Solomon made into a bridge. This is the wood from which the Cross was made. It was rediscovered by Helena, wife of the first Christian Emperor, Constantine. Later it was stolen by Chosroes, King of the Persians, but recovered in battle by the Emperor Heraclius who set it up in Jerusalem. Beside the large scenes, the death of Adam, the visit of the Queen of Sheba to Solomon, Constantine's victory over the pagan Maxentius, Heraclius's victory over Chosroes, and others, which gave scope for his dramatic gifts, there are also smaller scenes, like the night picture of Constantine's dream in his tent, in which Piero displays another and

Baptism of Christ,
Piero della Francesca, 1448-50 (National Gallery, London)

highly original example of his command of light.

The *Legend of the Holy Cross* was the fullest exposition of Piero's powers. In the *Resurrection* at Borgo San Sepolcro is one of the most arresting faces of the resurrected Christ which the Renaissance produced, a plain hard face staring at the onlookers with commanding power, worthy to be set beside the very different *Resurrection* which Donatello sculpted about the same time for San Lorenzo. Piero's art, which depended in part on the innovations at Florence, provided a very full application of Brunelleschi's sense of space and figure-painting which is solemnly classical. This was largely developed by the 1460s, before Laurentian art took off. It is an interesting variety of the humanist mode, different from the more influential line that painting was to take at Florence.

LAURENTIAN ART

In contrast to Piero della Francesca is the work of two central Florentine artists, a father and son, Filippo and Filippino Lippi, whose active lives between them span the

LEFT AND ABOVE Meeting of Solomon and the Queen of Sheba
from the Legend of the Holy Cross, *Piero della Francesca, 1452*
(San Francesco, Arezzo)

95

Madonna and Child with Saints and Angels,
Filippo Lippi, c.1437-41 (Louvre, Paris)

whole Medici period from the 1430s to the 1490s.

Filippo Lippi must have seen Florentine art in the 1430s in much the same condition as Piero saw it but he reacted to it in a different way. Instead of pursuing his own independent and individualistic interpretation of some of the inventions of Masaccio, Filippo was swept along by the influences that were attractive in the Florentine art world. Rather incongruously he was a Carmelite friar but it did not prevent him from being also a busy and highly paid painter. At one stage he imitated the colouring and light of Fra Angelico's works but he was also one of the first Italians to be profoundly influenced by Flemish painting.

Whether this was the result of a visit to Flanders or of seeing Flemish paintings that had been imported into Italy is impossible to say. Two famous paintings by Filippo, done in the late 1430s – the Tarquinia *Madonna and Child* in the Palazzo Barberini in Rome and the Santo Spirito *Madonna and Child with Saints and Angels* in the Louvre – make the Flemish connection clear. They both have the Flemish propensity to fit the figures into a rather tightly packed domestic interior that was foreign to the Italian tradition of more free-standing figures. This is the first sign of artistic influence swinging back across the Alps from north to south.

Filippo Lippi's openness to the influences around him enabled him to create a central Florentine style which we

RIGHT Madonna and Child,
Filippo Lippi, c.1453
(Galleria Palatina, Palazzo Pitti, Florence)

BELOW Annunciation,
Filippo Lippi, c.1442
(San Lorenzo, Florence)

Feast of Herod,
Filippo Lippi, c.1460-63 (Prato Cathedral, near Florence)

recognise immediately as belonging to Medici Florence.

One sees it already in 1442 in the *Annunciation* which he painted for one of the chapels in Brunelleschi's church of San Lorenzo. The Virgin reacts to the archangel not so much with innocence as with elegance. The buildings stretch away behind her in a long perspective sweep. The red patches in the background and foreground are set charmingly against the white and grey that predominate. It is a delightful painting in purely aesthetic terms if less inspiring in a religious sense.

Filippo's greatest commission was to paint frescoes in the choir of Prato Cathedral, a task that occupied him on and off from 1452 to 1466. On one wall are scenes from the life of St Stephen and facing them scenes from the life of John the Baptist. The stories are balanced: the saints' births face each other at the top, their life work in the middle range, their deaths at the bottom. The most famous scene illustrates the beheading of John the Baptist, Salomé dancing, and Salomé presenting the head to Herod. The fact that it shows three episodes does not destroy the unity of a single banquet scene, nor does the exceptionally gruesome story diminish the friendliness of the scene. We are clearly being permitted to witness a Florentine dinner party with charming, well-dressed people at the tables, presided over by an imposing major-domo, who is the only slightly alarming figure, with an attractive woman dancing, who happens unfortunately to be carrying somebody's head. This painting from the middle of the century carries us straight into the world of visual normality and elegance that makes up a great deal of the Florentine art world during the first period of Medici government.

Not very long after Filippo's work at Prato, another artist, much admired by the Medici, Andrea Verrocchio, made a bronze sculpture of *Jesus and the Doubting St Thomas* to be placed in a niche on Or San Michele. Made in the 1470s it was an extraordinary foretaste of the freedom of movement in sculpture that characterised later periods.

Jesus and the Doubting St Thomas,
Andrea Verrocchio, 1465-83 (Or San Michele, Florence)

Jesus stands with a raised hand drawing back his cloak to reveal the wound in his side. Thomas is outside the niche, one foot extending away from it, facing, as it were, Jesus in the doorway. The statues are not standing formally within the niche, as are earlier statues placed on Or San Michele; they are half in and half out of it, engaged in a free and flowing relationship of limbs and bodies. Verrocchio adapted the command of the human body, which he had inherited from Donatello, to a freer and more mobile

Triumph of St Thomas Aquinas,
Filippino Lippi, c.1488-93 (Carafa Chapel, Santa Maria sopra Minerva, Rome)

rendering of the figures.

Filippo's son, Filippino Lippi, was another artist of the late fifteenth century in Florence, whose work pointed forward to the sixteenth century, with its combination of Christian subjects and classical forms, and the liveliness and grace of his figures. These anticipations of 'Mannerist' art of the period 1520–50 were not, however, accompanied by much adoption of the new figure-drawing and inter-personal pattern-making of Leonardo that was to form the basis of the new school, the subject of the next chapter, which had begun to emerge in Leonardo's work twenty years before Filippino died. Filippino was born in 1457/8, the result of a liaison between Filippo Lippi and a nun, which was the subject of a misleading poem by Browning, and died in 1504 at the end of an energetic working life spent mostly in Florence.

His early manner was derived from his father, from Botticelli, in whose workshop he served, and from Verrocchio. His individuality can be seen in the 1480s in the *Vision of St Bernard* in the Badia at Florence. Bernard, seated at a rustic desk, confronts the Virgin before a complicated landscape that is indebted, like other Florentine landscapes of the period, to Flemish art. The donor appears in the corner, another Flemish touch, and around the Virgin is a group of childlike angels. Filippino shows his individual skill chiefly in the complex, flowing clothes, which are pleated into patterns and add to the grace of the figures.

In 1488 he went to Rome to paint a chapel in the church of Santa Maria sopra Minerva for Cardinal Carafa, an important and efficient ecclesiastical administrator whom Lorenzo de' Medici, anxious to secure his son's promotion to the cardinalate, may have wished to please by sending

100

Vision of St Bernard,
Filippino Lippi, c.1484-6 (Badia, Florence)

Exorcism of the Demon in the Temple of Mars,
Filippino Lippi, c.1487-1502
(Strozzi Chapel, Santa Maria Novella, Florence)

him one of the best Florentine painters. The paintings that remain are sibyls – pagan prophets of Christ's coming – on the ceiling, on the right-hand wall two scenes exalting St Thomas Aquinas, and on the back wall an altarpiece of the Annunciation with, above and to its sides, a triumphal presentation of the Assumption of the Virgin. St Thomas is shown in the miracle of the wooden cross that spoke to him, and then seated as a triumphant, enthroned philosopher-theologian with figures of the erroneous enemies of the true faith in dejection before him. These are serious scenes and the background is filled with elaborate heavy classical architecture. *Putti* balance on the arch above the saint and from a balustrade, above another arch, observers look down as they do from the classical balustrades of Veronese a century later. Here is the whole panoply of the classical setting as Italian art was to know it for a long time. There is still more vitality in the depiction of the Assumption. The Virgin rises on a cloud, accompanied by an oval ring of dancing angels playing musical instruments with great enthusiasm. Below, on either side of the altarpiece, the apostles look up from a delightful landscape, sometimes in evident classical poses. The chapel is filled with decoration copied from classical sculpture. The union of high-minded and learned theology with classical forms is complete. The visit to Rome seems to have filled Filippino with a new and extreme enthusiasm for the movement of his figures, which later grew even more intense.

Another step of a slightly different kind in this direction was taken in the 1490s when Filippino was allowed to go home to paint a chapel in Santa Maria Novella for Filippo Strozzi, a rich banker who wanted to turn the chapel into a funerary memorial for his family. The two main scenes in the Strozzi Chapel are, first, St Philip killing a dragon in front of a statue of Mars to prove the superiority of Christianity to paganism, and, secondly, St John the Evangelist bringing to life the dead Drusiana. The chapel is richly decorated with classical motifs of various kinds, allegorical figures and architecture. The two main scenes also have classical furnishing but of a less heavy kind than in the earlier St Thomas scenes. The god Mars stands splendidly before an elaborate and fantastic piece of Roman architecture. To the aesthetic observer the most remarkable feature of the scenes is the complicated nervousness of the figures. Drusiana has been surprised from sleep. The attendant figures lean to one side with flowing clothes like a crowd facing the wind. The miracle of St Philip was chosen because the saint's name was appropriate to the patron, Filippo Strozzi. In a sense the subjects of the paintings do not matter. The scenes, designed for a rich man who was perhaps not very devout but could pay for the most ostentatious religious setting in Florence, display a preference for style over content. They charm the eye by the sumptuousness of the decoration and the sheer vivacity of the figures. They are also witty. But they present only a pageant, without any really meaningful connection with the religious scenes they are meant to portray. This was a recurrent tendency in expensive art from which the Florentines were temporarily saved by the intervention of Leonardo and Michelangelo.

The combination of Florentine wealth, which sponsored frescoes and altarpieces in churches and convents, and the tradition of advanced art established by Masaccio, Donatello and Alberti, gave birth to delightful works of art in the Laurentian period. Between the high point of Donatello's art – he died in 1466 – and the emergence of Leonardo and Michelangelo at the end of the century, there was no single artist of equal stature. But there were a number of inventive painters and sculptors who maintained a lively interest in landscape, adopted under Flemish influence, in the imitation of classical models, and in the introduction of classical themes.

Florentine artists cooperating on a large scale could be best seen, however, in works subsidised by non-Florentine

Chapel of the Cardinal of Portugal,
Antonio Manetti, 1460-62 (San Miniato, Florence)

Greek cross with four equal arms. The arms are formed by deep niches in the walls of the square with round arches and above the centre of the chapel rises a round cupola. The vault was enriched by work of the ceramic artist Luca della Robbia and includes large terracotta *tondi*, circular plates, representing the cardinal virtues. To one side of the chapel, set under one of the four arches, is the sepulchral monument by the sculptor Antonio Rossellino. Like the architecture, it is entirely classical in its decoration, with *putti* holding up the sheet on which the effigy of the cardinal is stretched, and a Madonna and Child and angels above. On the altar stood formerly an altarpiece showing three saints, painted by the brothers Antonio and Piero Pollaiuolo, whose interest in the anatomy of the male nude contributed to the quality of their clothed figures in this painting. On the wall facing the tomb was an Annunciation painted by Alesso Baldovinetti. The chapel is a celebration of the cardinal's piety and his hope of eternal life. It is also an exquisite confection in which the Brunelleschian ideal of symmetrical church architecture with classical forms and detail has been expensively combined with a series of decorations in paint, stone and terracotta made by the best artists available in Florence.

The Sistine Chapel, famous primarily for the paintings by Michelangelo which will be described in a later chapter, was built by Pope Sixtus IV, an adversary of Lorenzo the Magnificent, at the time of the Pazzi Conspiracy, an attempt to kill Lorenzo. After the reconciliation which followed, however, in the years 1480–3, the lower walls were painted with a series of large frescoes by a team of principally Florentine artists: Perugino, Botticelli, Ghirlandaio, Cosimo Roselli and Signorelli. Whilst Perugino probably led the team, the most distinguished paintings were those by Botticelli. Within the limits imposed by work done for a strictly ecclesiastical purpose, the series as a whole displays the richness and virtuosity of advanced Italian painting at that period.

patrons, who were sometimes more generous than the normal patrons of simple altarpieces. Two examples of this kind from an earlier and a later period are the chapel of the Cardinal of Portugal built in the 1460s and the painting in the Sistine Chapel in the 1480s.

The Cardinal of Portugal died in Florence in 1459. In his memory a sepulchral chapel was added to the Romanesque church of San Miniato on the hill to the south of Florence. The chapel was built by Antonio Manetti, a pupil of Brunelleschi, working in a manner which developed out of his style. The chapel is in the shape of a

Charge to St Peter,
Perugino, 1481 (Sistine Chapel, Vatican, Rome)

The paintings on the end walls of the chapel have not survived. On the two long walls are two series facing each other: six paintings of the life of Moses and six of the life of Christ. The intention of the paintings is to express the claims of the papacy to authority. Christ is the inaugurator of the Eucharist and of priesthood, who confers on Peter the power of the popes. He springs from the tradition established by Moses, who was given authority and priesthood by God. Unlike Michelangelo's paintings on the ceiling, the meaning of which remains obscure in part because it is more personal, historians have interpreted the frescoes as designed to mirror contemporary theology. The painters must have been carefully controlled by clerics to make sure that they included the right episodes. They must also have exercised considerable freedom, however, in the structure of the scenes, the movements of the figures and the rich landscape settings of mountains, forests and seas which often show how much Italian painting by this time had accepted the Flemish landscape tradition.

The best known of the series, because of its plain structure, is probably Perugino's painting of the *Charge to St Peter*. Christ is handing the keys to Peter in the foreground flanked on both sides by a line of figures. Behind them is a broad paved area and behind that three buildings. The central one is an avant-garde, symmetrical, classical building, perhaps intended to be 'the Church', and on

105

Life of Moses,
Botticelli, 1481-2 (Sistine Chapel, Vatican, Rome)

either side are arches based on the Arch of Constantine in Rome, referring to the fact that Constantine was the first Christian emperor. A cursory observer might not notice that the much smaller figures on the paved square are playing out the stories of the tribute-seeker asking Christ for money and the stoning of Christ. But as a whole the painting is a clear, open, perspective-dominated vista that incorporates much of the obvious classicism and realism of the late fifteenth century.

In contrast to this, Botticelli's painting of the *Life of Moses* is at first sight a more complicated and obscure affair. Moses appears seven times within the same panel. The story runs roughly from right to left. Moses murders the Egyptian taskmaster, he flees from Egypt, drives away the robbers troubling the daughters of Jethro, helps them at the well, tends his flocks in Horeb, hears the divine call from God in the burning bush, and finally leads the Israelites towards Egypt. This is a fairly extreme example of compressed story-telling because all seven episodes are contained within what appears to be a single landscape in which the prominent features are the classical building on the right, the coppice in the centre with the well before it and the small hills behind extending to the burning bush on the right.

The most famous part of Botticelli's painting is the pair of daughters of Jethro in the centre foreground, one of whom was taken by Marcel Proust as the likeness of Odette because, of course, these biblical characters have the same charm as Botticelli's graceful figure-drawing in secular art. The figures and landscape are realistic. But the painting presents a curious mixture of realism and non-realism enforced by the combination, on the one hand of the developed Florentine artistic tradition, and on the other of the requirements of ideology. Moses has to appear seven times because he has to be shown, metaphorically, slaying a tempter, defending his church, obeying God and leading his people to salvation. Botticelli was able to accept this

convention which represents a stage in the history of art in which figure-drawing and landscape did not aim simply to portray the world as the artist knew it.

CLASSICAL PAINTING

The most important aspect of the painting of Laurentian Florence was not its proliferation of beautiful and powerful religious scenes but the introduction of paintings illustrating stories and personages taken from classical mythology. We have seen the sudden adoption of styles dependent on classical architecture and sculpture by Brunelleschi and Donatello. The mass of serious painting down to this period was largely ecclesiastical and its subjects were taken from the Bible and the lives of saints. The idea of employing a first-class artist to paint a scene of classical legend or of classical persons was an innovation of the second half of the fifteenth century. It was ideologically important because it opened up to the artist the possibility of original invention of a new kind: classical subjects enabled artists to deal with love and conflict, the preoccupations of secular life, in a more independent manner. It became possible for visual artists to deal with these subjects as Dante and Boccaccio had been able to deal with them in literature. At last art and literature were able to advance together to some extent in mutual interdependence.

Painters were not highly educated men and in the early days of this movement they painted what they were told to paint. The most powerful influence on the introduction of classical subjects was the taste of the Medici family. Some of the greatest early classical paintings – Botticelli's *Birth of Venus* and *Primavera* and Signorelli's *Court of Pan* – were painted at the request of the Medici to decorate the walls of their houses. But these were not the only cases and we must also allow some importance to the general development of domestic taste in Florentine society as a whole. The bourgeois of Florence, like their contemporaries the Montefeltro lords of Urbino and the Gonzaga lords of

ABOVE Adoration of the Magi,
Botticelli, 1472-5 (Uffizi, Florence)

RIGHT Primavera,
Botticelli, 1477-8 (Uffizi, Florence)

Mantua, built grander palaces and wanted to have the walls of their rooms decorated with paintings that suited their interests. Thus the expertise that had been acquired in generations of painting altarpieces for churches was turned into producing sophisticated panels of secular subjects.

Botticelli's *Primavera* was probably painted for Lorenzo di Pierfrancesco de' Medici, a relation of Lorenzo the Magnificent, perhaps at the time of his marriage to Semiramide, the daughter of the lord of Piombino, with whom Lorenzo was extremely anxious to have an alliance. Botticelli was then a well-established painter with twenty years' experience. In earlier days he had painted a number of important altarpieces. One of these was the *Adoration of the Magi*, probably painted between 1472 and 1475 for a chapel in Santa Maria Novella. The patron was not a Medici, but that family's prestige was illustrated because of

the presence of the Magi, and the bystanders around the Madonna and Child include a number of figures which are portraits of Medici: the dead Cosimo and Piero, Lorenzo himself and at one side Lorenzo's younger brother Giuliano, the hero of Poliziano's *Stanze*. In his earlier paintings, as we have seen in the case of the *Life of Moses* in the Sistine Chapel, Botticelli had also exhibited his mastery of the structure of a painted scene and his skill in the painting of female figures. These gifts were now applied to secular subjects.

Primavera contains a row of eight adult figures with a child Cupid above them. In the centre of the painting is the chaste and benign figure of Venus. On the right is a windy scene which shows Zephyr, the west wind, flying down to rape Chloris who flees before him in a transparent gown with flowers emerging from her mouth to show that as a

Birth of Venus,
Botticelli, c.1482 (Uffizi, Florence)

result of their love she will be transformed into Flora. Between her and Venus is Flora herself advancing and strewing roses for the advent of spring. On the other side of Venus the air is still. It is controlled by Mercury who stands on the far side with his caduceus raised towards the clouds. Between Mercury and Venus are three lightly clothed Graces, a trio of dancers. Cupid is firing his arrow at one of them and Venus is raising her right hand towards them in approval. The programme for the painting may have been supplied by Poliziano. It was certainly designed by someone who was familiar with Ovid and other classical writers. The intended meaning has remained obscure in spite of the efforts of many learned and ingenious interpreters. We can be sure, however, that the figures are meant to represent the contrast between the rape of Chloris and the chaste marriage of one of the Graces. More difficult to interpret is the connection between the lustful, flower-producing fate of Chloris on the one side and the calm May-time garden on the other. It is the presentation of spring as the season of love and marriage which gives the painting part of its charm.

Primavera introduces us to problems in the world of art history which are prominent throughout the Renaissance period after this time and which result primarily from the adoption of classical topics. The figures of *Primavera* – Chloris, Venus, Mercury – come from classical legend. There was no prescribed way of interpreting classical legend, as there was for interpreting biblical figures. The meaning of a painting depended in most cases on a programme approved by the patron, who might have consulted a literary expert. In the famous case of Mantegna's *Struggle between Chastity and Love*, the programme, which was laid down in January 1503 by Isabella d'Este, has survived. She said that the painting was to show Pallas and Diana fighting Venus and Love and various other details. For most paintings, however, including *Primavera*, no programme has survived. This has led to disputes about how far it was intended to represent a philosophical instruction, and how far it was a celebration of nature in the spring.

Primavera is the earliest of great classical pieces. A few years later Botticelli painted three more: *Pallas and the Centaur*, *Mars and Venus*, and the most famous of them all, the *Birth of Venus*. The nude figure of Venus is based on the model of the classical Venus Pudica, shielding her body with her hands, but she also has the face of appealing innocence which belongs to a new tradition and in fact repeats the faces of Botticelli's many Madonnas. She is blown across the water to the shore by Zephyr who carries Chloris at his side and a nymph waits to greet her with her cloak. The idea for the *Birth of Venus* was very likely supplied by Poliziano. Botticelli's success in converting it into a painting can only astonish us. We have a figure and a story derived from classical antiquarianism, perhaps infused with Poliziano's poetry. The stance of Venus is an imitation of a classical sculpture. She was painted by an artist trained in the school of ecclesiastical story-painting. But he created a figure which seems to represent the ideal of the innocence of womanhood in the setting of nature and which has never lost its appeal through all the changes of taste in the five centuries separating us from its maker. This is perhaps the best testimony to the success of the precarious balance of myth and naturalism that was achieved for a moment in the secularised Florence of Lorenzo. Classical legend, ecclesiastical painting, literary spiritualism and aristocratic enjoyment of the pleasures of life were all combined in a way that would become more difficult as secularism and scientific realism advanced further in later centuries.

In the 1490s Botticelli painted a much smaller picture which is certainly less attractive than *Primavera* and the *Birth of Venus* but in some ways still more interesting: the *Calumny of Apelles*. The source for this straightforward allegory was the Greek story-teller Lucian. The painting represents the victim dragged before King Midas by Perfidy, Fraud,

Calumny of Apelles,
Botticelli, 1495 (Uffizi, Florence)

Rancour and Calumny while Suspicion and Ignorance hold sway over the king and Truth and Remorse hang back, unable to intervene. The painting is delicate and precise on a small scale, almost closer to manuscript illumination than to panel painting, but Botticelli loses nothing of his command over figure and gesture. About the time that the picture was painted, Botticelli was accused of sodomy and the name of the Greek painter Apelles, the object of Calumny, was familiar to fifteenth-century humanists. It appears that the artist was using a classical story to make a statement relevant to his own personal life. Botticelli's works of the late 1490s – he died in 1510 – indicate that he was attached to the cause of Savonarola. His life contains

hints of art becoming a vehicle for the expression of ideas which are connected with his own personal emotions and attitudes and which may not have much to do with the wishes of patrons. Botticelli began his career as a craftsman in the traditional way. Perhaps his skill as a painter, which introduced him to the Medici circle, also introduced him to scholarly ideas that came to fill an important role in his imagination. If this is the truth it is an indication of the possibilities that were open in the exceptional environment of Florence at this time, a society in which the artist benefited from the dignity given to his trade by Alberti, in which patrons might be learned people who combined an interest in scholarship with an interest in art, and in which

Resurrection of the Dead,
Signorelli, 1499-1504 (San Brixio Chapel, Orvieto Cathedral)

the relatively open tumult of republican life allowed the individual the opportunity to follow his own instincts.

Another striking example of the direct influence of the Medici on classicising art was the *Court of Pan*, painted by Signorelli about 1490. Signorelli was from Cortona and worked mostly in that area rather than in Florence. His most remarkable surviving work is the extensive fresco decoration of the Chapel of San Brizio in Orvieto Cathedral, done later than the *Court of Pan*, which portrays the preaching of Antichrist, the end of the world, the condemnation of the damned to Hell and the resurrection of the redeemed, with an impressive display of a large number of male and female nudes. The main influences on

his style came from Piero and Perugino, painters only marginally connected with the Florentine scene, but who had themselves been influenced by the Florentine art of the early part of the century.

According to a single sentence in Vasari, which is all the information we have about the origins of the painting, the *Court of Pan* was probably painted about 1490 for Lorenzo de' Medici during a visit by Signorelli to Florence. It depicts Pan, half-human, half-goat with horns like crescent moons,

113

Court of Pan,
Signorelli, c.1490 (destroyed, formerly Kaiser Friedrich Museum, Berlin)

seated in the middle of the picture. The other figures are humans. To one side of Pan stands an old man holding a staff, apparently making a statement to the other youth playing a pipe. Before him are two male figures, one again an old man leaning on a staff, the other a younger figure reclining on the ground, and a striking young female holding a long pipe. The figure of Pan was connected in Medici circles at this time with Melancholy and the bucolic life of the country. Here he is linked with the failure of love in unsuccessful pursuit of the nymph Syrinx, who may be the female figure at the front of the painting. Interpretations do not carry us much beyond this general sense of the significance of the great god. The painting is still more obscure than *Primavera*. We cannot do much more than associate it with poetic melancholy and Lorenzo's desire to escape from Florence to his country villa in the last years of his life. The theme was, however, transformed by Signorelli into a splendid group of nude figures which shows again the capacity of ecclesiastical art to move easily into the secular field when a new kind of subject was called for by the patron.

A less spectacular example of the influence of classicism emanating from the Medici circle can be found in the Sassetti Chapel in Santa Trinita that was made in the 1480s for Francesco Sassetti, one of the managers of the Medici bank who had contacts with the humanist scholars. The

Adoration of the Shepherds,
Domenico Ghirlandaio, 1485 (Sassetti Chapel, Santa Trinita, Florence)

chapel was painted by Domenico Ghirlandaio, one of the most prolific mural painters of the period. His frescoes on the walls and altarpiece of the *Adoration of the Shepherds* suggest it might be a perfectly conventional chapel, but classical elements are spread about it profusely. The *Adoration* itself shows a Roman sarcophagus just behind the Child. The fresco of the *Confirmation of the Franciscan Rule* has a background which includes both the Piazza della Signoria at Florence and a building based on the basilica of Maxentius and Constantine at Rome, symbolising the new Florentine-Papal peace after the Pazzi Conspiracy. On the walls at the side are grisaille paintings that are copies of Roman coins. Above the entrance to the chapel is a painting of *Augustus beholding a Vision on the Capitoline Hill*. This is in fact not traditional chapel decoration but an elaborate attempt to express devotion to things Roman and the hope of concord between Florence and Rome.

The strangest figure of late fifteenth-century Florentine art was Piero di Cosimo (1461–1521) of whom Vasari reports:

He did not want the rooms to be cleaned, he wanted to eat when he was hungry, he did not want to dig or prune the fruits of the garden, but let the vines grow and the shoots spread over the ground and he never pruned the figs or any other tree but contented himself with seeing everything wild like his own nature, arguing that natural things should be left to look after themselves. He often went to see animals or plants which nature had made strangely and had a contentment and satisfaction with them ... Piero's works betray a spirit of great diversity distinct from those of others, for he was endowed with a subtlety for investigating curious matters in nature, and executed them without a thought for the time or labour, but solely for his delight and pleasure in art. It could not be otherwise, for so devoted was he to art that he neglected material comforts, and his habitual food consisted of hard-boiled eggs, which he

cooked while he was boiling his glue, to save the firing. He would cook not six or eight at a time, but a good fifty, and would eat them one by one from a basket in which he kept them. He adhered so strictly to this manner of life that others seemed to him to be in slavery by comparison. The crying of babies irritated him, and so did the coughing of men, the sound of bells, and the singing of friars.

This eccentric man was a painter who produced a number of conventional altarpieces. But he was also an imaginative illustrator of the classical theory of evolution that originated with Lucretius and descended through various authors to arrive in the Florentine world through Boccaccio.

The art that resulted from this unexpected adoption of ancient ideas can be seen in five paintings, now housed in galleries in England, Canada and the United States, which were done at the end of the fifteenth century. Two of them show a barbaric hunting scene in which skin-clad men and satyrs are attacking animals in a forest with wooden clubs, and a scene of return from the hunt with boats bringing the hunters back with their prey to be reunited with their women. The third, depicting a more advanced stage, shows a forest scene with animals, some of them with human faces, a forest fire from which the animals have fled and a cloth-clad human carrying a yoke. The fourth and fifth show scenes from the life of Vulcan, the inventor of iron-working, and in one of them he is working at a forge while Aeolus blows the fire.

These scenes of the early evolution of human society and of its arts and techniques have nothing to do with Christianity and arise from a tradition that is hostile to it. It is remarkable that fifteenth-century Florence should have given birth to a man with this taste for nature, natural history and speculation on the early history of man, of a kind that one would find more appropriate in the age of Voltaire. Piero's strange character and interests suggest a remote parallelism with Leonardo's natural science, though

Return from the Hunt,
Piero di Cosimo, c.1500
(Gift of Robert Gordon, 1875, Metropolitan Museum of Art, New York)

of course we have no suggestion that in Piero's case there was anything systematic: he seems to have been merely a nature-lover who found comfort in Lucretian naturalism and disliked church bells and the singing of friars. But his paintings – for instance the savages' boats on the wild shore in the *Return from the Hunt* – show a vivid and creative imagination applied to the history of man.

The Florentine world produced surprising things and one wishes that it could have prolonged its multifarious creativity instead of succumbing to the shrouds of orthodoxy and tyranny that eventually suppressed it after 1494. In spite of its relative brevity, however – twenty-three years from 1469 to 1492 – the Laurentian period in Florence was responsible for creating a secular culture, embodied most obviously in the philosophy of Ficino, the poetry of Poliziano, and the painting of Botticelli, which

profoundly influenced Italy and the rest of Europe.

This culture belonged essentially to the protected commercial city. Lorenzo de' Medici and Filippo Strozzi, two of the main patrons, were both merchants presiding over huge international companies, and Florence as a whole was a commercial city enriched by international finance. There is no reason to suppose that its prosperity had declined at this period. Its political independence, threatened after 1494 by the invaders of Italy, was still secure. We shall see Florentine ideas adopted at papal and French courts in the sixteenth century and becoming internationally important. The origin of this culture, however, was in a city where merchants lived by predicting the future rates of exchange and prices of cloth in European capitals, where thinkers and artists were protected from the tyranny of ecclesiastical intolerance and princely despotism.

117

VENICE AND THE ITALIAN DESPOTISMS

BROAD CULTURAL DEVELOPMENTS rivalling those of Florence took place in northeast Italy in the late fifteenth century. The centre of the region was Venice, which in 1500 and for some time before and after was the richest city in the world. The wealth was based on sea-borne trade, acting as the link between the industries of northern Europe and the luxury-suppliers of the Near East. Contacts with Europe were either by road across the Alps or by galleys sailing through the Straits of Gibraltar to Bruges; in the eastern Mediterranean the galleys sailed to Constantinople and Alexandria. Until the discoveries in the Atlantic carried trade away from the Mediterranean, which did not happen to a significant extent until the late sixteenth century, Venice's geographical position, judiciously exploited, brought untold wealth. A collection of houses built on a small, marshy island, the city of Venice was the medieval equivalent of a space station, unattached to the land, serving a purely commercial purpose.

Nevertheless by the end of the fifteenth century, when their arts began to be original, the Venetians had a considerable landed empire which made the city an important political power as well as a commercial centre. To be more precise there were two empires. The earlier of them had existed for centuries in the eastern Mediterranean, a collection of places that included at one time Cyprus, Crete and stretches of the Greek and Dalmatian mainlands. The other empire of the *terra firma*, which had been created entirely in the fifteenth century, embraced eastern Lombardy and was the result of the determination to safeguard Venice itself against Milan. Within its empire Venice exercised the same sort of rights that Florence did within its territory; cities like Padua which had once been independent and strong were by then merely subject.

Around 1500 the political tide was beginning to turn against Venice. The growth of powerful states on the edges of the city's dominions, the Ottoman Empire in the east and the Habsburg Empire to the north and west, meant that Venice was outclassed as she had not been earlier. A tremendous shock was given by the Habsburg Emperor Maximilian I's successful invasion of the Veneto in the War of the League of Cambrai in 1508, which marked the beginning of Venice's political decline. Both the political decline, and the ultimately more important economic decline following from the change of trade routes were, however, very slow. Venice was still a great power after the successful naval battle fought by her and the Habsburgs against the Ottomans at Lepanto in 1571. It is an interesting

RIGHT April,
Francesco del Cossa, c.1470-75
(Palazzo Schifanoia, Ferrara)

point, however, that the greatest age in Venetian art begins with Giorgione about the time that political decline sets in.

It is also significant that some of the most recognisable aspects of Venetian art, though they may be inseparable from city wealth, are connected with the mainland. The villas of Palladio were built for noblemen on the *terra firma*, some of them a long way from Venice. The cultivation of landscape was more prominent in Venetian than in Florentine art, though you could not reach the countryside without first having to cross the lagoon. City dwellers are more interested in the land, or at least find it more romantic, than those who live and work on it, and this accounts for the Venetian willingness to escape into landscape.

If we compare the Venetian aesthetic tradition with that of the Florentines, it is clearly less rich and complex because the Venetians lacked the long literary tradition and the serious intermingling of art and thought which marked Quattrocento Florence. Nor were they so closely in contact with Rome. By the end of the fifteenth century the Venetians were enthusiastic importers of humanism but they had contributed less than the Florentines to its creation. The agonised dialogue between thought and art which stood out in the Florentine worlds of Ficino and Michelangelo had no real parallel in Venice. Venice did not suffer the paroxysms of internal strife that contributed to the political thought of Machiavelli. Venice was more orderly, peaceful, richer, and intellectually duller. In the later fifteenth century, though less spectacularly than at Florence, Venetian patricians were keen patrons of humanism and classical art. Lorenzo sent Poliziano to Venice to look for manuscripts. The Grimani collection, facilitated by links with the eastern Mediterranean, had more genuinely Greek, as opposed to Roman, art than any at Florence.

In one respect the peculiarities of the Venetian political environment were important for the city's art. Venice remained a republic throughout the period from Giorgione to Tintoretto and for long after. This is a matter to be taken seriously when we consider that the great age of Venetian painting extended long after Florence had clearly passed its best. Venice had a wealthy republican government which engaged much of the time of its best painters in decorating the great halls of the Doge's Palace, but it never had a despotic government that absorbed the energies of the best artists and diverted them to the exaltation of the prince. Venetian art was organised in a different way from Florentine; its workshops tended to be family concerns passed on from father to son and this limited the possibilities of numerous enterprising innovators appearing as they did at Florence. But much of the large-scale patronage for Venetian art continued to come from independent noblemen, churches and the *scuole*, 'schools' akin to Florentine religious confraternities, as well as from the towns on the mainland. This allowed the continuation of a republican diversity of endeavours that was diminished in Florence by the coming of the Medici duchy in the sixteenth century, and it also permitted Venetians to work in a free-enterprise world of patronage by princes from other states, which was responsible for some of the most original art of the sixteenth century.

THE WORLD OF THE DESPOTS

Northeast Italy also had cultural centres that were not republics like Florence and Venice and had contributed very little to the early development of humanist thought and art. These were the despotisms of Mantua, Ferrara and Urbino, which were not great cities. Their cultural hubs were courts in which art and thought flourished through the patronage of artists and writers by princes. By the later fifteenth century the prestige of humanism, which originated in the city, made it attractive to princes to import and foster it. Principalities in Italy became secondary centres of Renaissance activity in very much the same way as the

Ceiling of the Camera degli Sposi,
Mantegna, 1465-74 (Palazzo Ducale, Mantua)

European monarchs outside Italy, Valois and Habsburg, imported Italian culture later in the sixteenth century.

Urbino, a small state to the east of the Appenines, was ruled in the mid-fifteenth century by the Montefeltro family, whose most famous member, Federigo da Montefeltro (1422–82), was a patron of Piero della Francesca. Ferrara, farther north, between Romagna and the Veneto, was ruled throughout this period by the Este family, who were the patrons in the early sixteenth century of the poet Ludovico Ariosto. Mantua, in Lombardy, was ruled by the Gonzaga family who were patrons of the painters Mantegna and Giulio Romano, and into that family married the most prominent of the female patrons of the arts in Renaissance Italy, Isabella d'Este. All three

principalities were ruled from huge palaces. If one is looking for an impression of the despotic world of Renaissance Italy, the vast, sprawling palace of the Gonzaga at Mantua or the still-beautiful palace of the Montefeltro at Urbino are perhaps the best places to find it. The particular contribution of the principalities lay in the combination of princely aggrandisement and the life of the court which produced a despotic society quite different in character from the city republicanism of Florence, even during the incipient lordship of Lorenzo the Magnificent.

A mixture of the myth and reality of life in the despotic court is conveyed charmingly by the frescoes with which Francesco del Cossa decorated the Palazzo Schifanoia at Ferrara and which Andrea Mantegna painted at the palace at

Gonzaga family, Camera degli Sposi (detail),
Mantegna, 1465-74
(Palazzo Ducale, Mantua)

Mantua in the 1460s and 1470s. Cossa painted scenes representing the months of the year with illustrations for appropriate classical gods and astral deities, including a scene of young courtiers devoting themselves to the pleasures of Venus. The vault of Mantegna's *Camera degli Sposi* has an illusionistic opening at the top from which the ladies of the household are apparently about to drop a tub playfully on the lord and lady below. In both cases the main function of the paintings was to glorify the despot and his family. Court life had this combination of serious politics and entertainment; festivities and allegorical displays were features of all courts. From the cultural point of view the fundamental thing was that some of the despots were seriously interested in art and literature and therefore became valuable patrons. With their inherent ambition to absorb and display Renaissance culture, principalities of this kind provided a bridge between the world of the commercial city and the world of the agricultural state, not only in Italy but also in Europe as a whole, and this was their contribution to European ideas.

LITERATURE IN THE HIGH RENAISSANCE PERIOD

A range of original literary creations was produced in northeast Italy in the period on either side of 1500. Here we shall find a literary culture in a sense parallel with the literary world of the Medici circles at Florence under Lorenzo: a new secularised expressiveness that liberated a state of mind intent on individual character and the naturalistic depiction of life.

Pietro Bembo (1470–1547) was a well-to-do Venetian patrician who failed to secure himself an important role in the administration of his native city and devoted himself instead to literature. Fascinated by the tiny court maintained at Asolo in the Veneto by Catherine Cornaro, a member of one of the great Venetian colonial families who called herself Queen of Cyprus because she had married the last Lucignan king of the island, Bembo composed his *Asolani* (1502), which vulgarised Ficino's Neoplatonism. This philosophy was presented as a defence of love as a force capable of elevating human beings towards the divinity. This was in fact the version of Ficino's ideas that most commonly penetrated the literary world, where they were widely accepted in the early sixteenth century, and Bembo was later adopted as the imaginary expounder of them in Castiglione's *The Book of the Courtier*. Bembo also established himself as a new arbiter of literary taste, laying down influential precepts for the use of Latin and Italian that helped to rescue the vernacular from the subservient position in which it had been placed by the humanists' obsession with Latin and Greek in the fifteenth century.

One of the features of the Renaissance period was the attempt to adapt medieval romance to modern taste. The romance stories, dominated by King Arthur, Charlemagne and other such figures, had provided the main subject matter of imaginative narrative since the twelfth century.

Gonzaga family, Camera degli Sposi (detail),
Mantegna, 1465-74
(Palazzo Ducale, Mantua)

123

Isabella d'Este,
Titian, 1534 (Gemäldegalerie, Vienna)

They offered many poets opportunities to tell stories of war, love and magic, often fantastic, sometimes subtle, characteristically long, with rambling successions of episodes. Romance literature was still alive at the time of Thomas Malory, who wrote *Morte d'Arthur* in England in the mid-fifteenth century. It was a type of literature inseparably connected with the world of nobility and gentry because it dealt with the customs of chivalry and courtly behaviour that were a kind of ideology of the noble and landed classes. In the course of the sixteenth century these ideals were eroded by the development of large national armies, gunpowder and the greater importance of commerce, but the process was slow. Chivalric attitudes and indeed jousts were still common. The novel did not yet exist and writers with narrative instincts often adopted the form of the romance. Luigi Pulci and Matteo Boiardo in fifteenth-century Italy and Rabelais and Cervantes in sixteenth-century France and Spain wrote romance stories, partly or entirely satirical, which were particularly suitable for the environment of despotism with its host of courtly knights and squires.

The greatest Italian writer of romance was Ludovico Ariosto, a gentleman attached to the Este family at Ferrara. His *Orlando Furioso*, first published in 1516, became one of the most popular books of sixteenth-century Europe and one of the links between Italy and the rest of the continent. Its origin in Ferrara was understandable because that was a courtly society in which the romance ethos was less strange than in the republican commercial cities of Florence and Venice. *Orlando Furioso* is a long and complicated poem which relates stories about a bewildering number of characters. Ariosto spent some twenty-five years on the work and included much superb poetry. The war between Charlemagne and the Muslim invaders of Europe provides the general framework. Most of the interest is centred on two couples: Orlando and Angelica, Ruggiero and Bradamante. Ruggiero and Bradamante are supposed to be

imaginary early members of the Este family. Their story is one of faithful love that is ultimately successful. Orlando's long pursuit of Angelica, on the other hand, ends in her final betrayal of him which drives him into madness.

Ariosto does not treat the romance material in a straightforward fashion. He makes frequent references to contemporary people and events and adopts an outwardly casual tone: 'He spurs on his horse, seizes his trusty sword, and makes straight for the place where the noise is coming from: but I will put off till next time telling you what happened, if you want to hear.' We have the impression that his attitude to the stories he is telling is ironical. But, on the other hand, a satirical purpose is much less obvious than it is in Rabelais or Cervantes. Ariosto is not jeering at the society around him.

Ariosto's series of fantastic episodes, either taken over from earlier romances or invented, conceals the fact that his mind was stocked with a vast range of literature, including not only the romance traditions but also the works of Homer, Virgil, Dante and the humanist writers Ficino and Bembo. His stories contain complex reminiscences of classical and Italian writing, deceptively reintegrated by a poet's imagination into forms that are difficult to disentangle. The description of the web woven by Cassandra in canto 46 reminds one of Renaissance painting in which classical legend, Christian doctrine and romantic figures are interwoven:

Here the Graces, gaily attired, are attending a queen in child-bed. A babe is born, of such beauty the like of which the world has never seen from the First Age to the Fourth. Jupiter, eloquent Mercury, Venus and Mars are there: with a generous hand they scatter over him celestial flowers, sweet ambrosia and heavenly perfumes. 'Hippolytus' reads an inscription in minute characters on the swaddling bands. Grown a little stronger, he is taken in hand by Adventure,

125

while Virtue leads the way. New arrivals are portrayed, wearing long hair and garments: they have come on Corvino's behalf to ask the tender lad's father for him.[1]

'Hippolytus' refers to Cardinal Ippolito d'Este, Ariosto's patron. 'Corvino' is King Matthias Corvinus of Hungary, a well-known patron of humanists. Contemporary personages are woven into the romantic picture.

In some cases the themes are poetic reworkings of Renaissance ideas. Ruggiero's release from the spell of the bad sorceress Alcina to the power of the good sorceress Logistella, who redeems him, is an allegory of the choice between luxury and virtue. The whole work reaches its climax with Orlando descending into madness when he discovers that Angelica, the beauty whom he has been pursuing since the beginning of the poem, has fallen in love with, and given herself to, a common soldier. Ariosto interrupts the story with a few lines which probably reflected his own experience:

If you have put your foot in the birdlime spread by Cupid, try to pull it out, and take care not to catch your wing in it too: love, in the universal opinion of wise men, is nothing but madness. Though not everyone goes raving-mad like Orlando, Love's folly shows itself in other ways; what clearer sign of lunacy than to lose your own self through pining for another?

The effects vary, but the madness which promotes them is always the same. It is like a great forest into which those who venture must perforce lose their way: one here, another there, one and all go off the track. Let me tell you this, to conclude: whoever grows old in love ought, in addition to Cupid's torments, to be chained and fettered.

You, my friend, are preaching to others, someone will tell me, but you overlook your own failing. The answer is that now, in an interval of lucidity, I understand a great deal. And I am taking pains (with imminent success, I

hope) to find peace and withdraw from the dance – though I cannot do so as quickly as I should wish, for the disease has eaten me to the bone.

Ariosto is rarely so self-revelatory. But, in spite of his ending the poem by introducing his Este friends and the admired writers of the epoch, and in spite of the theme of the origins of Este grandeur, *Orlando Furioso* impresses one chiefly as a 'great forest'. This is a complex image in which lovers are running wildly, hither and thither, in pursuit of loves that are mostly disastrous. It is a panorama of love-folly in which Ariosto himself was experienced, and no doubt he transferred the varieties of love, male and female, that he himself had suffered and witnessed, into the world of romance adventure in which they could be depicted in extreme forms. Critics have suggested parallels with the 'folly' that his contemporary Erasmus presented in *In Praise of Folly*, as the description of the better sides of human character, contrasted with the viciousness of calculating reason. Ariosto does not, however, present any explicit scheme of human behaviour as Erasmus does. His aim as a poet was to tell a story. His poem appealed to its readers because it told romance stories not as mythical examples but as expositions of the realities of human behaviour exaggerated in a mythical setting. In that sense his work was a narrative expression of the realistic grasp of human characteristics developed in the Renaissance world. The setting of chivalrous activity within the web of courtly relationships made the work acceptable to the gentlemen of the sixteenth century, who lived in, or hankered after, a social setting of that kind on a more mundane level.

The man who came to symbolise the world of the sixteenth-century court, not only in Italy but throughout Europe, drew his inspiration from the court of Urbino. He was Baldassare Castiglione, who came from a wealthy family near Mantua and whose mother was a Gonzaga. In his youth, he studied at Milan and was in contact with the

Baldassare Castiglione,
Raphael, 1514-15 (Louvre, Paris)

Sforza court. From 1504 to 1516 he worked for the rulers of Urbino, first Guidobaldo Montefeltro and then Francesco Maria della Rovere, a relation of Pope Julius II placed there by the Pope. In his later years Castiglione took orders and became a servant of Pope Clement VII. By profession he was a courtier. Apart from living at the court he took part in war and went on embassies, one of them to England to collect the Order of the Garter for the Duke of Urbino. He was also a learned man who had absorbed the Latin and Greek culture of the humanists.

The combination of personal charm, evident in the portrait of him painted by Raphael, of experience of the courtly world, and of humanist scholarship, enabled him to write *The Book of the Courtier*. Following the tradition of Latin dialogues written by the humanists, this dialogue, written in Italian, consists of imaginary conversations in which different speakers present different ideas. The discussion was supposed to take place between people at the court of Urbino over four evenings, and it was about the best way of life to be followed by a courtier:

So all day and everyday at the Court of Urbino was spent on honourable and pleasing activities both of the body and the mind. But since the Duke always retired to his bedroom soon after supper, because of his infirmity, as a rule at that hour everyone went to join the Duchess, Elisabetta Gonzaga, with whom was always to be found Signora Emilia Pia, a lady gifted with such a lively wit and judgment that she seemed to be in command of all and to endow everyone else with her own discernment and goodness. In their company polite conversations and innocent pleasantries were heard, and everyone's face was so full of laughter and gaiety that the house could truly be called the very inn of happiness.[2]

The first three books contain a wide-ranging discussion about life at the court and how courtiers should behave. It deals, among other things, with chivalry, honour, styles of speech, and the games that should be played. Attention is paid to the characters of women, who play a substantial part in the conversation and are clearly important at the court, and to problems of love, in which weaknesses of both men and women are resolutely attacked. The impression conveyed is of a circle of intelligent and lively people with wide experience and a good capacity for telling stories.

Although the form of the book grew out of the humanist dialogues, the manner is much closer to reported speech and the substance closer to the content of everyday witticisms:

'So it would be very fitting, madam, if since you are a woman and ought to know what pleases women, you undertake the task yourself and put everyone in your debt.'

'But you enjoy such universal favour with women,'

replied Signora Emilia, 'that you must surely know all the ways in which their favour can be won. So it's fitting that you should teach them to others.'

'Madam,' replied the Unico, 'I should give a lover no more useful advice than that he should ensure that you have no influence on the lady whose favour he seeks; for such good qualities as everyone once thought were mine, together with the sincerest love that ever existed, have not had as much power to make me loved as you have had to make me hated.'[3]

In the fourth book of *The Book of the Courtier* Castiglione advanced to a more serious subject: the political philosophy of the princely state. He accepted throughout, without much question, that the state he was talking about was a monarchy. But he applied an essentially Aristotelian approach to the subject. Rulers should be encouraged to lead a contemplative life which would equip them better to encourage subjects to practise the arts of peace. They should take the advice of the nobility and the people, so as to make the state as far as possible a combination of monarchy, aristocracy and popular rule. Castiglione was adapting principles of political analysis devised for a republican city state to a despotism and, in so doing, he defended the view that the prince's aim should not be chivalric success in war, but the betterment of his subjects.

Finally, Castiglione rose to a panegyric expressing the idea that the lover's enjoyment of beauty could be elevated into an awareness of the essential goodness of God and the universe. A rational approach to beauty would lead to a rational appreciation of its true value and thus ultimately to the kind of contemplation of the divinity which Plato and St Francis had been able to achieve. This was a somewhat simplified expression of the Neoplatonic philosophy developed at Florence by Ficino, put here into the mouth of Pietro Bembo as one of the courtiers assembled at Urbino. Bembo was in real life, like Castiglione, associated with the court of Urbino and an actual populariser of Ficino's ideas.

It provided a grand climax to the discussions, which had mostly been concerned with much more down-to-earth aspects of human behaviour.

The Book of the Courtier, in the Italian in which it was written and in translations into the other European languages, was reprinted at least 110 times between 1528 and 1619. It shared with Erasmus' works the capacity to nourish the whole European mind. Via the Italian court, it transmitted to Europe the delicate perception of human relations and the social and political philosophy that had arisen in the Italian cities, providing a range of attractive observations and ideals acceptable to the nobility and gentry of monarchical states. From a social point of view the works of both Ariosto and Castiglione were important as adaptations of city ideas that made them acceptable in the broader seignorial society of Italy and Europe.

Bembo, Ariosto and Castiglione created a new world of polite literature suitable for the educated gentleman of the sixteenth century, in rather the same way as the novels of Balzac and Dickens appealed to the bourgeoisie of their era. The new literature was Italian, not Latin; and whilst it owed much to the humanists, it presented a range of naturalistic portrayals of character and society which constituted a new stage in the literary imitation of life. The authors were principally at home in the society of the court but their familiarity with city humanism enabled them to act as intermediaries between city culture and the external world.

VENETIAN ART: MANTEGNA AND BELLINI

There were many connections between Florentine and Venetian art, some of them straightforward, such as the visit of Andrea Verrocchio, one of Lorenzo de' Medici's favourite artists, to Venice to erect the equestrian statue to Bartolommeo Colleoni, a favoured Venetian *condottiere*. In the later fifteenth century the outstanding figures in the tradition of Venetian art were Andrea Mantegna (1430-1506) and Giovanni Bellini (d. 1507). Mantegna, who was

Bellini's brother-in-law, came from Padua, a Venetian city not far from Venice, and the early influences on his mind must have included the learned classicism available in that university city, sometimes regarded as Venice's *Quartier Latin*. In 1460 he entered the service of the Gonzaga family at Mantua and was a well-paid servant for the rest of his life, an exceptionally close connection between a notable artist and a court. He was placed in a triangle of influences from Padua, Venice and Mantua and his most famous compositions, the frescoes in the Camera degli Sposi and the *Triumphs of Caesar*, would have been unthinkable without Gonzaga patronage.

Mantegna's figure-drawing and use of perspective, his command of colour and his attention to minute detail, which led Ruskin to advise that his paintings should be examined with a powerful looking-glass, made his work immediately pleasing. In another sense, however, his most striking characteristic was the classicism that encouraged him to paint classical mythology and to give particular attention to the painting of real or imaginary Roman buildings. Botticelli and Mantegna can be regarded as the two parallel, independent innovators who introduced classicism into paintings, but they were in many ways very different. Unlike his contemporary, Mantegna does not seem to have been an expert painter who then received classical instructions from his patrons. A record has survived that includes him in a humanist jaunt to Lake Garda in 1464 in which the participants amused themselves by copying Roman inscriptions. Clearly Mantegna had pretensions to some classical scholarship of his own.

The instinct which the feeling for classical models had inspired appeared already in an early work, mostly destroyed in World War II, the frescoes of the lives of St James and St Christopher in the Ovetari Chapel in Padua. Mantegna had taken pains to fill his frescoes both with elaborate perspective vistas and accurate presentations of Roman buildings. In the *Trial of St James* King Herod is

Trial of St James,
Mantegna, 1454-5 (destroyed, formerly Ovetari Chapel, Padua)

seated on a raised throne with the saint looking up to him. Behind them is a passable imitation of a Roman triumphal arch with a genuine inscription on it. Roman soldiers appropriately clad stand about. Beyond and through the arch the landscape stretches in the far distance. The painting is a successful combination of antiquarianism and realistic space. In the *Martyrdom of St Christopher* Mantegna essayed a still more adventurous design when he joined together two separate panels, dominated by a mass of Roman architecture, with an illusionistic column that seems to be part of the space of the panels.

Mantegna's most famous construction was the *Triumphs of Caesar*, painted much later between 1485 and 1492. The series of nine panels was designed to celebrate a victory of a *condottiere* Gonzaga, an example of the typical way in which Renaissance military prowess could attach itself to purely

classical illustration. The panels portray the procession of a Roman triumph, including soldiers, captives, booty and Julius Caesar himself drawn on his chariot. Mantegna painted a complex line of people moving in front of a landscape and the stances of his figures make it an attractive display, but it is clear that his main interest was the complexity of the miscellaneous antiquarian paraphernalia that makes the paintings look like a museum on the march. A more attractive classicism is to be seen in the two paintings of *Parnassus* and *Pallas expelling the Vices* that he did in the 1490s for the rooms of Isabella d'Este, who was married to a Gonzaga. These paintings illustrate classical mythology, rather as Botticelli's *Primavera* did, though they are less obscure and less ambitious, and the subject matter was mostly specified by the patroness, a lady with scholarly tastes. *Parnassus* shows Mars and Venus, signifying chaste love, while to one side a cupid fires darts at the genitals of Vulcan to destroy his jealous lust. Below, the Muses dance to Orpheus' lyre and Mercury stands to the side with Pegasus. The figures are more awkward than Botticelli's: Mantegna was better at soldiers than nymphs. Nevertheless this delightful scene is another early case of the liberation of painting through classical myth.

Mantegna painted a number of altarpieces too, often magnificent for their figure-drawing, harsh landscapes and distant walled cities, like the *Agony in the Garden*. His concentration on classical themes somewhat distorted his art but it also gave him his striking individuality. Of all the artists of the late fifteenth century he was the most wholeheartedly devoted to antiquity. Employment by the Gonzaga saved him from the lifelong church-painting that was the fate of many good artists and provided the most striking early example of the beneficent laicisation that could result from the patronage of a noble household.

Giovanni Bellini was nevertheless a more significant painter than Mantegna because his efforts were principally directed towards the improvement of the technique of

130

ABOVE Bearers of the Statues of the Gods,
from the Triumphs of Caesar, *Mantegna,*
c.1485-92 (Hampton Court, London © Her Majesty the Queen)

BELOW Parnassus,
Mantegna, c.1495 (Louvre, Paris)

St Francis,
Giovanni Bellini, c.1475 (Frick Collection, New York)

painting rather than the pursuit of original subjects. His success in painting figures and faces within a realistic space produced a refinement that can only be described as revolutionary for Venice and was to some extent parallel to the advances Leonardo da Vinci was making at the same time in Florence and Milan. As with Leonardo, Bellini's skill with the brush was inseparable from his acceptance of Flemish influence, both in the introduction of oil painting and in his more sensitive attention to landscape. Unlike Leonardo, however, Bellini was a modest man who left hardly any record of his thoughts outside his paintings. We do not know what he imagined he was aiming at and the obscure iconography of some of his works gives few clues. He was one of the more mysterious of the Renaissance

painters, whom we have to interpret on the basis of visual work without any other assistance. In his work of the 1460s and 1470s the ruggedness of the figures and the stratified rocks suggest the influence of Mantegna. Later he seems to have been impressed by the German artist Dürer, who visited Venice in 1506, and the acute sadness and sharpness of some of his Passion scenes may reflect a Northern influence. Despite his receptiveness, Bellini seems to have been able to absorb external forces without transforming his essential instinct for the loving presentation of human sadness in the environment of nature.

Oil painting began to be used under Flemish influence in the 1460s and the effect it had can be seen slightly later in two of Bellini's major works of the 1470s. The *Coronation of the Virgin* at Pesaro is an original attempt to place the coronation within a single space. The Virgin and Christ are on a square marble seat. Outside the arms of the seat are four saints. Behind them rises a classical structure like an altarpiece, through which we see, as through a window, an elaborate landscape scene of a hill with three towers: an identifiable scene near Pesaro but perhaps also intended to refer to the Trinity. The whole painting, figures and landscape, begins to be endowed with the warm quality of light and colour that oil allows. Shortly after this, Bellini painted one of his most famous creations, the *St Francis*, in which the light and the landscape played a still more interesting role. The saint stands in the open, his hands, already bearing the stigmata, outstretched as though the

stigmatisation were taking place. Most of the painting is an elaborate landscape including rocks, fields, plants, trees, animals, distant buildings and an onlooking shepherd and is suffused with light whose source is not clear, though it may be coming from the sun somewhere beyond the top left-hand corner. Are we being shown the stigmatisation, without the traditional rays directed by the seraph to the saint's body, or is this a painting of Francis glorying in the multifarious wealth of nature which he adored? We are given no clue. Whatever the answer, this was perhaps the greatest landscape of fifteenth-century Italy, a painting that expresses Bellini's sense of the identification of man and nature.

By the 1490s Bellini was fully in command of the total

Madonna and Child with Two Female Saints,
Giovanni Bellini, c.1500
(Accademia, Venice)

Madonna of the Meadow,
Giovanni Bellini, c.1500-1505
(National Gallery, London)

presentation of human features which he had developed. One of the best examples is the *Madonna and Child with Two Female Saints*. The three female faces are set against a dark background but brightly lit, as from a candle or fire before them. The chiaroscuro of fully rounded faces was a successful experiment with a new kind of painting. Bellini's skill in handling religious scenes was carried forwards to its height in the first decade of the sixteenth century. About the same time he painted the *Madonna of the Meadow* in which the Madonna and Child are seen against an elaborate agricultural setting, including cows, a swain, a maid and a well, as though the innocence of the mother and babe were being connected with the realities of country life.

It was probably in the 1490s that Bellini painted his strange *Sacred Allegory*, which has lent itself to various interpretations. It consists of a fenced and stone-floored platform at the centre of which is a fruit tree with four infants playing below it. At one end are two nude men, one of whom is St Sebastian; at the other end are three ladies, one of whom, though it has been disputed, may be the Madonna. Two figures looking like Peter and Paul lean across the fence from outside and a turbaned figure, presumably a Muslim, walks away. The platform is by a lake beyond which an extensive landscape stretches back. It is probably an allegorical picture of the Church in relation to the world but its exact meaning remains hidden. It is clear, however, that Bellini was playing sensitively with the romantic landscape that pleased him in order to establish a relationship between the natural and the spiritual worlds. When Isabella d'Este was trying to negotiate with him through Pietro Bembo for the production of a painting, Bembo reported that she must not tie him down, 'because

Sacred Allegory,
Giovanni Bellini,
c.1490 (Uffizi, Florence)

he is accustomed to move as he wishes in his work'.

In the last twenty years of his life Bellini spent a great deal of time on paintings in the Doge's Palace which were destroyed by fire later in the sixteenth century. Much of his work is unknown to us and we may have a one-sided view of him. Based on what we do know, it seems that at the very end of his life Bellini was dragged out of his normal religious preoccupations – everything suggests that he was a pious man whose altarpieces were deeply felt – and persuaded to do paintings of a different kind connected with other currents in the later development of the Venetian style.

There are two notable pictures in this new class. One is the *Lady Combing Her Hair*, a charming painting which was certainly a nude given to someone for the erotic pleasure it provided, foreshadowing Titian's great Venuses. The other

is the much debated *Feast of the Gods*, an unusual case of a picture that was originally painted by one supreme artist, Bellini, and then substantially altered by another, Titian. The *Feast of the Gods* is based on a story in Ovid's *Metamorphoses*. The gods fell asleep under the trees of Ida after a feast. Priapus, seeing the beautiful Lotis asleep, seized his chance of lifting the robe that covered her, but at that moment Silenus' ass brayed and the gods woke up. Bellini painted the picture for the private apartments of Alfonso d'Este at Ferrara, as the first of a series of paintings about classical subjects that Alfonso hoped to receive from leading contemporary artists. It was finished in 1514. Some years later, when Titian had done other paintings for the same room, the *Feast of the Gods* did not fit into the series. Titian therefore painted over quite large portions of Bellini's original work. His main change, as X-rays have

135

Lady Combing Her Hair,
Giovanni Bellini, 1515
(Kunsthistorisches Museum, Vienna)

Feast of the Gods,
Giovanni Bellini, 1514 (Fletcher Fund, 1936, National Gallery of Art, Washington)

shown, were to remodel completely the landscape on the left-hand side. More important than Titian's intervention is that this painting is an example of the refinement of Venetian art applied to a classical subject to suit the taste of a despot. It marked the beginning of the sixteenth-century taste for pictures with narrative subjects drawn from mythology, which was to become prominent under the leadership of Titian.

THE AGE OF GIORGIONE 1500-10

The idea that the moment of acceleration in Venetian art came with Giorgione was first stated by Vasari, who described him thus:

Though he was of very humble origin, his manners were

gentle and polished throughout his life. Brought up in Venice, he displayed very amorous propensities, and was exceedingly fond of the lute, playing and singing so divinely that he was frequently invited to musical gatherings and meetings of noble persons. He studied drawing and was so fond of it, Nature assisting him to her utmost, and he was so enamoured of the beauty of that art, that he would never introduce anything into his works which he had not drawn from life. So closely did he follow Nature, and so carefully did he imitate her, that not only did he acquire the reputation of having surpassed Gentile and Giovanni Bellini, but he competed with the Tuscan masters, the authors of the modern style. Having seen and greatly admired some things of Leonardo, richly toned and exceedingly dark, Giorgione made them his model, and imitated them carefully in painting oils… Nature had so richly endowed him that he succeeded wonderfully both in oils and fresco, making certain things so soft and harmonious and his shadows so vapourous, that many artists of recognised standing admitted that he was born to infuse his figures with spirit and to counterfeit the freshness of living flesh better than any painter, not in Venice alone but everywhere.

Vasari, who was writing nearly half a century after Giorgione's death, may have been too remote to know much about him, but the description of his life and work fits the impressions conveyed by the paintings now commonly attributed to him. Complaints about the lack of sources for Renaissance artists are common, but Giorgione remains the most enigmatic artist of his rank. He came into prominence about 1500 and certainly died in 1510 but not much is known about the intervening short life beyond what we attempt to deduce from the paintings. He did most of his painting for a limited, rather sophisticated lay clientèle. Vasari may be correct in thinking that Leonardo was one of his inspirations. His patrons may have had a taste for the gentle atmosphere of autumnal sadness that fills his paintings. He created, at any rate, a style in which the freedom of subject matter, in combination with advanced painting, went further than it had before at Venice.

To place Giorgione in perspective, one should probably set him against the background of a growing interest in classical visual art in late fifteenth-century Venice before Giorgione appeared. An example of this is the sculpture of Tullio Lombardo. His *Adam*, which was prepared for the tomb of Doge Andrea Vendramin in the 1490s, is an upright, beautifully proportioned figure of a man, which looks like an imitation of the antique. Some have suggested that it may have been a contributory model for Michelangelo's *Bacchus and David*, the former sculpted only a few years after Tullio's work. The wish to imitate the classical world had already become strong and refined at Venice.

Print from Hypnerotomachia Poliphili, 1499

One of the most remarkable publications of Aldus Manutius, the greatest revolutionary publisher and printer, at Venice was the *Hypnerotomachia Poliphili*, printed in 1499, probably written by a friar, Francesco Colonna. This was a romantic story of a dreamlike search by Polifilo for his beloved Polia which takes him through various adventures and encounters with nymphs and goddesses to final success. The story is full of classical allusions and descriptions of classical buildings and objects, and it was illustrated by an unknown artist who was quite clearly an expert. The classical drawings attract the attention more easily than the text. The book implies an interest in a kind of classicising romance and, taken together with the work of Bembo, makes it somewhat easier to understand the background to the painting associated with Giorgione and early Titian. This was a society which, like Lorenzo's Florence, had a

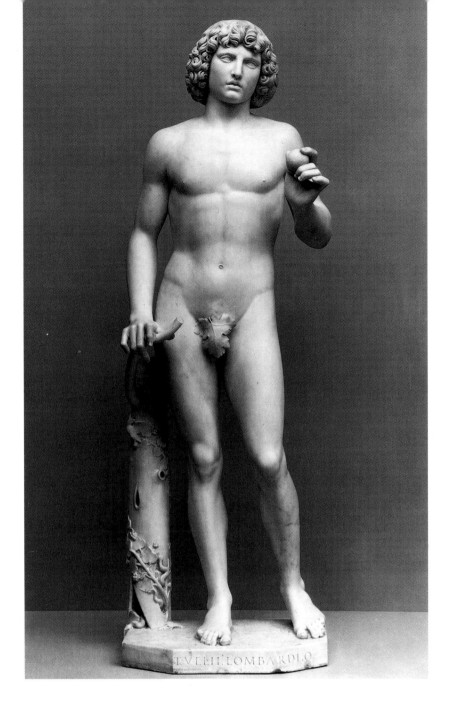

Adam,
Lombardo, 1492-5
(Metropolitan Museum of Art, New York)

secular culture that was ready to appreciate new kinds of secular art.

Giorgione's most famous paintings, and those most confidently attributed to him, are the *Tempest*, the *Three Philosophers*, and the *Sleeping Venus*. They all to some extent conform with Vasari's description of the artist. The *Tempest* was perhaps connected with reactions to Venice's political and military plight in the period of invasion by the League of Cambrai 1508–9. The soldier and the nursing mother in the foreground have been identified by some as representing Fortitude and Chastity in a time of trouble, and the streak of lightning in the thunderous sky of the background as the work of Fortune which the city must suffer. Giorgione may well have entertained ideas like these. But many conflicting interpretations have been offered, including the idea that the man and woman are Adam and Eve. This is difficult to fit with the city walls behind and also with the fact, revealed by X-rays, that the man was originally a female figure. Giorgione incorporated his figures in a painting of nature in

139

Three Philosophers,
Giorgione, c.1500-10
(Kunsthistorisches Museum, Vienna)

a thunderstorm, capturing not only the landscape, but the atmospheric feeling that pervaded it, in the range of greens and blue-greens with which he painted the plants, the river and the sky. It is his most interesting landscape.

The subject of *Three Philosophers* is also difficult to determine. The painting was certainly related to philosophy because mathematical and astronomical allusions are indicated by the young man's pair of compasses and the drawings on the old man's sheet of paper. A Platonic interpretation is suggested by the fact that the youngest of the three is staring into a dark cave like the non-philosophers in Plato's *Republic*, instead of looking at the marvellous landscape that stretches away from him behind the tree. Perhaps the turbaned figure refers to Arab exponents of classical thought. Perhaps the old man, not unlike Raphael's Plato in the *School of Athens*, is the wise philosopher king himself. The figures, especially the ingenious side view of the reflective youth, are among Giorgione's best and they are placed again in a marvellous landscape. The most convincing interpretation is that they are the three Magi at the moment of observing the star that is to lead them to Bethlehem. It is difficult to explain the importance of philosophical content and landscape in a painting like this, for which we know nothing of the programme.

The *Sleeping Venus* was the first and most attractive of reclining nudes in the Venetian Renaissance tradition, less provocative, more mellow and more directly a presentation

Tempest,
Giorgione, c.1500-1510 (Accademia, Venice)

Sleeping Venus,
Giorgione, c.1510 (Gemäldegalerie, Dresden)

of the beauty of a woman than Titian's Venuses. Like them it must have been painted for an erotic purpose but its approach to the female form was more serious. The landscape was partly painted by Titian, who seems in the last years of Giorgione's life to have rivalled his master. He perhaps upset the older man's temperament, and may finally have taken over the completion of some of his works. Looking back to the *Tempest*, however, it is not difficult to identify the particular wayward romanticism which was characteristic of Giorgione and helped to make him a more attractive and original painter than the ambitious

professionals who were commoner in the Venetian scene.

The style of painting that Giorgione introduced was fundamentally different from the Florentine tradition. He emphasised colour and light rather than the shape of figures and objects, and did not follow preliminary drawings but allowed his design to develop as he proceeded with his brushwork. This approach became common among later Venetians, notably Titian and Tintoretto, and it produced a kind of painting in which the creation of a unified ambience of colour was dominant. Venetians had of course long taken over the sense of spatial depth invented by the Florentines

Concert Champêtre,
Giorgione, c.1510-15 (Louvre, Paris)

and continued to use it, but the design of space was less important to them. Flemish oil painting and Flemish landscape also had a more obvious effect on the Venetians and, in spite of the parallel of Leonardo, fitted better with their aim of reproducing a world of subtle and rich colouring rather than precisely delineated forms seen in perspective.

Giorgione's little-known career is only a part of the general obscurity that veils Venetian art at the beginning of the sixteenth century. The limits of Giorgione's *oeuvre* are disputed and several major paintings are difficult to assign to individual painters. Perhaps the most famous is the so-called *Concert Champêtre*, a scene of two musicians in a landscape, apparently conversing and unaware of the presence of two nude female figures. Are they muses existing only in another world? The *Concert Champêtre* is unquestionably one of the outstanding paintings of the Renaissance and one of the greatest works created in Venice in the early sixteenth century but we have no independent information to help us to interpret it. Another painting, the attribution of which was much disputed in the past, though it is now clearly given to the young Sebastiano del Piombo,

Judgment of Solomon,
Sebastiano del Piombo, c.1509-10
(National Trust, Kingston Lacey, Dorset)

is the *Judgment of Solomon*. This is remarkable for its impressive use of the vista of classical architecture and the assurance of the clearly delineated figures, all successfully related to each other. Painted when he was still in Venice, which he left in 1511, it has already the commanding impressiveness that marks his later works.

In Venice during the period from 1500 to 1510 there was an atmosphere, partly derived from literature, which cultivated a taste for the Theocritan country idyll, associated with the Greek poet Theodotus, for landscape and for classicism. The precise nature of the movement is unclear but we would probably be right to link it, like the artistic movements at Florence, with an educated aristocracy, devoted to classical literature and willing to patronise artists capable of satisfying a secular romanticism. At Venice there was no figure as dominant as Leonardo, and the broader spread of an original cast of mind makes this in some ways a more striking movement, though the lack of good evidence renders it more difficult to observe. The city of Venice had a more naturally secular society than Florence, farther away from the pope at Rome, and less willing to accept ecclesiastical interference. When Florence was anxiously trying to placate Pope Julius II (1503-13), Venice was at war with him. It was this secular setting that provided the background to the broad romanticism associated with Giorgione and the young Titian, creating a Renaissance art comparable in magnitude and originality with the art of Laurentian Florence.

CHAPTER SIX

THE HIGH RENAISSANCE IN FLORENCE AND ROME

THE LAST GREAT REVOLUTION in the Florentine tradition of painting and, to a lesser extent, sculpture, occurred in Florence and Rome between 1490 and 1530. The source of the inspiration was the broad and complex tradition of Florentine art, with which the Roman tradition could not compare. But although Rome had to import its artists, the connection between the two cities was essential. Two important popes of the pre-Reformation period, Julius II (1503–13) and Leo X (1513–21), were devoted to the embellishment of their see and prepared to pay for it on a scale with which there was nothing comparable in Florence. At the same time the cities were intimately connected politically. The Medici were turned out of Florence in 1494 but returned to dominate it from 1512 to 1527 and again in 1530. Leo X and Clement VII (1523–34) were both Medici popes, the first a son, the second a nephew of Lorenzo the Magnificent, and they took a keen interest in what was happening in both Rome and Florence.

Throughout this period Florence was deeply troubled by revolution, war and religious conflict, in complete contrast to the relatively stable, laicising society of the age of Cosimo and Lorenzo. One reason for this was that from 1494 onwards Italy became, as against the isolation of the period 1454 to 1494, a place of repeated warfare between the kings of France, the kings of Spain and the Habsburg Holy Roman Emperors, who in the person of Charles V added Spain to their empire as a result of the accidents of marriage. It was beyond the capacity of the small Italian states to deal with these rulers on equal terms. They became the victims of super-power rivalry.

After the expulsion of the Medici in 1494 the Florentines attempted to return to republicanism but did not succeed in doing so. In the years from 1494 to 1498 they fell under the control of the idealistic and puritanical Dominican, Girolamo Savonarola, who carried many of them into excesses of religious austerity very different from the tolerant secularism of Lorenzo. Savonarola's prophetic voice affected most Florentine artists of this period; least of all perhaps Leonardo da Vinci, who spent most of his working life abroad developing a highly personal philosophy. Botticelli repented of his earlier secular art and one of the new masters, Fra Bartolommeo, burned his nude drawings and joined the Dominican order. It is difficult to know how much Savonarola's example affected Michelangelo or how much it encouraged the increased seriousness and grandeur often found in Florentine art of the early sixteenth century.

After Savonarola the Florentines attempted to introduce a permanent head of the republic in imitation of the Doge of Venice. In 1512 the Spanish returned the city to the keeping of the Medici. It was unfortunate for the Medici and for Florence that the two chief Medici managers of the city, Giuliano Duke of Nemours and Lorenzo Duke of Urbino – the two men commemorated by figures in Michelangelo's New Sacristy – both died within a few years. The final attempt to restore republicanism came between 1527 and 1530 and is associated with Michelangelo's management of the city's fortifications. After that the Medici returned permanently, as rulers.

The internal upheavals of Florence in the early sixteenth

Niccolò Machiavelli,
early sixteenth century
(Palazzo Vecchio, Florence)

way that will secure their power, disregarding the moral prohibitions that are observed in private life. He introduces us to real figures, whether they are Moses or Alexander from antiquity or Cesare Borgia or Julius II from contemporary life, glimpsed briefly as out-and-out politicians rather than as patterns of virtue or vice, and uses them as examples within a rational argument. This approach presented political theory in a different literary form from the works of medieval philosophers and even early Renaissance humanists. Machiavelli gave it a sharper focus as the activity of fallen humanity seen in individual lives.

Machiavelli can be regarded as the successor of Bruni and Alberti. Like many Florentine civil servants he was a classicist who believed in the value of lessons to be learned from the Roman past. He was also a satirist who stood on its head the traditional milk-and-water advice given to rulers by the authors of handbooks for princes:

A prudent ruler cannot keep his word, nor should he, when such fidelity would damage him, and when the reasons that made him promise are no longer relevant. This advice would not be sound if all men were upright; but because they are treacherous and would not keep their promises to you, you should not consider yourself bound to keep your promises to them...

[Pope] Alexander VI was concerned only with deceiving men, and he always found them gullible. No man ever affirmed anything more forcefully or with stronger oaths but kept his word less.[1]

Machiavelli wrote comic plays whose literary extravagances seep into his political thought. He was also,

century were the background to the essays in political thought composed in the Renaissance period by Niccolò Machiavelli, the *Discourses* and *The Prince*. Machiavelli was a civil servant who lost his job because of the overthrow of the republic in 1512. He went on to write his two most famous books which contain observations inspired by bitter experience of political dilemmas. The *Discourses*, which takes the form of a long commentary on Livy's history of Rome, is a series of reflections on the difficulties of maintaining a republican government. *The Prince*, which is brief and pithy, exerted great influence in the next two centuries, though it was probably designed specifically as advice to one of the Medici on how to establish effective control in a newly acquired city. Machiavelli is famous for his realistic advice to rulers to conduct themselves in the however, an experienced and perceptive observer of politics in an environment appropriate for realistic candour: republican Florence imperfectly controlled by the Medici under the aegis of the tolerant papacy of Leo X. He examined the behaviour of politicians realistically in the same way as the sixteenth-century realism of painting and drama examined other kinds of characters.

The *Discourses on the First Ten Books of Livy*, to give it its full title, is a book about republics. It is based on Livy's account of the history of the Roman republic, seen as a political story that offers lessons for other times and places. Machiavelli had particularly in mind the recent history of Florence. The experiment of giving the Florentine republic an elected head of state, the Standardbearer for Life, on the model of the Venetian Doge, had come to a bad end. Machiavelli had been attached to that system of government and was deeply involved in its administration. Therefore the Roman republican polity, the historical situation in which in spite of ancient traditions and popular willingness it seemed impossible to maintain a stable electoral system, was of great interest to him. Like the earlier humanists he accepted the doctrine that the movement from republican Rome to the empire was a decline. Ancient Rome could shed light on the problems of modern Florence.

The *Discourses* reveals that Machiavelli was acutely aware of the problem of 'corruption' in a republic, whereby private gain was placed before the good of the whole state. Machiavelli accepted with charming naïveté the idea that there were states in which, as the stories of Roman heroes like Fabricius showed, men thought and acted in terms of the good of the state even if that conflicted with their private interest. In the later Roman republic and in the political world that Machiavelli had experienced in Florence, public interest was subordinated to the interests of classes or individuals and the republican polity became unworkable. The security of the state could ultimately be rescued only by the intervention of a despot. This concern

with the tendency of states to move from republicanism through corruption to despotism led Machiavelli to adopt a cyclical view of history that was inspired by the Greek historian Polybius. All political systems tended to go through the same cycle of change, returning at the end of it to the despotism from which the republicans had first freed themselves and thus going through the cycle again. A cyclical theory was the natural implication of the city-state political theory formulated by Plato and Aristotle in the ancient world because they assumed that there was a standard range of constitutions – aristocracy, democracy, monarchy – through which states might pass. By adopting this cyclical theory, Machiavelli introduced a classical concept into modern thought partly because of Italian veneration of Rome, partly because of genuine similarities between ancient and modern city states. This approach to political theory was not easily transferable to the very different world of the Northern monarchies but Machiavelli's prestige was such that it was later transferred, with quite considerable implications for European political thought up to the eighteenth century.

Though much concerned with classes and systems, the *Discourses* pays considerable attention to individuals both ancient and modern and there are obvious links between this book and the advice given to despots in *The Prince*. For example, in the *Discourses* he describes the conquest of Perugia by Pope Julius II in 1505 as a case of the impetuosity of the victor, who rashly went into the city ahead of his army, triumphing over the inadequacy of an opponent, Giampaolo Baglioni, the ruler of Perugia. Observers were puzzled by Julius's success, wondering why a criminal like Baglioni had held back:

They could not believe that it was any good motive, or his conscience, that held him back, for the heart of a criminal who had committed incest with his own sister and to gain the throne had put to death his cousins and his nephews, could scarcely be influenced by any pious consideration. So they concluded it must be due to men not knowing how to be either magnificently bad or perfectly good.[2]

In *The Prince* the same episode appears again, this time to illustrate the significance of Julius's actions rather than Baglioni's. 'Julius by his impetuous move achieved what no other pontiff with the utmost human prudence would have succeeded in doing.' The point of the story here is that

Fortune is a woman, and if you want to control her, it is necessary to treat her roughly ... She is always well disposed towards young men, because they are less cautious and more aggressive, and treat her more boldly.

The interpretation of politics in terms of 'Fortune', the power of external circumstances, and 'Virtue', the inner resources of the individual with which he holds out against external pressure, was inherited by Machiavelli from humanist predecessors such as Alberti and Petrarch. *Virtù*, a key word for Machiavelli, has a less ethical implication and more relevance to the internal capacity of the individual than its English equivalent. The idea of Virtue also acquired an enlarged significance in his writings because he applied it to whole societies as well as to individuals. Successful republics are virtuous, decayed republics corrupt; it is virtuous to have a native militia of citizens fighting for their country rather than a mercenary army of paid foreigners. Looking at Machiavelli's work from the standpoint of the twentieth century, one is struck by the crudeness of his sociology where individuals and peoples are classified by the application of simple descriptions that clearly have no scientific value.

Machiavelli was an essayist giving us his reflections on political events as the fruit of personal experience. *The Prince* is a series of acute observations on how states can be managed, drawn partly from seeing notable contemporary

politicians – Savonarola, Julius II, Cesare Borgia – in action. Written by a bureaucrat who had perhaps decided that republicanism was no longer viable, it was intended to help the Medici in the problem they faced to keep control of Florence.

Machiavelli's machiavellianism, his advocacy of political ruthlessness, was in part the product of a genuine dislike of Christianity and of its enthusiasts:

The people of Florence were persuaded by Friar Girolamo Savonarola that he had converse with God. I do not propose to decide whether it was so or not...

Christianity had serious political defects. It encouraged men to be meek and to seek their rewards in the afterlife. This was harmful to political life because it made it easier for the wicked to gain power. How much better was the religion of antiquity which 'did not beatify men unless they were replete with worldly glory: army commanders for instance and rulers of republics'. Machiavelli admired ancient religion for being at one with the state, unlike modern religion which worked against it. In this respect he foreshadowed the attitudes of writers in the distant future such as Gibbon and Nietzsche. Though suspicious of Christianity he had of course to accept the fact that the Pope and Church had political importance in Italy. *The Prince* ends with a chapter on the freeing of Italy from the barbarians, addressed to the Medici in general but presumably thinking primarily of Pope Leo X. These observations on Christianity and the Italian nation are arresting but Machiavelli's distinction between private and political morality was his most notable innovation. This too must be seen as a product of the tolerant Italy in a period in which lines of religious conflict had not yet encouraged states to be as suspicious of rebellious opinions as they later became during the Reformation.

His other great innovation was to accompany the

presentation of his political heroes and villains with a realistic estimation of their aims and characters. Whilst the consideration of political structure and political principle was traditional, this was quite novel. It is an innovation parallel to the development of portraiture, the precise revelation of a single person. Individuals were pulled out of the mass of symbolic and systematic generalisation in which they had previously been embedded. They became *personae* in a theoretical argument but also clearly individual characters with their own peculiarities. This was another audacious step that could only have been taken in Italy. When he fell from office Machiavelli had been tortured by the agents of the Medici, to whose honour and advancement he wrote *The Prince*, but it remains true that the work was a product of the freedom and irreverence characteristic of Florentine city society.

Machiavelli should be seen in company with another prominent commentator on the Florentine scene, Francesco Guicciardini. The two men were complementary in the sense that Machiavelli preferred a fairly wide extension of popular power while Guicciardini thought the city would be better served by strengthening aristocratic power. But Guicciardini was in the long run still more important for his development of the art of writing political history, following the earlier successes of Bruni and others. He wrote a *History of Florence*, covering the post-Medician period, and a very long *History of Italy*. The modern reader of their works feels immediately that he is in a recognisable literary environment, where political events are connected by causal chains. This was indeed the summit of the effort to recreate history, imitating the ancient models. There will not be much development beyond Guicciardini's method before the much later expansion of history into the economic and cultural fields in the eighteenth and nineteenth centuries. Machiavelli and Guicciardini wrote when republican Florence, which they loved, was becoming impossible to maintain and was shortly to fall finally under the sway of the Medici dukes. It is a historical irony that the high point of republican political thought and republican history was reached at that time.

LEONARDO DA VINCI

The visual artists of this period achieved three things in their treatment of the human figure. First, the depiction of the face with a fuller and more affective sensitivity. Second, the depiction of the human body in a more complex range of movements. Third, a relationship between figures that was more satisfying in both an aesthetic and an emotional sense. All this constituted an advance well beyond the comparatively static painting of the age of Botticelli, and the figures of this period can strike the modern eye as catching the extremes of physical action and inner emotion in a way that had not been achieved before.

The originator of the new movement in painting, Leonardo da Vinci (1452–1519), stood in an odd relationship to it. After 1481 he spent little time in Florence and hardly any in Rome, and much of his time was devoted to scientific interests which were not shared by other artists and which had a rather tangential relation to painting, though for him it was an important relation.

Leonardo's most important early work was the *Adoration of the Magi* which he started in 1481 but left unfinished. His inability to finish what he had started was a feature of his whole career and the number of completed works by him is small. But his sketches or cartoons were sometimes so original that they made a profound impression on the artistic world. In this early case Leonardo had achieved a new kind of design for an old subject. The ingredients were the same: the Virgin and Child, the visiting Magi, the crowd of admiring onlookers, the hint of the decayed classical past in the background in contrast with the new promise of the incarnation. The novelty lay in the figures and their arrangement. The Madonna is in a central position in the lower part of the painting. She is seated on the edge

Adoration of the Magi,
Leonardo da Vinci, c.1481-2
(Uffizi, Florence)

of a round platform of earth or rock from which a tree rises. The four Magi are kneeling at four corners around her. Outside them are the faces and in some cases the figures of onlookers and, beyond them, passing horsemen. At the two lower corners are symmetrically placed erect figures, one a pensively observing elderly man, the other a young man looking outwards and connecting the painting with the outside world. The faces, although unfinished, already have the spiritual depth which Leonardo introduced and which he was later to develop with such subtlety by complicated and delicate shading. The circle around the

Madonna consists of figures that are interconnected in a rhythmical manner. They are not merely a random collection of people but a number of convincing individuals relating to the scene and to each other by gestures and expressions. The meaning of some parts of the painting is not clear but its evident nobility made it an object of wonder even in its unfinished state.

In 1482 Leonardo left Florence to work for the Duke of Milan and it was in Milan that he painted the first great works of his maturity which are well-known milestones in the history of European art: the Louvre *Virgin of the Rocks*, the *Lady with an Ermine* and the *Last Supper*. Like many other artists in the service of despots, Leonardo spent much time on solemn, symbolical or jocular pageants, creating ephemeral displays. His reflections on mathematics,

Lady with an Ermine,
Leonardo da Vinci, c.1483 (Czartoryski Museum, Cracow)

geology, the human body and other scientific subjects, however, were recorded on thousands of manuscript pages that were preserved after his death and are now scattered through the libraries of Italy, France, Spain and England. Their survival has allowed historians to piece together, very laboriously, the wanderings of a unique mind of enormous power grappling with an extraordinary range of problems. Leonardo was an autodidact who struggled throughout his life to absorb the scholarship of professional mathematicians and philosophers and to add to it, studying mathematical problems and using the special advantages that he had as an artist. His drawings of anatomical dissections, weight-lifting machines and the movements of water had little importance in the history of science, but as manifestations of a mind with great originality and vision they were astonishing. His combination of outstanding capacity as an artist with deep interest in the problems of natural science made him still more exceptional than if he had been merely the author of the *Last Supper*. Italian Renaissance artists were often expected in addition to have an expertise in architecture and the construction of fortifications. Michelangelo and Brunelleschi, for example, also served the city of Florence as military engineers. Leonardo's interest in scientific problems may have arisen in part out of this side of his profession. But his development of a consuming interest in mathematics and technology was exceptional. It marked him off from other artists, who tended to absorb passively the intellectual environment around them.

Apart from anatomy, in which all Renaissance artists were bound to have an interest, there are also some other areas in which one can see connections between science and painting in Leonardo's work. The haunting landscapes of water and huge caverns that lie at the back of the *Virgin of the Rocks* and the *Mona Lisa* were quite different from the landscapes that many Italians had taken over from Flemish art. They arose out of a personal fascination with the movement of water, flooding and the history of the earth's geology. Leonardo connected currents of water with the entwining of strands of hair and this interest can be seen in the hair of Leda in *Leda and the Swan* (lost and known only from copies) and in his *St John the Baptist*. These were parts of a general intensification of the connection between nature and painting which carried him far beyond the simpler perspective and anatomical accuracy of the fifteenth century, so that his pictures seemed to be sections taken out of an emotionalised natural world.

The Louvre *Virgin of the Rocks* consists of a group of two adults, the Madonna and the angel, and two children, St John and Christ, set against a background of water and rocks. It is impossible to know what Leonardo intended by this juxtaposition of the holy figures and a vision of the structure of the earth. Perhaps it points to some idea of the centrality of the incarnation. The more obvious innovations in the painting lie in the softly rounded features of the figures and the satisfying pyramidal structure of the group in which they all participate. In the later version of the same subject in the National Gallery, London, the figures were given a clearer religious significance by the addition of haloes and a cross, and the treatment of the group was improved by removing the angel's rather awkward, outstretched right hand as well as by a parallel established between the garment of the Madonna and the blue waters behind her. By comparison the *Lady with an Ermine* is a lighthearted portrait of the Duke of Milan's mistress, which presents a charming young woman with a naturalness and an accuracy of characterisation unknown to earlier artists.

The *Last Supper* at Santa Maria delle Grazie in Milan is notoriously difficult to assess because it is badly damaged as a result both of Leonardo's experiments with pigments and of natural decay. But it was in a sense his most ambitious work. The *Last Supper* had been painted with the same characters in much the same positions a thousand times before. What Leonardo added was in part the same as could be seen in his earlier paintings: a greater depth in the depiction of face, figures and emotion. But this was also his most complicated scene, in which thirteen individuals, each with their own thoughts, were interacting at a given moment, and the movement of each one had to be caught.

RIGHT Virgin of the Rocks,
Leonardo da Vinci, c.1483-5
(Louvre, Paris)

Last Supper,
Leonardo da Vinci, 1495-8 (Santa Maria della Grazie, Milan)

The problem was to some extent the same as it had been in the *Adoration* and one that Leonardo did not take up again. But here the individuals had more normal faces; they had to some extent known characteristics, and their intercourse could be presented as the reaction of known people to Christ's sudden announcement, 'Verily I say unto you that one of you shall betray me.'

Leonardo returned to Florence in 1500 during the republican experiment and stayed there off and on until 1508. The years between 1508 and his death in 1519 were to be spent in Lombardy, in Rome, and in France. The Florentine period from 1500 to 1508 was peculiarly important because Leonardo's presence in the city enabled

him to have an impact on other Florentine artists which set them off in a direction that in effect constituted the High Renaissance School of Florence and Rome.

This effect was caused, as far as we can tell, largely by seeing Leonardo's works and realising that his example must be followed. Of the two works which we know caused great excitement, the first was a lost cartoon of the Virgin and St Anne that was exhibited and seen by crowds in 1501. Although it is lost we can gain some idea of its character by looking at two related surviving works: the cartoon of the *Virgin and Child with St Anne and St John* in the National Gallery and the painting of the *Virgin and Child with St Anne* in the Louvre. The London cartoon shows the Virgin seated

Virgin and Child with St Anne,
Leonardo da Vinci, c.1508-10 (Louvre, Paris)

beside St Anne, partly on her knee, the Child stretched across their legs and the infant St John almost upright to the right leaning on Anne's other knee. The Louvre painting has the Virgin seated across Anne's knees, bending forward to grasp the Child who is playing with a lamb. It is perhaps the most satisfying of all Leonardo's surviving paintings. The onlookers of 1501 were presumably captivated as we are by the fullness and freedom of the forms, by the deep

inscrutability of the expressions of the Virgin and Anne, and by the pleasing pattern of forms that was achieved by the relationships of faces and limbs. Humanity was presented realistically but with a greatly heightened attractiveness, and figures were effectively related to each other.

The other influential painting was the result of the republic of Florence's intention to build a new Great Hall for meetings of the council. The room itself was ready by

Michelangelo's Battle of Cascina,
copy, Aristotile da Sangallo, early sixteenth century
(Holkham Hall, Norfolk)

1503 when it was decided to commission frescoes for its walls. These were to be paintings of two great battles in the earlier history of the republic, the Battle of Cascina in 1368 and the Battle of Anghiari in 1440. The commission of Cascina was allotted to Michelangelo, Anghiari to Leonardo. No love was lost between these two masters: Leonardo thought painting a superior art to sculpture and did not admire Michelangelo's religious muscularity; Michelangelo was offended by Leonardo's detached observation of the natural world. The painting of the Great Hall was not a competition, but the rivalry of the two artists in the High Renaissance presented a faint parallel with the competition of Brunelleschi and Ghiberti for the bronze doors of the Baptistery a hundred years earlier. The presence in Florence of two such great artists, both working at the same time on schemes designed to glorify the revived republic, provided a contrast with the conditions of patronage by a superior family which we have noticed as characteristic of the production of great works in the Laurentian period. In this case the commune itself was the patron paying for the room in which its main council was to meet. Both artists prepared designs for the Great Hall and Leonardo was one of the experts whose advice was sought – and it has survived – when the commune was deciding where to place Michelangelo's *David*. It may not have been disastrous for Michelangelo or Leonardo that they were called away from Florence to work for the Pope and the King of France respectively. But it is worth reflecting on whether art would have been better served if Florence had survived as a republic instead of succumbing to the powers that also stole its most brilliant offspring. According to Condivi's biography of Michelangelo, the artist was urged

LEFT Virgin and Child with St Anne and St John,
Leonardo da Vinci, c.1500
(National Gallery, London)

157

Leonardo da Vinci's Battle of Anghiari,
Rubens, c.1615 (Louvre, Paris)

by Piero Soderini, the Standardbearer of Florence, to obey Julius II's command to return to his service for fear war would break out between Florence and the Pope, no doubt an exaggeration either by Condivi or by Soderini, but also a genuine indication of Florence's relatively weak position in relation to greater powers.

Neither of the Great Hall paintings survived but their importance is certain and some of their character is known. Michelangelo's *Cascina* never got beyond the stage of a cartoon, which is lost. Part of Leonardo's *Anghiari* was

painted. Though it was destroyed after the republic fell, copies give an impression of its power. The part which was painted was the meeting of two small groups of mounted soldiers. Mounted men and fallen horses were intertwined. They met in a furious collision of realistically portrayed energy such as no one had succeeded in painting earlier. The battle scene in Uccello's *Rout of San Romano* fifty years earlier, for example, looks static in comparison. This was an extension of Leonardo's technique in the direction of force and fury which was not paralleled in his other works but was also connected with his interest in the fury of nature exhibited in torrents and earthquakes. Once again man was part of nature.

Mona Lisa, which later became Leonardo's most famous work, was painted during the Florentine period. She was given once again the background of water and rock inspired by Leonardo's scientific interests. The pose of the figure was a novelty. But attention is fixed on the womanly face, a confection of infinite mysteriousness and the most extreme example of Leonardo's power to convey a depth of expression that cannot be defined. It is not, as in Rembrandt's portraits, a complexity of easily imaginable regrets, but an expression to which no name can be attached; the same is true of the Virgin and St Anne. Leonardo worked on *Mona Lisa* for years, adding complexities that had little connection with the original sitter.

Leda and the Swan, which we know only from copies, was a sensual presentation of the female nude as well as a reaction to Renaissance cultivation of classical myths. Its beauty pointed forward to innumerable exquisite female figures in the painting of the sixteenth century. *St John the Baptist* in the Louvre, Leonardo's last known painting, is as mysterious as *Mona Lisa*, and its subject has a similarly inscrutable expression. St John's half-figure looms out of a very dark background with raised arm and finger, a soft smile beneath the heavy, curled hair, a feature whose artistic potential always fascinated Leonardo.

The expressions on Leonardo's faces leave us, increasingly as he grew older, with the feeling that we are never likely to understand him fully and that his sympathies lie with the mysterious and inexplicit rather than with the world of common emotions. His rather abstract interest in form and movement carried him away from the common world of human intercourse to an inner world of enquiry and contemplation that was in turn reflected in his faces. His earlier portraits were more human and less enigmatic

Study for the Kneeling Leda,
Leonardo da Vinci, c.1504-6 (Chatsworth)

than *Mona Lisa*. His strange remoteness was in the end inseparable from his stature as an artist. His detachment did not reduce the impact made by his revolution in painting and that impact had little to do with the particular emotions he attempted to convey, but reflected instead the development of the expressiveness of the face and form and the realistic connection of figures to a new level of sensitivity and complexity.

Leonardo believed that painting was superior to sculpture because it involved the total creation of an illusion, whereas sculpture was an imitation of a piece of nature:

The sculptor is not able to achieve diversity using the various types of colours. With respect to these painting is

159

Pope Julius II,
Raphael, 1511-12
(National Gallery, London)

not deficient in any way. The perspective used by sculptors [in reliefs] never appears correct whereas the painter can make a distance of one hundred miles appear in his work. Aerial perspective is absent from the sculptors' work. They cannot depict transparent bodies, nor can they represent luminous sources, nor reflected rays, nor shiny bodies such as mirrors and similar lustrous things, nor mists, nor dreary weather – nor endless other things.[3]

This is a judgment with which the detached reader is inclined to agree. Sculpture may have preceded and inspired painting in its depiction of the human form, but it was not capable of reaching the same heights of imaginative fiction. If the visual arts of the Renaissance can be thought to be

superior to those of antiquity and the middle ages it must be chiefly because of the development of painting to a level of expertise not imagined earlier and in this movement Leonardo himself was the outstanding inventor.

'O anatomical painter,' said Leonardo, in a piece of advice very likely intended as a taunt to Michelangelo, who certainly did sometimes exaggerate the muscularity of his nudes, 'take care that excessive attention to the bones, chords and muscles does not cause you to become a wooden painter in your desire that your nude figures should exhibit all their emotions.'[4]

ROME

In its last republican period, 1494–1530, Florence was still a city of artisans, businessmen, trade guilds and religious confraternities in which the patronage of art was quite widely distributed, though for some of the time, as in the days of Lorenzo the Magnificent, the Medici were particularly important. In Rome there was one great patron, the pope. The papacy of the age of Julius II and Leo X was in better control of the papal state than before: still untroubled by the Reformation – Luther was of no importance before 1517 and the English and Calvinist reformations were yet to come – and still drawing revenues from the European clergy. The works commissioned in these years – the tomb of Julius II, the rebuilding of St Peter's, the ceiling of the Sistine Chapel and the rooms in the Vatican palace – were on a splendid scale. They attracted to Rome artists whose aesthetic roots were in the Florentine tradition but who found here more generous patrons than they could have found in Florence. As a result, many of the artistic ideas that had their roots in Florence – Leonardo and Michelangelo were both products of Lorenzo's patronage – found their culmination at Rome.

Julius II had exceptionally ambitious ideas for the glorification of the papacy both in the political and in the aesthetic sphere. He was the only pope to act as the

160

commander of his armies, attempting to strengthen his control of the papal state as far north as Bologna and to free Italy from the invading French. At the same time he hoped to set up monuments in the city itself: he wanted to create a vast papal palace, to rebuild St Peter's, to prepare a tomb for himself grander than any built by a Christian before. Leo X was a less commanding personality but he was a Medici and his sharp aesthetic instincts encouraged him to continue patronage on a large scale. The years 1503-21 were therefore a great cultural period in Rome. The patronage was halted by Leo's death, but artistic activity continued on a lesser scale in the 1520s, and then was dealt a terrible blow in the Sack of Rome by the German troops of Charles V in 1527, which temporarily devastated the city and drove out the artists.

The heart of Julius' plans for Rome was the rebuilding of St Peter's and this design looms over the whole artistic history of the city in the sixteenth century. As the pope's see, St Peter's was the most important church in the Christian world but it was a much less impressive building than Hagia Sophia at Constantinople. That was to be remedied. St Peter's was to be rebuilt in a classical style, fitting the tradition of Brunelleschi and Alberti, and to be the centre of a rebuilt Rome fit for the capital of Christianity. The presiding genius chosen for the new Rome was the architect Donato Bramante who came from Lombardy. The foundation stone of the new St Peter's was laid in 1506. It was to have the form of a huge Greek cross with four equal arms topped by a dome, the successor of Brunelleschi's at Florence. The building had only been begun when Julius II died in 1513 and Bramante in 1514. But the start which had been made was at the crossing, the focal point of the building, embodying Bramante's grand idea of a dome resting on four huge pillars. This survived through many changes of plan and architect until Michelangelo took up the role in 1546. He devised the scheme which was partly followed thereafter, and which

Tempietto,
San Pietro in Montorio, Rome, Bramante, 1502-11

added to Bramante's crossing a long nave and a façade towering over the square below. The façade that we see nowadays was not in Michelangelo's plan but the high wall concealing the essential structure of the building behind it was. Inside, under the crossing, on the other hand, one is closer to the sense of classical space that Bramante had intended.

Bramante belonged to the generation of architects following Alberti who were developing classical styles both for churches and for secular palaces. In ecclesiastical architecture their main interest was the concentric church, of which St Peter's was to be, according to Bramante's wishes, the culminating example. In his earlier years in Rome he had already designed one particularly delicate

161

Laocoön,
first century AD, copy (Vatican Museum, Rome)

concentric chapel at San Pietro in Montorio, a circular building. Classicism was also invading the world of the aristocratic palace with, for example, Lorenzo de' Medici's country seat at Poggio a Caiano, designed by Antonio da San Gallo, and the new Strozzi Palace in Florence; and Rome was to offer an extensive field for palace architecture, with many cardinals competing to live in the finest buildings. This movement reached a climax under Leo X with Baldassare Peruzzi's Farnesina Villa built for the banker Agostino Chigi and Raphael's Villa Madama, for the pope, conceived as a halting place for large diplomatic missions about to enter Rome.

The painting of Michelangelo and Raphael took place against a background of extensive rebuilding. Whilst Bramante was an architect concerned with a setting, painters and sculptors were concerned directly with the human figure and the human personality. They had behind them and could take for granted the spatial realism and figure-drawing developed in fifteenth-century Florence. They retained and increased their attentiveness to the lessons of classical art. Rome itself was a classical inspiration through its surviving buildings and sculptures which had a profound influence on artists working there. The statue of *Laocoön*, dug up in Rome in 1506, was declared by Michelangelo to be 'a singular miracle of art' and, like many other Roman remains, it was much copied. Although they were not scholars, the artists were to some extent influenced by the Neoplatonism of Ficino, which gave spiritual importance to beauty, and by the religious earnestness of Savonarola. They were also influenced more than their predecessors by the more complex designs of Netherlandish and German art that began to be known in Italy in the late fifteenth century and knowledge of which was assisted by the multiplication of prints. The influence of the Northern interest in landscape backgrounds and in complex designs involving landscape can be seen, for instance, in the Florentine school in the work of Leonardo,

Battle of the Centaurs,
Michelangelo, c.1492 (Casa Buonarotti, Florence)

Piero di Cosimo and Pontormo. The two main artists working at Rome in the High Renaissance period, however, were Michelangelo and Raphael.

MICHELANGELO

Michelangelo was influenced by the example of Leonardo. However, his contribution was largely independent not only because it was primarily in sculpture, but also because it expressed a different kind of personality. Leonardo might be described as essentially a naturalist, absorbed by the relations he could establish between humanity and the world about it. Michelangelo, on the other hand, was, in spite of his immense capacity for physical labour, essentially a spiritualist, interested in various forms of the body's expression of the soul and in this sense a truer descendant of the more intellectual aspects of Laurentian Florence than

his great rival.

Michelangelo's earliest works, the *Battle of the Centaurs* and the *Madonna of the Staircase*, both relief sculptures, were made in Florence in the early 1490s. They showed clearly enough two of the features that were going to be important in his art throughout his life: the fascinated devotion to the male nude and the interest in religious symbolism. The *Battle of the Centaurs* is the more remarkable of the two. It was intended to portray the classical legend of the battle between Centaurs and men but in fact it concentrates on the upper parts of the centaurs and shows a struggle between two groups of nude men, depicted with an advanced command of their anatomical structure. They are shown moreover in a complex pattern of related bodies and limbs, dominated by one central figure facing outwards. The scene is a turbulent scrum in which power, violence

163

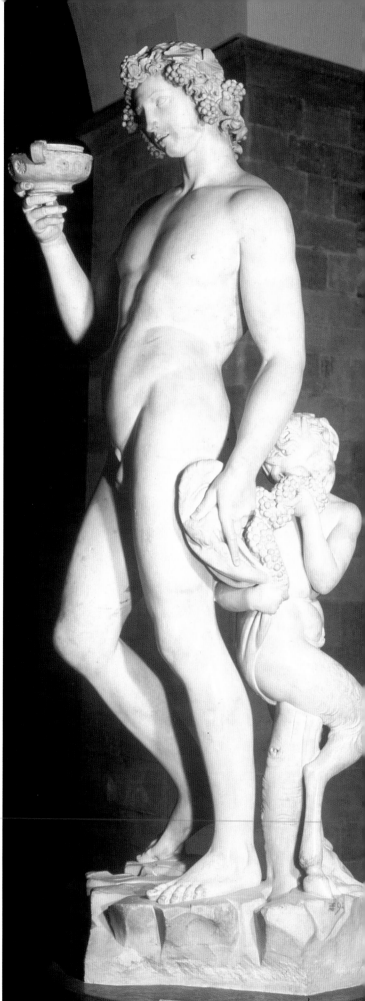

and movement prevail. The relief embodies the novel capacity for representing energetic figures that Michelangelo had acquired before he was twenty and points forward to the Sistine ceiling and the battle scenes of the future.

The *Madonna of the Staircase*, in contrast, is a rather mysterious low relief depicting the Madonna and Child seated at the foot of five steps at the top of which are angels. It represented the doom intended for the child and also the means that were offered of ascent, by the steps, towards heaven and truth. Michelangelo was often to create works that would puzzle the observer with the unexplained obscurity of the religious symbolism governing his subjects, and here, early in his career, this characteristic is present.

From 1496 to 1501 Michelangelo was in Rome and came under the influence of the wealth of ancient sculpture visible in that city. In this environment he sculpted his *Bacchus* for a patron who admired classical art. The intoxicated god, stumbling forward, was a highly original figure not only because of its apparently un-Christian significance but also because of the ambiguity and complexity of its form, which demands to be seen in the round and which is accompanied by a smiling faun fully integrated into the composition. The contrast with the *Pietà* at St Peter's, also made during this Roman period, could be seen as a repetition of the difference between the two earlier Florentine reliefs. This *Pietà* is a strange subject: the young and beautiful Madonna has stretched over her lap the body of a Christ of the same age as herself, if not older. But it allowed Michelangelo's gift for transforming marble into drapery and human form to find its fullest expression.

Michelangelo went back to Florence soon after

164

Doni Tondo,
Michelangelo, c.1504 (Uffizi, Florence)

Leonardo had returned there and, like other artists, seems to have been strongly influenced by the cartoons of the Virgin and St Anne. The desire to compete with these was probably the inspiration behind his several attempts to paint or sculpt the Virgin and Child in the period approximately between 1503 and 1505. The *Doni Tondo* painting shows the child on the shoulder of the Madonna with St Joseph behind, and in the background a line of nude figures whose significance is obscure. The painting is Michelangelo's attempt to make a satisfying pattern of figures and clothes out of the three main figures. Although very different from Leonardo's cartoon of the Madonna and St Anne, it was

inspired by it and an early example of the hundreds of experiments with small groups of the Holy Family that were to be made by artists in succeeding decades. The sculptured *Taddei Tondo* is more obviously related to Leonardo because, although it shows no St Anne, the child lies across his mother's lap in a manner reminiscent of the Leonardo cartoon.

The major product of these years, however, was the *David*, commissioned by the commune of Florence and placed after debate prominently in front of the Palazzo della Signoria. It now resides in the Accademia. The *David* was accepted as a symbol of the republic's struggle against

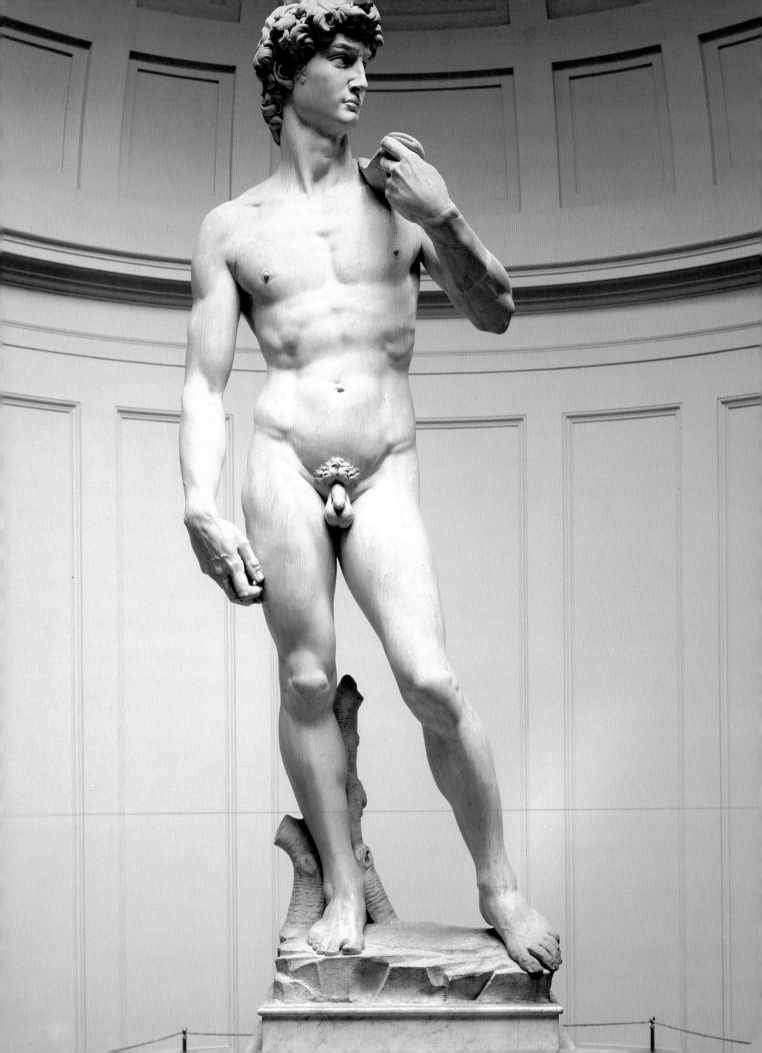

LEFT David,
Michelangelo, 1501-4 (Accademia, Florence)

superior odds and it is a gigantic statue which established Michelangelo as the supreme sculptor of his time. In his hands it acquired other characteristics apart from its political symbolism. It is obviously an imitation of the antique and a development of the traditional pose with the weight of the body on one leg and the other stretched out to the side. The face, which is not very clearly visible because of the height of the statue, is that of a man facing the world with a mixture of puzzlement and controlled strength. Though its familiarity makes it difficult to appreciate, we should probably imagine it as related not only to Michelangelo's interest in the male nude but also to his own stance facing external fortune.

After the *David* Michelangelo began work on another piece of patriotic art, the painting of the *Battle of Cascina* for the Great Hall. He got no further than a preliminary cartoon which is lost but which we know from copies to have been a complex picture of nude men bathing before the battle, a development of the tangled mass of bodies that he had produced earlier in the *Battle of the Centaurs*. Michelangelo was condemned both by fortune and by his own restless temperament to leave a trail of unfinished works. The most troublesome of them was the Tomb of Julius II which Julius summoned him to Rome to begin in 1505. Julius and Michelangelo planned an unprecedently large, free-standing tomb whose outer walls and roof were to show no less than forty figure statues. It was to be an adaptation of classical sepulchral designs to Christian ideas, celebrating the great pope who saw himself as the defender of the arts and restorer of Italy. Michelangelo went to work enthusiastically. Characteristically his plans were too vast to be realised. Julius lost interest and when he died the project was scaled down successively to the relatively poor thing we see in San Pietro in Vincoli in Rome today. However, a few remarkable statues came out of it. The *Moses*, which is at

Dying Slave,
Michelangelo, 1514-16
(Louvre, Paris)

167

ground level in the tomb, had been intended to stand high up and be seen from below. In that position its presentation of a powerful, dominating figure, no doubt related to the personality of Julius, would have been even more impressive than it is now. Still more remarkable were the two *Slaves* that were to be placed in niches or on pedestals around the foot of the tomb. These two beautiful male figures show clearly the artist's pleasure in his depiction of the smooth strength of muscles, relaxed in the *Dying Slave* and tensed in the *Rebellious Slave*. They were sculpted after Julius died in 1513, by which time Michelangelo had turned aside again to produce his most famous work of art, the only one of his great projects ever to be properly completed, the ceiling of the Sistine Chapel. Paradoxically, it was painting not sculpture.

The Sistine ceiling was done for Julius II to complete the painting of the huge chapel near St Peter's which had been built and partly painted some thirty years earlier under the patronage of his uncle, Pope Sixtus IV. The general meaning of the design is unclear. We do not know for certain why those precise subjects were chosen or how the artist imagined the scenes as being related to each other. Starting from the east end where the swirling figure of the prophet Jonah rises above the *Last Judgment*, which was painted on the east wall much later, the main scenes in the middle of the ceiling are early episodes from the Old Testament running from the *Separation of Light from Darkness* to the *Drunkenness of Noah*. They tell the story of the origins of the world and original sin. Around these scenes are seven prophets and five sibyls, the Jews and pagans who foretold the coming of Christ. Above these, at the corners of main scenes, are the Nudes, which cannot be fitted into any biblical pattern. Below them in the spandrels and lunettes are the Ancestors of Christ. We do not know how far the ceiling was conceived by Julius himself, by theologians from the influential school of the Augustinian order in Rome or, as Michelangelo claimed, by himself. The Nudes, however,

were clearly a contribution by the artist.

The development of Michelangelo's style of painting can be seen without knowing the metaphorical meaning of what he was portraying because his main interest was the human body and the individual episode. The ceiling was painted in a sustained outburst of furious energy in four years from 1508 to 1512 with a break in the middle. Michelangelo started from the west end and the break came between the *Creation of Eve* and the *Creation of Adam*. In the second half of the ceiling Michelangelo approached his work in an abandoned manner, freeing himself from his earlier caution. This later part of the work was therefore more strikingly original. The main scenes of the *Separation of Light from Darkness*, *Creation of Sun and Moon*, *Separation of Land from Water* and *Creation of Adam* are of course imprinted on our minds as the images of Genesis. These visions of weightless divinity are astonishing creations of an artist working at the very heart of the Church, freed from its potential restrictions by his own determination and by the pope's approval. Still more important in some ways are the prophets and sibyls and the male nudes, because Michelangelo treated these as an opportunity for developing his portrayal of the human form. They are presented with dramatic contortions and gestures which have some relation to the subject but are mainly expressions of the artist's delight in the anatomy of complex postures of the body. To take three examples: the Libyan sibyl twists round from her seated position to open a huge book with wide-stretched arms, presenting her back but looking over her shoulder; the Nude above the Persian sibyl, again seated, recoils with exaggerated horror, his hair falling over his face; and finally the figure of Jonah, emerging from the whale, throws back his head, discovering the world anew in a gesture that recalls the scenes in the creation of the world behind him. In those paintings Michelangelo outshone even *Laocoön* and created a series of figures that were memorable as religious images as well as for the stylishness with which they were

Jonah, detail,
Sistine Chapel ceiling, unrestored, Michelangelo, 1511
(Vatican, Rome)

169

Sistine Chapel ceiling, restored,
Michelangelo, 1511 (Vatican, Rome)

so vigorously and brilliantly imbued.

In the second and third decades of the century Michelangelo, like other artists, became involved in work for the Medici family in Florence and out of this came two buildings, conceived in the 1520s, though in part executed later, both connected with the Medici church of San Lorenzo in Florence. The first, and more important, was a New Sacristy to balance Brunelleschi's Old Sacristy on the opposite side of the church. Like the Old Sacristy, this was a square building intended principally as a funerary monument to members of the Medici family: Giuliano, Duke of Nemours, and Lorenzo, Duke of Urbino, who had been in charge of Medici Florence between 1512 and 1519. Both were now dead and the Medici were represented among the living by Giulio who became Pope Clement VII in 1523. In the New Sacristy Giuliano and Lorenzo, as elegant seated warriors, one alert, the other pensive, sit in niches in opposite walls at some height. Below them are the sarcophaguses and reclining on these the four figures of Night and Day (female and male, below Giuliano) and

Tomb of Lorenzo de' Medici,
Michelangelo, c.1520-34 (New Sacristy, San Lorenzo, Florence)

Dawn and Dusk (female and male, below Lorenzo). We do not know exactly what Michelangelo intended to symbolise and in this case the uncertainty is not about papal theology but about the artist's own attachment to Neoplatonism. Giuliano and Lorenzo are certainly highly idealised figures, not portraits. The four times of day represent the inexorable passage of time. But it is the quality and imaginativeness of the sculpture that matter most. In Night and Dawn Michelangelo created two marvellous images of the reclining female nude, one a woman past her prime, the other with all the smooth contours of youth. Night is quite closely related to the figure of Leda in the act of intercourse with a swan that was painted by Michelangelo about the same time, though known to us only from copies. *Leda and the Swan* may have represented Death for Michelangelo and we should regard Night as containing for the artist a complex of meaning, now indecipherable, in which night and time, death and sexual action are all involved.

The sarcophaguses and figures are set in walls of a

chapel, the same shape as the Old Sacristy, with architecture Michelangelo had developed out of Brunelleschi's plainer style to provide an intricate pattern of highly artificial sculptured niches. This style was developed with still more freedom in another building, the Laurentian Library, designed to house the Medici collection of manuscripts. In the vestibule to the library, with its elaborate staircase and walls decorated with prominent pillars and velouts, Michelangelo created an architecture of pure style, as far removed as one can imagine from functional architecture. The huge architectural features were detached from any utilitarian aim of holding up the building and created a fantastic, almost absurd, world of stone. Walking down the staircase one has nevertheless a strong sense, as in some Rococo buildings, of moving in a space of satisfying shapes. Whether this is a summit of architectural invention or the abandonment of pleasing good sense is a matter of opinion. Stylishness was perhaps not as appropriate for building as for representations of the human figure. In his later years, which were much concerned with architecture, Michelangelo moved into more rational designs in his replanning of the Capitol at Rome and his substantial changes to the plans for the new St Peter's.

Around 1530 Michelangelo was also making elaborate drawings of a new type, such as the drawing of the *Fall of*

Entrance Hall of the Laurentian Library,
Michelangelo, c.1524 (Florence)

172

Phaethon in which the movements of the figures are much more important than the realism of the space, a tendency evident in his paintings from the beginning. Michelangelo had achieved a very early command of realism and was always therefore drawn to go beyond it to a refinement of the body's movements in an unreal weightless space. This tendency found its consummation in the last of his great paintings, the *Last Judgment* on the east wall of the Sistine Chapel. Michelangelo's figures provided the chief source of inspiration for the movement which art historians have called Mannerism, and in the last forty years of his life from 1520 to 1560 he lived alongside it, acting both as a mentor to younger artists and as a repository of respected sincerity.

After 1533 Michelangelo spent most of the last thirty years of his life in Rome, where he bitterly regretted the final destruction of republicanism which he had worked hard to defend. We are better informed about his inner life during the 1530s because of the literary records of his intense relationships with the young man Tommaso dei Cavalieri and the Marchioness Vittoria Colonna, whom he accepted as a confidante and religious authority. He appears to have moved in the direction of more orthodox religious beliefs and a more exclusive interest in religious subjects. Though he had never had a developed philosophy or made any serious attempt like Leonardo to educate himself in learned thought, he subscribed to general Florentine ideas about the power of artistic beauty to liberate the soul from its physical chains.

Apart from the overwhelming obsession with the male body that dominated most of his life, he was moved by the significance of father and mother figures in ways that we do not clearly understand. At the end of his life he was concerned with the mystery of Christ's broken body and his relationship with the Madonna, as he showed in the unfinished sculpture *Deposition*, on which he was still working in 1564, and over which his own hooded face looms as Nicodemus. A sad piety is characteristic of his later years.

The huge *Last Judgment* was conceived and painted between 1533 and 1541. Though the general scheme of the division between those who are redeemed to reassume their bodies and those condemned to be sent down into hell is traditional and plain enough, there are puzzling features which make it difficult to interpret the painting. The Apollonian nude who commands the universe looks like a Greek god or hero, not like any ordinary Christian's picture of the Saviour. Why does the Madonna crouch submissively at his side and why does a skin with Michelangelo's face painted on it hang prominently from the hand of St Bartholomew? There is apparently an obscure personal interpretation behind these things, unless we are to assume, which is not impossible, that Michelangelo has extravagantly painted figures that interested him as figures and included a simple confession of the sinful state of his own soul. Except at the lowest level, the *Last Judgment* has no 'space' in the sense of figures in a landscape. They are carried in the void like the figures in the last main scenes of creation on the ceiling. Michelangelo was in his later years less concerned with grace. The figures, men and angels, declare their physical reality but it is a gross world populated by burly, overdeveloped muscles. What he has given us is a picture of humanity moving in massed crowds. But it is of course humanity in which each individual figure was painted with an ability to portray muscular movement and foreshortened limbs. That and its sheer scale made it an awesome model for other artists, though it seems to us now that its plain humanity is rather remote from the atmosphere of later religious painting and that, like Dante's *Inferno*, it is about the terrestrial, not the celestial, world.

Michelangelo's life has carried us well beyond the early sixteenth century. He produced great works from a commanding position for sixty years and lived through changes of style, on some of which his personal influence was considerable, extending from Laurentian Florence to the world of the Counter-Reformation. Michelangelo established his power and independence as no other artist had done before him; popes and rulers competed for his services. Federigo Gonzaga, Marquess of Mantua, instructed his agent to obtain a work by Michelangelo whatever it might be: 'We do not think of any one material rather than of another, nor have at heart one subject rather than another, if only we can have an example of his unique art.' Michelangelo submitted to some patrons because only they had the money necessary for the expensive schemes of which he dreamed. In this respect he was not unlike twentieth-century architects, who also depend on patronage, and he was placed in that position because of the grandeur of his designs. He differs from painters and sculptors of earlier periods because he was determined to express his vision and his world was prepared to accept it. He remained exceptional. Most of his contemporaries were still craftsmen-lackeys and the arts were a long way from their twentieth-century role.

To explain his achievement we have to take two developments into account. The first was the enhanced position given to artists in fifteenth-century Florence by Alberti's writings and by the intense patronage in that society. The second was the spilling out of that attitude into other parts of Italy and Europe which made artists international figures whose services might be sought by a number of patrons from Paris to Rome. That development was assisted by the tolerant, open, art-loving atmosphere of high society before the Reformation and Counter-Reformation brought in the iron curtains. It was not to be improved upon for a long time.

RAPHAEL

After Leonardo and Michelangelo the third of the great trio of names associated with the visual art of the High Renaissance was Raphael. His entry into the highest level of the artistic world was different from theirs because he was not in quite the same manner an independent creator of a new style. Raphael came to Florence in 1504 when he was twenty-one and already an expert painter of the school of Perugino. He was in Florence on and off from 1504 to 1508, when the first impact of the new inventions of Leonardo and Michelangelo was strong in the city, and he was changed by them. He copied their work in drawings and attempted to imitate their style in paintings. The results can be seen, for example, in the painting of 1507 known as *La Belle Jardinière*, a pyramidal composition showing the Madonna and Child and St John the Baptist which, though it is not as powerful, shows the influence of the full figures and realistic positions of Leonardo's paintings of the Madonna and St Anne. It is also present in a different way in the *Entombment*, a group of figures, two of whom are carrying the dead Christ, which have some of the new tension and flexibility in the arrangement of active and emotional human beings that Raphael derived partly from the work of Leonardo and Michelangelo on the walls of the Hall of the Great Council.

In 1508 Raphael went to Rome, where he remained until his death in 1520. It was an ideal environment, because Rome was the best place in Europe to observe classical remains of sculpture, painting and architecture for which he developed a keen archeological enthusiasm. And also there had never before been patrons who combined more wealth and enthusiasm for the latest fashions in the visual arts. The city that disgusted Luther and disturbed Erasmus was Raphael's natural home. The most important patrons were Pope Julius II, followed by Pope Leo X and the wealthy Sienese banker, Agostino Chigi, who was involved in the management of papal finances. It was a revival of the situation that had existed seventy years earlier when Cosimo de' Medici had been banker to humanist popes.

Raphael was working in Rome during and after the time when Michelangelo painted the Sistine ceiling, which had a

Transfiguration,
Raphael, 1517-20 (Vatican Museum, Rome)

strong influence on his receptive imagination; he is a striking case of an artist who was open and ready to absorb other people's good ideas, very different in that respect from the self-obsessed Leonardo and Michelangelo. Raphael's prodigious output of painting was not entirely done for Julius, Leo and Chigi. The *Donna Velata* is supposed by some to be a portrait of one of his mistresses. Whether or not that is true, it contains one of the many women's faces painted with a haunting softness which abound in his work and also a remarkably delicate depiction of clothing in her dress, especially in the elaborately cut and modelled sleeve. The *Transfiguration* on which he was working when he died, on the other hand, is an ambitious

and inventive altarpiece for a church in France. Raphael fitted together two separate gospel subjects, the Transfiguration and the failure of the apostles to heal a possessed boy, in a large double composition of the kind that was common in the sixteenth century, emphasising the distinction between the celestial world above and the earthly world below. Though it may not have been a promising direction for the design of single panels, Raphael's painting, especially in the lower half, which depicts men and women in attitudes of emotion around the

175

Parnassus,
Raphael, 1510-11
(Stanza della Segnatura, Vatican, Rome)

boy, is a splendid adaptation of pose and gesture to a dramatic scene. The *Donna Velata* and the *Transfiguration* illustrate the range of subjects that he was able to command.

For Julius II Raphael painted the walls of the Stanza della Segnatura, in the Vatican Palace, which was actually the pope's private library, with scenes appropriate to Theology, Philosophy, Poetry and Jurisprudence. Theology has the *Disputa*, with the Host at the centre, again a double scene showing Father and Son above with prophets and apostles, below a congress of Fathers, heretics and others, probably including some irrelevant portraits of known contemporaries like Bramante. For Poetry, in contrast, he provided *Parnassus*, the mountain on which the poets, including Sappho, another of Raphael's memorable female figures, are assembled, with a music-making Apollo at the centre. The array of beauty and literature ranges from the muses and Homer to Boccaccio.

Philosophy has the most famous of Raphael's paintings, the *School of Athens*, in which Plato and Aristotle stride through the hosts of ancient thinkers in a classical building that looks as though it were rather distantly related to the plans for St Peter's. In its subject matter the Stanza della Segnatura is perhaps the best expression of the balance of pre-Reformation Rome, the doomed but glorious attempt to hold together the Christian faith and classical paganism. What is remarkable pictorially is Raphael's success in placing numerous figures within a large space. The varied

176

Miracle of the Mass at Bolsena,
Raphael, 1512
(Stanza di Eliodoro, Vatican, Rome)

postures of the figures in the *School of Athens* – standing, twisted, sprawling – convey a sense of both grandeur and a delightful physical appropriateness against the classical spaciousness of the architecture.

Over the next few years, extending into the pontificate of Leo X, Raphael also painted the room beside the Stanza della Segnatura, the Stanza di Eliodoro. This time he was concerned with themes of a different kind, emphasising papal power. The *Deliverance of St Peter from Prison* fitted into this theme because the position of the papacy was based on the apostolic succession from Peter. It was important in the history of painting because of its depiction of the brightness of the angel in the darkness of night, which represented a new step in the exploration of the treatment of light. The *Miracle of the Mass at Bolsena*, in which the Host was found to be bleeding, illustrated the devotion of the pope to the

Eucharist because Julius II himself is kneeling before the celebrating priest with his Swiss guards below him. The *Expulsion of Heliodorus* shows an Old Testament scene in which a thief is driven out of the temple in Jerusalem, watched by Julius II on a litter. In the *Repulse of Attila*, which was intended to refer to papal temporal power in Italy, the victorious Pope Leo I appears as a portrait of Leo X. The last two paintings in particular are of lively and dramatic episodes in action, different from the more stable groups of figures in the Stanza della Segnatura. They gave Raphael the opportunity to develop his gift for figures in motion. An example is the attacking horseman on the right of the

177

Expulsion of Heliodorus, followed by angels who are in effect leaping men, and the characteristically Raphaelesque figure of the kneeling, recoiling woman on the left. A few years after the Stanza di Eliodoro Raphael painted for the pope a series of paper cartoons depicting scenes from the lives of Peter and Paul, intended as models for tapestries to go into the Sistine Chapel, defending the justice of papal authority by showing its origins. The medium deprived the cartoon of the finished perfection of fresco or panel painting but again provided opportunities for presenting events expressed by dramatic postures in environments that gave them majesty by the fictional use of confections of ancient architecture.

Raphael's commission from Agostino Chigi was a challenge to exploit still more fully the classicising side of his interests. Chigi had built the Farnesina Villa on the outskirts of Rome and wanted it decorated in the manner of the ancients. Raphael's first fresco showed the Nereid *Galatea* riding the waves on a shell drawn by dolphins, a debased sequel to Botticelli's *Birth of Venus* but still a glorious depiction of triumphant female beauty. When he came a few years later to design paintings for the ceiling of the Loggia of Chigi's villa, Raphael took as his subject Apuleius' story of Cupid and Psyche in which Cupid fell in love with her against the wishes of Venus. When Cupid fled from her she pursued him and was eventually immortalised and married to him by Jupiter. The story offered an

ABOVE Expulsion of Heliodorus,
Raphael, 1511-12
(Stanza di Eliodoro, Vatican, Rome)

RIGHT Galatea,
Raphael, c.1511-12
(Farnesina, Rome)

178

opening for a thorough treatment of the female nude and Raphael took a full part in preparations for this, as one can tell from his drawings. The paintings themselves are generally thought to be mostly by assistants – perhaps Raphael was too much occupied by a variety of different commissions in the hectic last years of his very active life – and they may seem to observers to show a decline from the high seriousness of the paintings of Leonardo, the Sistine ceiling and the Stanze. The greatest age was past.

In the Farnesina paintings the pursuit of luxurious eroticism had taken over and seems to point forward to less impressive art, both religious and secular, in the future. This change took place because the quality of the painting is not as good, since it is not by Raphael, rather than because the painting dealt with a risqué love affair. We may reject the idea that painting designed obligingly to suit the taste of a pleasure-loving millionaire necessarily lacked the impulse to originality and greatness. Nevertheless, the highly successful tension between patronage and genius, Christian doctrine and classical style, which had been achieved in the pontificate of Julius II, had passed and was not to be repeated.

Raphael was also a great portrait painter. The approach to the art of the portrait had been revolutionised by Leonardo in his earlier years, when he had first endowed portraits not merely with a likeness to the sitter but with a complex investigation of human personality. Raphael continued this approach. The portrait of *Baldassare Castiglione*, a courtier, writer and friend of Raphael, is a picture of a sensitive and mellow contemplator of the human scene, as Castiglione appears to have been by his own writing in *The Book of the Courtier*. Its lifelike portrayal of Castiglione's friendly, open expression made it a supreme example of Italian Renaissance portraiture. The most surprising of Raphael's portraits was that of *Julius II*. The old man, worn out by his intensely ambitious life, is simply seated in a chair. There are various items in the painting which denote the papal office and Julius' family, but the main impression it conveys is of a tired and ruminative old gentleman. Such a personal portrait of a pope was a novelty; popes had been painted as donors and as holders of their office but never before simply as individuals. That such a portrait could be painted is evidence both of Raphael's skill in depicting character and also of his close relationship with the pope that allowed him to act in this way. It is one of the many indications in this period of the newly elevated status of art.

Raphael's attractiveness results from the fact that, unlike Leonardo and Michelangelo, his paintings present a harmonious and balanced view of life. They reflect neither homosexual nor spiritual nor scientific obsessions. The charm of the *Fornarina*, the portrait alleged to be of the mistress of his last years, with bared breasts, and the charm of symbolic figures, such as Sappho in *Parnassus*, both arise from a natural and completely understandable reaction of man to woman. It is this sympathy with the feminine which makes him a supremely good portraitist and which also allowed him to construct a range of new female figures in a variety of often exaggerated but beautiful poses. Lacking the psychological eccentricities of the other two masters, he was able to place their discoveries within a world of human normality. Though he succeeded by understanding and taking over the innovations of Leonardo and Michelangelo, Raphael was unique in his power to give uncomplicated pleasure by conveying the warmth of a face, the delicacy of skin or the elegance of a pose. He captured the technique of painting as it rose to a peak of excellence and conveyed in supreme fashion the poetry of the sensuous. Many other painters copied the two great innovators. None grasped the simple possibilities now open to the artist as Raphael did.

MANNERISM

The work of Leonardo, Michelangelo and Raphael was the last of the creative revolutions in the Florentine tradition.

La Fornarina,
Raphael, c.1518-20 (Galleria Nazionale, Rome)

We cannot, however, leave Florence without looking briefly ahead into the consequences of the Renaissance in the fifty years after Raphael's death to observe sketchily how the discoveries of the great triumvirate were adopted, and sometimes exaggerated and distorted, by a series of considerable artistic talents in the age of Mannerism.

Among the painters associated with Florence rather than Rome in the early sixteenth century, the most remarkable was Andrea del Sarto, who devoted himself persistently to essential characteristics of the new art: the monumentality of the human figures, natural relationships between the figures, and the expression of personality. He had a strong sense of colour and a sensitive feeling for children that manifests itself in a number of Holy Family groups. He was capable of treating themes of high seriousness as he showed in 1517 in the *Madonna of the Harpies*. The Madonna is a softly feminine but authoritative figure holding the laughing naked child raised on a sculptured pedestal with St John the Evangelist and St Bonaventure below her. The painting owes its attractiveness to its monumentality and to the very successful juxtaposition of colours. He also became involved in some much larger and more ambitious enterprises. He was drawn into the plans for the Medici villa at Poggio a Caiano, where he was probably the chief designer in the early stages of painting the interior. There he painted the fresco of the *Tribute to Caesar*, a grand classical scene taking place on steps leading up to an imposing building which probably owed something to Raphael's frescoes in the Stanze at Rome. But Andrea's animals and roughly dressed plebeians added a different kind of humanity which could be seen as a joke at Raphael's expense.

Andrea del Sarto demonstrated one possible direction that art might have taken after the explosion of the early sixteenth century. It was not the road that the most considerable artists of the next half-century followed. They were interested in the refined and elegant treatment of the human form which they had witnessed in Michelangelo's Sistine Chapel and in Raphael's Stanze, and they wished to carry this approach further as an exercise in pleasurable design rather than as an investigation of human reality. This tendency is what art historians have labelled Mannerism. It developed particularly in Rome during the period between 1520 and the Sack of Rome in 1527. The dispersal of artists at that date meant that for most of the mid-sixteenth century one must regard Florence as the capital of Mannerism, but it also spread widely over Italy as a result, for example, of Giulio Romano's move to Mantua, where he built and decorated the Palazzo del Tè, and also to some extent to France with Rosso Fiorentino's emigration to Fontainebleau.

The wealth of Italian artistic production in the period after 1520 is overpowering, because of the large number of cities and courts where patronage was available – England and France in contrast had only one court and one great city each – and also because of the strong artistic traditions spilling out from Florence, Rome and Venice, and the continued wealth and sophistication of Italian urban society. A reader of Benvenuto Cellini's *Autobiography*, which was written about 1560 and covers the previous half-century, finds that Italy was still as lively and as capable of being irreverent as it had been in the time of Machiavelli. As well as being an autobiographer, Cellini was a considerable sculptor and goldsmith.

In concentrating on the trio of Leonardo, Michelangelo and Raphael in this chapter, at the expense of other central Italian artists who flourished during Michelangelo's lifetime, we are omitting a number of stars of considerable magnitude: Sebastiano del Piombo, who came from Venice but fell under the influence of Michelangelo in Rome; Rosso Fiorentino, a pupil of Andrea del Sarto who emigrated to Fontainebleau; Beccafumi of Siena; Correggio of Parma; Parmigianino, who came from Parma but was drawn for a time to Rome and Bologna – and many others.

These men were also all connected with Mannerism.

An early example of the tendency towards Mannerism is the fresco of the *Deposition* painted for a chapel in Santa Felicità in Florence by Jacopo Pontormo, who had been associated with Andrea del Sarto but then moved in a different direction. The figures are lanky, painted in light blues and pinks. They swoon and float. Some of the lower figures stand on the floor but for others there is little sense of a realistic support; the figures appear to hang in mid-air. The aim of the painting seems to be to exhibit the pattern made by the relationship of the figures to the dead Christ. The painter has advanced beyond the conquest of realistic human form to an enjoyment of an elaborate pattern of poses with limited reference to their placement in real space. This is a remarkable painting which in one sense moves away from the direction followed by Michelangelo and Raphael in the previous decade, but in another carries forward tendencies that were present in their work.

Bronzino's famous *Allegory*, painted about 1545, is another example of the novel departures of Mannerist art. It illustrates the despair caused by illicit love and, some have suggested, the syphilis that results: the brightly lit forms of Venus, Cupid and Folly; behind, and less clearly visible, are the agonised figures. This is a severely moral picture. It is also plain that Bronzino's chief pleasure is in the graceful nude Venus and the charming boy Cupid with his hand fondling Venus' breast. We are in a world of fairly outspoken eroticism in which the characteristics of nude painting have to be refined and exaggerated to give the maximum pleasure to the observer.

In sculpture we might consider as Mannerist the bronze Perseus cast in about 1545 by Benvenuto Cellini, the author of the *Autobiography*. The *Perseus* shows the hero standing on the body of the dead Medusa, sword in one hand, head of the victim in the other. Compared with, for example, Donatello's *Judith*, also a sculpture of a decapitation, it is a

Deposition,
Pontormo, c.1526
(Capponi Chapel, Santa Felicità, Florence)

work with little psychological significance. Its aim is to demonstrate the sculptor's command of Perseus' dramatic and athletic posture. A late example of Mannerist sculpture is Giambologna's *Rape of the Sabines* (1579–83) in the Accademia at Florence, which is a successful upward-moving triad of figures, one kneeling, one standing, and one lifted. It derives from the model offered by Michelangelo's *Victory* and exhibits the same interest in the twisted nude but developed in a much more complicated manner. It is, however, a piece of elaborately decorative posturing rather than an advance in artistic invention or understanding.

After the magical period ended with the death of Raphael in 1520 Italy remained wealthy. Florence became a despotism with the Medici harnessing the arts to their own purposes. Venice, to be examined in chapter 9, was more grandly inventive because it remained a republic. Roman society was genuinely shattered by the Sack of 1527 but it recovered to some extent and the artistic censorship associated with the Counter-Reformation in mid-century was slow to develop. But the great period in Florence and Rome was over. Later artists did not make innovations that involved such striking breaks with the past.

The sense of achievement in the visual arts in the mid-sixteenth century and the consciousness of the historical development lying behind it were enshrined in the writings of one of the Florentine Mannerist painters, Giorgio Vasari, who produced a series of *Lives of the most excellent Italian painters, sculptors and architects* published in two editions in 1550 and 1568. Vasari was himself a distinguished painter and architect – he designed the Uffizi in Florence – and was much patronised by the Medici. His *Lives* provide much of the information we have about the biographies of artists from Giotto to Michelangelo. They are interesting, however, not only as a source of information that would otherwise have been lost, but also because Vasari expressed a point of view about the history of art. His book is concerned mainly with the school of Florence and he divides it into three ages: the first starting with Cimabue and Giotto, the second at the beginning of the fifteenth century, the third with Leonardo. He believed that art had improved through observing the models of the ancients, through better imitation of nature and through development of the skill of drawing. He thought the last age was the best, because a kind of perfection had been attained by Michelangelo, and many artists were performing better than their predecessors before Leonardo.

Vasari's view of the evolution from Giotto to Michelangelo has some similarity with ours, which descends from it. But it begs the question, which he did not ask, of whether it makes sense to think of art as 'improving'. Leonardo might be said to have painted better than Giotto; in another sense he was doing something different. A modern observer might be hard put to decide whether one was better than the other. He would think of them as expressing different ages and states of mind and therefore not comparable. He would also appreciate the value of the medieval art, produced between the Romans and Giotto, which Vasari despised. The modern historian would, however, share with Vasari a consciousness of the extraordinarily prolonged series of creative achievements of the one rather small society of Florence over the three centuries since Giotto. Florence was not the biggest or most typical city in Renaissance Europe but it was certainly the city that contributed most to the development of the European imagination, not only in the visual arts but in literature and thought as well. It is the most striking case in modern history of a society with a creative tradition and a repeated capacity for producing new ideas that the European mind could accept with enthusiasm. In the sixteenth century Florence lost both its republican independence and its outstanding commercial and financial position. Leadership passed to other cities as Tuscany declined, eventually into backwardness.

THE NEW EUROPE OF THE SIXTEENTH CENTURY

Columbus' voyage to the New World,
Theodore de Bry, c.1590

SIXTEENTH-CENTURY EUROPE WAS a very different place from Europe in the age of Donatello and Van Eyck. The first and most obvious reasons were the geographical discoveries that changed the shape of the world. In 1492 Columbus landed in America. In 1497 Vasco da Gama sailed round the Cape of Good Hope to India. In the early years of the sixteenth century Venice, the place most obviously threatened by the discoveries, since it depended on the trade of the land-locked Mediterranean, was already greatly alarmed as Indian spices flowed into Lisbon and from thence to Antwerp, undercutting Venetian goods. Great empires were built up by Portugal in Brazil and by Spain in the rest of South America. By the middle of the century gold and silver were flowing into Spain to give that kingdom its hundred years of greatness. By the end of the century English, Dutch and French expeditions to the

185

Portuguese carracks off a rocky coast,
Joachim Patinir, c.1521 (National Maritime Museum, London)

Americas and the Far East were laying the foundations of new trading empires based on northern Europe.

Another major change was the acceleration of population growth and the connected revival of the monarchies. This destroyed the independence of those towns that had been outstanding in the period of population decline. The great powers of the sixteenth century were the houses of Valois in France, and Habsburg based in Germany and Spain. The Habsburg Emperor Charles V (d. 1556) became ruler of Spain in 1516. In a long reign he controlled much of Germany, the Low Countries, Spain and Lombardy, an empire unparalleled since the time of Charlemagne. For much of the first half of the century European politics centred on the duel between Charles V and Francis I of France (d. 1547). In the later part of the century France was rent by the Wars of Religion and the chief European power was undoubtedly the Spain of Philip II (d. 1598). One of the results of this revival of the monarchies was that from 1494 Italy was no longer a safe and insulated family of states but a country repeatedly invaded and desolated by foreign powers. The Sack of Rome by Charles V's army in 1527 was only the most striking event in a series of wars. Francesco Guicciardini, writing his long *History of Italy* in the 1530s, was aware of the changes that had transformed the world, and particularly his Italian world, in his lifetime. The voyages of Columbus, he said, had opened up new lands which 'have so much space that they are beyond any comparison far greater in size than the habitable earth previously known to us'. For Guicciardini, as no doubt for most of his Italian contemporaries, however, it was the invasion of Italy which loomed largest and with which he began his book. In 1494

186

Money-changer's shop,
Vocation of St Matthew (detail), *Jan van Hemessen, c.1540 (Alte Pinakothek, Munich)*

'those whose profession it is to foretell the future by means of science or divine inspiration unanimously affirmed that more frequent and greater changes were in store, and stranger and more horrible events were about to occur than had been seen in any part of the world for many centuries.'

Guicciardini may not have been aware that the world of the cities of the fifteenth century was doomed by the revival of monarchical power and in the long run by the shift in trade routes. The latter process took a long time to be effective and the Mediterranean remained the centre of civilisation through the sixteenth century. But the suppression of the cities can be shown, at least symbolically, by the fate of Ghent and Florence in the 1530s. The revolt of Ghent in 1539 was the last of the rebellions with which the Ghenters had asserted their restless contempt for their seigniorial superiors. It did not impress the World-Emperor Charles V, who determined to suppress them finally. His envoy, the Comte de Roeulx, told the Ghenters that 'rebels and disobedient subjects have never been victorious against their good princes,' conveniently forgetting the notable successes of that kind Ghent had enjoyed several times in earlier centuries. This time the people were powerless and the constitution that Charles imposed in 1540 made the *échevins* the nominees of the prince and removed all independent power from the bourgeoisie. Earlier, in 1529, the same Charles had agreed with Pope Clement VII to return the Medici to Florence, still obstinately republican and employing Michelangelo to design its fortifications. In 1530 Charles's representatives entered the defeated city and imposed Alessandro de' Medici as duke, to be followed in 1537 by Cosimo I, from whom the later dukes of Tuscany descended. That was the end of republicanism at Florence.

187

View of Antwerp,
Jan Wildens (Private Collection)

By that time Bruges, formerly the wealthiest of the Flemish cities, had suffered a decline for a different reason – the silting up of its port – and lost its position as the entrepôt of northwest Europe to Antwerp, which never had the same degree of independence in a world ruled by the Habsburgs. For most of the sixteenth century, until it was suppressed by the army of Philip II in the 1580s, Antwerp was northwest Europe's great trading centre, drawing goods from the Portuguese empire as well as the Mediterranean. But it never developed an international commercial empire of its own to rival those of Florence, Venice and Genoa earlier, or later London and Amsterdam. Its position in the world was therefore somewhat more limited. Though it housed a considerable artistic tradition, most obviously represented by Pieter Bruegel in the mid-sixteenth and Rubens in the early seventeenth centuries, it never achieved the independent accomplishment of the essential Renaissance cities.

Venice remained an independent republic and the chief home of city creativity, which will demand separate attention in a later chapter. Apart from Venice, the world of the independent cities of the fifteenth century, based on a particular set of trade routes in the Mediterranean and the eastern Atlantic and on freedom from monarchical intervention, was no more. That phase of city creativity had come to an end. The history of the Renaissance in the sixteenth century therefore becomes a different kind of story. We are no longer concerned with a separate and sheltered creation of new ideas in a few favoured centres. The story of the Renaissance becomes the story of the export of those ideas to widely distributed centres of patronage, mostly in the monarchical world, and their intermingling with other ideas drawn from other traditions. The intellectual and artistic prestige of Italy and Flanders

ABOVE Old port of Antwerp,
Sebastien Vranck (Musée Massey, Tarbes)

BELOW Taxpayers,
Bruegel the Younger, c.1600 (Musée des Beaux Arts, Ghent)

189

remained impressive: witness the attention paid to Leonardo da Vinci and other Italians by Francis I of France or to Titian by Charles V and Philip II; the visits of Rabelais or Bruegel to Italy, drawn by the strength of its traditions. But outside the old creative centres Renaissance attitudes, separated from their original comfortable cradles, were diluted.

That was the situation in the middle years of the sixteenth century. By the end of the century a further development had taken place: new commercial empires, centred on London and Amsterdam, were superseding those of Florence and Venice and establishing a creative Northern Renaissance world, similar to the old Italian pattern in that it had a powerful human creativity based on the rapid expansion of wealth derived from long-distance commerce.

The new commercial empires, however, were fundamentally different from the old ones in several respects. Their trade was partly world-wide, extending to the East and West Indies, not confined to the Mediterranean and Atlantic Europe but stretching far over the Atlantic and Indian Oceans. They were cities of a different type from Florence and Venice. The Italian Giovanni Botero, who published the first great book on cities in the late sixteenth century, envisaged a city differing from Florence and Venice as London did. This was a city in which the concentration of wealth was determined not only by trade but also by three other factors: the residence of the

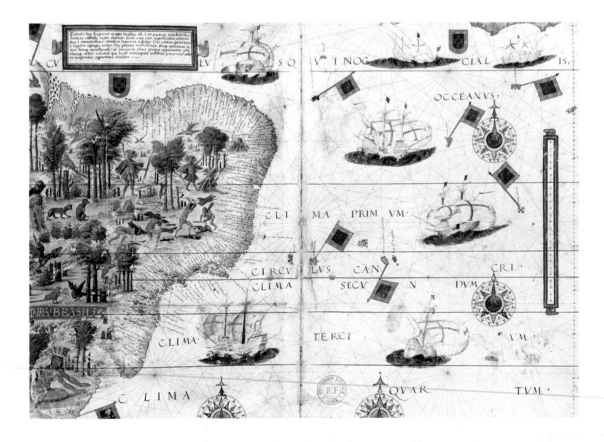

'Brazil'
from the Miller Atlas, *Pedro Reinel, c.1519*
(Bibliothèque Nationale, Paris)

190

Defeat of the Spanish Armada,
1588 (National Maritime Museum, London)

prince, the courts of justice, and the nobility bringing their dependents. London's make-up was determined not only by the wealth of its native patricians, important though that was, but also by the combination of a trading community with the personnel of the royal court and the inns of court; it was a capital as well as a wealthy mercantile community.

The relationship between London and England also was different from the relationship of Florence or Venice to its subject dominions. London's wealth was based partly on the improvement of agriculture and the extensive growth of new industries in southeast England: London society was partly made up of visiting nobility and gentry. London was the apex of a kingdom, not an imperial city owning and repressing its empire as Florence and Venice had been. Nevertheless the internal conditions of city life encouraged, as in the Mediterranean, a rapid interchange of concepts between the intelligent freemen. The Globe Theatre and the royal court were different from the Medici Palace but

they served an analogous function as social and intellectual centres of a wealthy urban community. It remained true, as it had been in the fifteenth century, that the motive power for original conceptions of humanity was linked with the concentrated wealth of cities drawn from commercial empires. The old commercial empires had come to an end by 1600 and had been replaced by new ones in the North.

In 1600 London's population was probably approaching 200,000 and it was possible for a writer in 1615 to describe it as 'the greatest or next the greatest city of the Christian world'. Its wealth was based on several factors. There was rapidly increasing external trade. The greatest part of this was still directed to neighbouring parts of the Low Countries. London merchants benefited from the collapse

191

of Antwerp after 1585, which followed the Dutch rebellion against Spain, and by the end of the sixteenth century alien merchants in London had become much less prominent. There was also expansion outside the North Sea. English maritime activity – pirateering against the Spaniards, circumnavigation by Drake, attempts to sail to the northwest and the northeast of the Atlantic – was intense in the reign of Elizabeth. The Levant Company was founded in 1592 to trade with the Eastern Mediterranean, and the East India Company in 1599 to trade around the Cape of Good Hope with southern Asia. Early seventeenth-century London contained a fairly large community of merchants deriving wealth from the old trade in the export of cloth, and from the import of an extended range of goods for a market of increasing prosperity and sophistication.

The last point was perhaps the most important. People poured into London from a countryside in which agriculture and industry were being diversified – the growing of woad and the manufacture of pins and stockings were replacing more traditional agriculture. King James's efforts at the beginning of the seventeenth century to stop the gentry flocking into London and the court testified to the attractions of an urban centre that offered delights irresistible to the fancy of countrymen. The growth of London and its market was the result of a complicated interaction of economic and social factors, the presence of merchants, nobility and administrators of a kind that tends to operate in capitals. Because English economic life was growing and expansive at that period, its central city became wealthy and the mass of population in one place was able to afford the shops, brothels and theatres that sprang up.

In the period around 1600, therefore, London became a fully developed metropolitan city with the accompaniment of an extremely complex mass of writers of pamphlets and actors of plays emphasising the endless interaction of wealth and corruption, the city of *A Chaste Maid in Cheapside*,

Thomas Middleton's comedy of 1615. The pamphleteers Thomas Nashe and Robert Greene and the playwrights Christopher Marlowe, Ben Jonson, Middleton and Thomas Dekker may be taken as the obvious representatives of this rich and violent society. London was no doubt similar to many other great cities but it happened to throw out from its literary maelstrom, without which he could not have existed, the greatest writer of the late Renaissance, Shakespeare, the last and most splendid mouthpiece of Renaissance innovations.

The nearest parallel to early seventeenth-century London was Amsterdam. It was not the capital of the Dutch republic, which was at The Hague, but it was easily the weightiest of the Dutch cities, both in population and in commercial wealth. Like London – and like Florence and Venice – it was a city without a university, a condition that was probably important for creative Renaissance centres by preserving them from the excessive effects of scholastic tradition and allowing them to cultivate original pursuits. In London it was the theatre, in Amsterdam painting, which enabled the imagination to venture into novel forms of expression without the danger of being restricted by censorship. Amsterdam was naturally much more republican in atmosphere, since the Stadtholder was elsewhere, and the city councillors constituted a more serious political body than anything in London except the intermittent parliament. Even more than London in the early seventeenth century, Amsterdam was a powerful commercial capital, housing the main directors of the Dutch East India Company, a stock exchange and a large population of financial brokers.

The Dutch, and especially Amsterdam's, prominence in international commerce, which had outstripped that of all other cities before 1620, had developed very rapidly out of the extremely unpromising situation of the Netherlandish provinces' rebellion against the might of Spain in 1572. As in the case of London, it was based on an active native

Port and town of Amsterdam,
Hucquier, sixteenth century (Private Collection)

economy that produced an increasing variety of manufactures and, much more than in London, by a long tradition of shipbuilding and seafreight, in which the Dutch towns had already been prominent in the later Middle Ages. But an equally important factor was Holland's geographical position between the Northern world of the Baltic and Russia and the Mediterranean and Eastern worlds. The Dutch developed a prominent role in the North in trade with the Baltic and Russia. In the period around 1600 they opened up commerce with the Mediterranean, South America and, around the Cape of Good Hope, with the East Indies. The Dutch East India Company was founded in 1602. By that time the Dutch were moving towards their 'primacy in world trade' that was to be a feature of the seventeenth century and the essential background to the golden age of Dutch art. Amsterdam was ahead but early in the seventeenth century – and this is as far as we shall go – London and Amsterdam were both cities with a growing international trade, the centres of companies whose many shareholders included both active merchants and passive investors, and the homes of large, untidy populations, including a few individuals whose artistic perceptions were creating new levels of expression.

Our examination of the later Renaissance will have to take account of three subjects: first the spread of ideas from Italy into the Northern world in general (chapter 8); secondly the continuation of a creative Italian tradition in Venice (chapter 9); thirdly the establishment of new

Renaissance enterprises in the two greatest cities of the North Sea, London and Amsterdam (chapter 10). Are we justified in defining this final movement, so far from Laurentian Florence, as part of the Renaissance? One argument in favour of this approach is that, as we shall see, both the English dramatists and the Dutch painters depended heavily on Renaissance assumptions derived ultimately from Italy. The dramatists would also have been very different without the models of Plautus and Seneca, the stories of Plutarch, the reflections of Montaigne. The painters would have been equally deprived without the inspiration of Raphael and Titian. What they achieved in both cases was a creative transplantation of Italian traditions into a Northern idiom, native to the European world of later centuries, broader than the now decaying Mediterranean civilisation.

We go no further than 1630 at the latest. By that time the Mediterranean had lost its primacy, the Italian cities are no longer where one should look for new ideas and new art. We can no longer speak sensibly of the Renaissance as a sector of the European mind because it had gradually been generalised to the whole of Europe. At the same time man's idea of an earth-centred universe had been overtaken by a heliocentric system, astrology had lost much of its authority, the unitary tradition of philosophy and magic stretching from the Greeks to the present had been shown to be imaginary. The intellectual as well as the physical environment of the Renaissance was being seriously undermined.

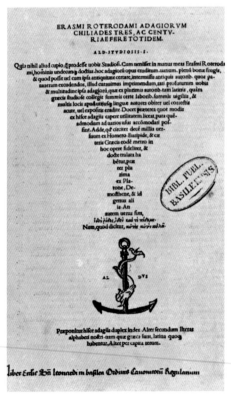

Frontispiece of Erasmus's Adages,
printed by Aldus in Venice, 1508 (Kupferstichkabinett, Basel)

The intellectual world of the High Renaissance period depended on particular conceptions of space and time, the universe and history which made Ficino's Neoplatonism acceptable. The universe was centred on the earth, affected by the encircling spheres of planets and stars that revolved around it. History stretched back to the pre-Socratic period, which had seen the origins of magic and the hermetic philosophy, after which there was a continuous line of thought. These underlying beliefs were upset in the early seventeenth century by the discovery that the solar system centred on the sun and that the hermetic writings dated only from the time of the Roman Empire. The High Renaissance world-picture, which had lingered on in the European mind, finally became untenable. These discoveries were quickly followed by the philosophy of Descartes, which established the material world as an independent subject for scientific calculation and therefore cast into serious doubt the harmony of spirit and matter, science and magic, that had been characteristic assumptions of Neoplatonic thought.

The late Renaissance world, it seems in retrospect, was notable for the contradiction between extreme irrationality of beliefs and a powerful impulse towards rational analysis. On the one hand this was the great age of witch-hunts, when the belief in the maleficent powers of humans in communion with devils caused immense cruelty in some parts of the continent. It was also the period in which violence based on religious belief was at its height in the many wars and persecutions caused by the

194

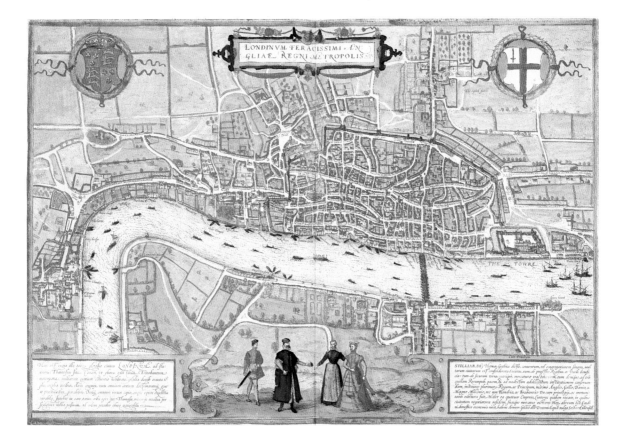

Plan of London from Civitates Orbis Terrarum,
Braun and Hogenberg, 1572 (British Museum, London)

conflict between Catholics and Protestants. This kind of irrationality was more obviously present in early modern Europe than it had been in the Middle Ages. It would clearly be mistaken to suggest that religious belief at that time caused more misery than nationalist, racialist or class hatred in the twentieth century, but the late Renaissance was distinguished by the simultaneous presence of intense and conflicting beliefs leading to war and persecution whose hold on the human mind is now difficult to explain. At the same time physicians and astronomers were making continual and ultimately successful efforts towards rational, physical explanations of the operations of the human body and the movements of the planets and stars. Francis Bacon,

who believed, as a precursor of modern scientists, in a system that 'derives axioms from the senses and particulars, rising by a gradual and unbroken ascent, so that it arrives at the most general axioms last of all', was Lord Chancellor under King James I, who certainly believed in witches and who narrowly escaped being blown up by the Gunpowder Plot planned by religious fanatics.

This coexistence of the rational and the irrational was in a less violent manner essential to the general philosophy of the Renaissance, which was highly scholarly in its investigation of ancient history and texts, but highly irrational in its tendency to believe in magic and astrology. The period around 1600 was marked by an intensification

195

however, was to undermine the assumptions of Neoplatonism. By about 1615 Kepler and Galileo were making it clear, whatever scholastic theologians might urge to the contrary, that the heavens could be investigated by telescopes and mathematics and that the solar system was not earth-centred. With this new astronomy, the idea of the closed interdependent universe, in which angels, stars and planets affected the destinies of men on earth, became impossible to maintain. About the same time, in 1614, the classical scholar Isaac Casaubon published his refutation of the theory that the hermetic writings and the sibylline oracles dated from the early Greek period; they were in fact post-Christian, from the period of the Roman Empire. In effect Casaubon demolished the continuous philosophical theology in which Ficino had believed and the importance of the sibyls enshrined on the Sistine ceiling.

The 'end' of the Renaissance which we postulate thus involves two things: the total absorption of some Renaissance attitudes into northern Europe and Europe generally, and the intellectual destruction of the unified world-picture that had been assumed by Ficino and his followers. This may sound contradictory, as if the Renaissance had been both undermined and generally accepted. What was accepted was a series of Renaissance ideas separated from the main Ficinian philosophy that had supported them: the writing of history, the emphasis on individual character in art and literature, philosophy as ethical and epistemological analysis as opposed to scholasticism, veneration for the legacy of the classical world. These became essential parts of the European mind. The last three chapters of this book will describe a few outstanding stages in this process. As the Renaissance spreads into Europe we cannot describe the evolution of its ideas with the relative completeness that was possible in the early stages in fifteenth-century Florence. We shall have to pick out only a handful of strikingly creative figures who provide an indication of its direction.

Columbus,
Ridolfo Ghirlandaio, early sixteenth century
(Museo Civico Navale di Pegli, Genoa)

of the contrasts within the European world-picture as scholars and scientists became increasingly competent against a background of great religious violence in the French Wars of Religion, the Anglo-Spanish conflict, and the beginning of the Thirty Years War. This was to be followed eventually by the triumph of reason and science and a relaxation of religious belief in the late seventeenth and eighteenth centuries.

One of the early results of scientific and scholarly effort,

RENAISSANCE IDEAS SPREAD TO THE NORTH

Self-Portrait,
Dürer, 1500 (Alte Pinakothek, Munich)

197

THE FIRST NORTHERN ARTIST artist to be profoundly influenced by first-hand contact with Italian art was Albrecht Dürer (1471–1528). He came from Nuremberg, a wealthy and independent city on the edge of Bavaria, which benefited from the expansion of industry and commerce at the end of the fifteenth century. He was apprenticed to a leading Nuremberg painter at the age of fifteen and travelled in Western Germany, visiting Colmar, Basel and Strasburg to work temporarily for famous masters in those cities. He was therefore well trained as a young man in the German tradition, not only in drawing and painting but also in making woodcuts, a type of art that was much more developed in Germany than in Italy.

Between 1494 and 1495, however, he made a visit to Venice. This was a natural direction for a southern German to take. Commercial connections with Venice were strong and the Germans had a centre there, the Fondaco dei Tedeschi, in which merchants from Nuremberg were to be found. Dürer visited Venice again between 1505 and 1507 but the first trip had already been decisive. He was consumed by a passion for the unfamiliar art that he found there and immediately began to copy it.

Dürer was a theorist as well as an artist. At an early age he had been introduced to the classics by friends with humanist interests in Nuremberg. As a result of his Italian excursions he became familiar with the writings of Italian theorists of art from Alberti onwards and made Italian artistic theory available to the German reader for the first time. His own writings included highly technical discussions of perspective and the proportions of the human body, and were printed at the end of his life, with a practical emphasis on their usefulness to the artist. Like the Italians, Dürer believed that the purpose of the artist should be to copy nature but his approach to this aim was less idealistic than theirs. He was less interested in the ideal figure and more in figures that actually existed, even if they were ugly: 'Life in nature manifests the truth of these things. Therefore observe it diligently, go by it and do not depart from nature arbitrarily, imagining that you can find something better by yourself … Art is embedded in nature; he who can extract it has it.'

Dürer was a deeply reflective and rather unhappy man who took his mission in life with great seriousness. This is reflected in his self-portraits: the charming portrait of 1493 of a serious and handsome young man, well dressed and carrying an eryngium flower, symbol of conjugal fidelity; the extraordinary portrait of 1500 in which he presents himself as Christ with hair cascading below his intense face onto his shoulders; the portrait of 1522 as the Man of Sorrows, naked to the waist with scourges in his hands ready for self-flagellation. Whilst the self-examination of Leonardo and Michelangelo was intense, his expressions of introspection, connected with the highly developed Northern tradition of portraiture, in which Dürer also excelled when he painted other people, have no real parallel in Italian art.

In later life Dürer was won over by the principles of Luther's Reformation, as indeed was the rest of the city of Nuremberg in which he lived. This conversion is usually believed to explain two of his later works. One is a woodcut of the *Last Supper*, which shows Christ and the apostles around the table without Judas. Dürer's interpretation of the scene, with Christ guarding the recumbent St John, was intended to emphasise the love in their relationship at the expense of the betrayal and the eucharistic significance of the scene. The other is the double painting of the *Four Apostles*, John, Peter, Mark and Paul, which he presented to Nuremberg, a city recently converted to Luther. The *Four Apostles* gives prominence to the two figures standing in front, St John the Evangelist and St Paul. They are picked out because John's gospel and Paul's epistle were so important to Luther. Also the four gospels have been given the four humours (sanguine, choleric, phlegmatic and melancholic) with John as the sanguine and Paul as the

Alpine landscape,
Dürer, c.1495 (Ashmolean Museum, Oxford)

melancholic; a combination of art, theology and medicine. Dürer should not be regarded as a religious fanatic but his earnestness found roots both in the tradition of pious art, which he inherited from his Northern predecessors, and in the Italian grace and naturalism that he found at Venice. The two strains were mingled, each retaining an original purity, to create an outlook different from either.

Dürer was also a notable figure in the history of landscape. The watercolours, which he made on his journeys over the Alps and elsewhere in Germany, convey an impression, stronger than in the backgrounds of earlier Flemish paintings, both of charm and simple reportage, without a dramatic purpose, and seem to usher in a new world of the romantic traveller. This basic imitative skill, however, is far from being the main tendency in Dürer's work. In his woodcuts and engravings, rather than the paintings, he emerges as an artist with an intellectual and visionary inspiration, whose artistic creations were meant to carry an idea in which the detailed depiction of human forms and nature was really subordinated to the urgency of his message.

The impact of the Italian world on Dürer began to show

199

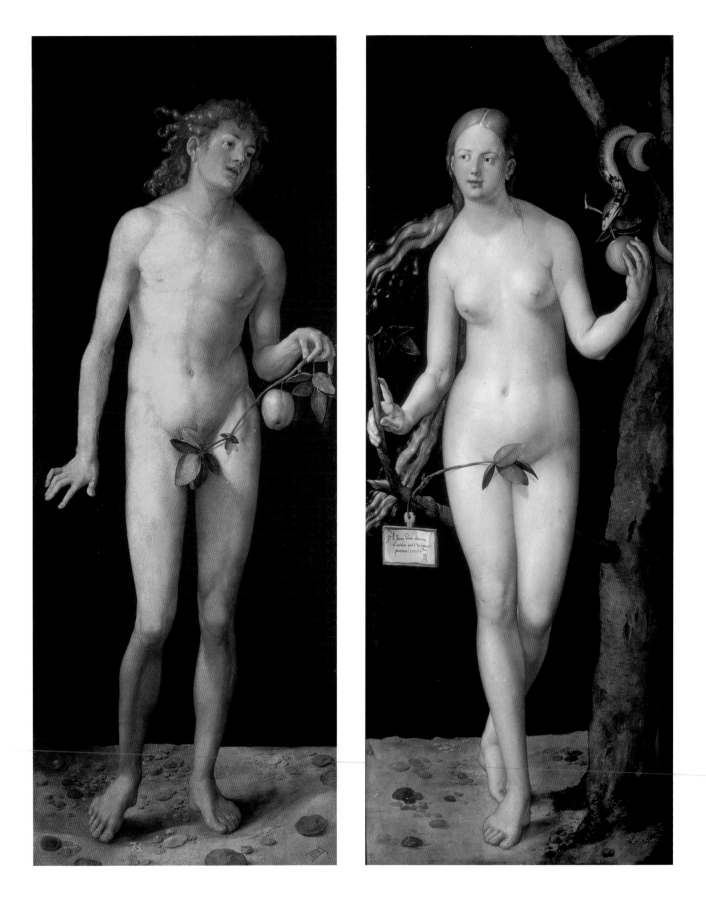

LEFT Adam and Eve,
Dürer, 1507 (Prado, Madrid)

specifically after 1494 in his imitations of classical and Renaissance models, and in the long run by his laborious attempts to develop the Vitruvian teaching on the relations between different parts of the human body. The process of adaptation can be seen by comparing the engraving of *Adam and Eve* of 1504 with his later paintings of the same subjects made in 1507. The 1504 engraving contains a number of symbolic details but its main purpose is clearly to present idealised male and female figures. They are the result of a large amount of preparatory work inspired both by the nudes of Pollaiuolo and others, and by looking at classical monuments. Adam is connected with the pose of the Apollo Belvedere that was owned by Julius II. The Adam and Eve of 1507, in contrast, incorporates the skill in figure-drawing Dürer derived from following the Italians, but the figures are no longer imitations of the classical models. Both Adam and Eve are people with a complex and hesitant character. The classical inspiration has been worked into Northern types. Incidentally, Dürer's command of another aspect of Italian art, perspective, was demonstrated

Adoration of the Magi,
Dürer, 1504 (Uffizi, Florence)

Melencolia I,
Dürer, 1514 (Guildhall Library, London)

in his painting of the *Adoration of the Magi*. This impresses one with its typically delightful contrasts of reds, greens and blues and by the emphasis on lines marking clear divisions. It is also a good example of the perspective scene in the Italian manner in which the figures are firmly placed in a setting outlined by buildings.

The atmosphere created by Dürer's work as a whole is best conveyed by three engravings of 1513–14: the *Knight, Death and the Devil*, *St Jerome in his Cell*, and *Melencolia I*. The *Knight, Death and the Devil* is a drawing of a resolute

knight in armour, set on a magnificent horse, advancing with intrepidity before a mountainous landscape. Behind him looms Death bearing an hourglass and to his rear is the menacing but also slightly absurd figure of the Devil as a hairy goat. The engraving presents Christian determination striding through the world, superior to perils natural and supernatural. It was influenced by Erasmus's *Manual of the Christian Soldier* published a few years earlier. But the mounted knight and his horse, taken in themselves, are based on the equestrian statues of Renaissance Italy and the whole scene, in visual terms, marks an entry of Renaissance man into Northern landscape and Northern piety.

Melencolia I depicts a seated winged woman, lost in dejection, surrounded by objects connected with geometry, architecture and craftsmanship. The complex picture relates to ideas drawn both from medieval conceptions of melancholy and the melancholy part of the human temperament as understood by physicians, and from the idea of melancholy as an expression of the influence of the planet Saturn, the melancholic temperament, as developed by the Italian Neoplatonists. How these ideas were related to Dürer's own elusive personality is not clear, but he was probably drawing a picture of himself as a melancholy artist with aspirations that he was unable to realise with the artistic materials at his disposal.

The *Knight, Death and the Devil* and *Melencolia I* were both supreme examples of the engraver's art. An engraving, unlike an oil painting, could be reproduced in many copies. Throughout his life Dürer lived in circles in which the printing of works of art was common and he made

Knight, Death and the Devil,
Dürer, 1513 (Kupferstichkabinett, Berlin)

203

Four Horsemen,
Dürer, c.1497 (British Museum, London)

substantial advances in the adaptation of this kind of reproduction to the needs of more sophisticated artists. In the last years of the fifteenth century, he produced a series of fifteen woodcuts of scenes from *The Apocalypse* which endowed his figures with some of the solidity characteristic of naturalistic paintings. The famous woodcut of the *Four Horsemen*, which shows them galloping with visionary fury through the air, trampling the mortals in their path, is the best known of the series, and created a vivid and lasting new image.

Dürer developed an interest in engraving, which offered much better opportunities than the woodcut for the delicate delineation of figures, and he used this in part for classical stories. The Roman *Hercules*, for example, illustrates the story of Hercules at the cross-roads facing the choice between Virtue and Pleasure, which had long been a favourite expression of moral choice. Here Hercules faces Pleasure as a dangerously attractive reclining female nude and Virtue as an upright and determined woman properly dressed. Dürer's figures are derived from the paintings of Mantegna and Pollaiuolo, transferred to the form of engraving. Here again Italian Renaissance ideas are incorporated into a Northern setting and a Northern style.

Dürer was not the only artist of his generation in whom the Northern and Italian traditions were combined in various ways. We have already, in chapter 3, looked at two contemporaries, Bosch and Grünewald, in whose works Northern styles appeared in an extreme form. Farther east in southern Germany the influence of Italian styles was stronger. Several notable artists in the early fifteenth century can be seen grappling with inspirations from the South whilst at the same time turning them into visual forms in which the power of the Northern background is also obvious.

Albrecht Altdorfer (*c.*1480–1538) had a lifelong link with Regensburg on the Danube and his paintings were made mainly for churches and noblemen in Bavaria. The power of the German landscape is clear in many of them. For instance, *St George and the Dragon* shows the saint on horseback with the menacing monster, apparently just before the fight is to begin. But the figures of man, horse and dragon are at first sight difficult to detach from the huge trees that rise above them, filling more than nine-tenths of the panel with the rich greens of their foliage. Is this a holy legend or a landscape? What we see in the painting is above all the overwhelming luxuriance of the German forest, in which the small man and animals are almost lost.

St George and the Dragon,
Altdorfer, 1510 (Alte Pinakothek, Munich)

Susanna Bathing,
Altdorfer, 1526 (Alte Pinakothek, Munich)

Altdorfer had a romantic German fondness not only for landscape and natural vistas but also for architectural backgrounds in which the buildings, drawn with attention to perspective form, stretched into the distance, leaving small figures dwarfed by the half-mystical structures behind them. One of his strangest paintings was *Susanna Bathing*. In the foreground Susanna is having her feet washed by handmaidens before a fountain. The painting is dominated, however, by a vast palace, constructed in a classical style but with much additional ornament, and topped by a rounded tower and spire far above the earth. Dozens of small figures

are talking, buying and selling at ground level and looking out from balconies three levels above the square. The painting is not so much an Old Testament scene as an architectural fantasy.

Altdorfer's most extraordinary creation was the *Battle of Alexander*, a pictorial representation of Alexander of Macedon's battle with the Darius, King of Persia, in Syria in 335 BC, a story worked out by a classical scholar. It was commissioned by Duke William of Bavaria when he was on the point of taking part in a campaign against the Turkish invaders of Central Europe. Altdorfer sees the Greek-

Persian war and the German-Turkish struggle as similar episodes in the world-historical confrontation of East and West. He has therefore painted an epic struggle in a vast landscape in which the eye is drawn backwards over distant seas and mountain ranges. We are looking at the world divided between armed civilisations. In the foreground are armies of men, each figure minutely drawn, with Alexander on horseback pursuing Darius in his chariot, just discernible in the mêlée. This is a panoramic vision of worlds in conflict.

Altdorfer lived in a Catholic Germany whilst Lucas Cranach (1472-1553) spent much of his working life in Protestant Wittenberg and was a close friend of Luther, the reformer. The spirit of reform was to be hostile to Renaissance eroticism. However, the court of the Electors of Saxony, for which Cranach worked, at some periods accepted it and Cranach painted a number of illustrations of classical stories, *Apollo and Diana, Venus and Cupid* and *Lucretia* in which he developed his own version of the female nude, an adaptation of erotic painting for an aristocratic taste adapted to a Northern, Protestant court. A good example is the *Judgment of Paris*. To the left are Mercury and Paris, dressed very inappropriately in sixteenth-century armour; on the right the three goddesses who are being judged, Minerva, Venus and Juno, are naked except for their necklaces and offer their beauty to the judge. The type of nude which Cranach created and which he repeated in many paintings was connected with the medieval miniature tradition rather than with the classic Venuses of Giorgione and Titian: slim with small, high breasts and rounded belly and hips. But the incorporation of the female nude in a serious painting was an Italian idea, and Cranach was expressing very clearly, if unintentionally, the combination of Northern and Southern lines of development that preceded him.

Another great southern German, Hans Holbein, came from the independent city of Augsburg, again close to

Judgment of Paris,
Cranach, c.1520
(Rogers Fund, 1928, Metropolitan Museum of Art, New York)

Bavaria. His life was bound up with the Reformation. He spent the years 1526–8 in England, before the Reformation had really got going, and returned there in 1532, when it was in full swing, to remain until his death in 1543. Before his periods in England Holbein became associated with Erasmus at Basel. His first visit to England was under the patronage of Thomas More, Erasmus's friend. It is a curious fact that on his second visit Holbein's introduction to court circles appears to have been through Anne Boleyn, Henry VIII's new queen, married in defiance of the pope at a time when More, staunch in his Catholicism, was in disgrace.

Holbein came to England, presumably because of chances of employment, and worked extensively both for the court and those connected with it, and for the community of German merchants in London. He remained South German, as far as his painterly skill was concerned, and seems to have been successful in riding through the storms of Reformation from one confession to the next.

The complexities of which Holbein was capable are shown in *The Ambassadors* which is a double portrait of two Frenchmen who came to England in 1533 with diplomatic proposals relating to Henry's marriage to Anne. The painting contains many symbols relating to their mission:

The Ambassadors,
Holbein, 1533 (National Gallery, London)

208

Artist's Wife and Two Children,
Holbein, 1528 (Öffentliche Kunstammlung, Basel)

the lute with a broken string, indicating disagreement; the text of a work of Luther, indicating sympathy with reform; the *cosmati* pavement from Westminster Abbey, the shrine of the English kings; the crucifix hidden behind the curtain; the distorted skull rising from the floor. Holbein's fame rests, however, chiefly on his portrait painting. It appears with great delicacy in the *Artist's Wife and Two Children* which captures a gentle sadness, possibly related to the fact that the artist was so much separated from them. His sitters included many of the great figures of this period, which makes him a frequently reproduced illustrator of the pre-Reformation and post-Reformation worlds: *Erasmus* at Basel, *Thomas More* in London, *Henry VIII* and *Thomas Cromwell*. *Christina of Denmark*, painted as a potential wife for Henry VIII, and *Sir Richard Southwell*, an unscrupulous member of Henry's court and an enemy of Holbein's friend More, show the delicacy with which Holbein painted courtiers.

The portraits, for which Holbein is famous partly because some of his larger compositions have disappeared,

209

Christina of Denmark,
Holbein, 1538
(National Gallery, London)

have earned him the reputation of being second only to Dürer among German artists of this period. They recorded the personalities of individuals with a refinement that carried forward the traditions of Flemish rather than Italian painting.

ERASMUS, MORE AND NORTHERN HUMANISM

When Dürer was visiting Venice and importing ideas of the Italian painters into the North, a flood of contacts between Italian and Northern scholars was spreading Renaissance humanism over Europe. This was a movement which, because it depended on reading printed books rather than on the transportation of works of art, could spread widely in a comparatively short time. In the early sixteenth century there were groups of humanists in every European country: Conrad Celtis's 'College of Poets and Mathematicians' at Vienna; the Greek and Hebrew scholar Johannes Reuchlin at Wittenberg; the philosopher Jacques Lefèvre d'Etaples at Paris; Francisco Ximenes producing the polyglot Bible in Spain; John Colet and Thomas Linacre in England. All were enthusiasts for the Italians' classicism and, with its help, they created local schools with interests in literature, philosophy, theology, law, history and the sciences, which transformed the European mind.

The most remarkable of the Northern humanists was a Dutchman, Desiderius Erasmus. In 1488 he took vows in the order of Augustinian Canons but a few years later he entered the service of a bishop and in 1495 got the chance to go to Paris. He did not abandon his monastic vows but never went back to the convent and remained for the rest of his life in a slightly awkward position, half in and half out of monastic life. In Paris he studied theology and developed an intense dislike of scholasticism that stayed with him until his

210

death. 'No one can understand the mysteries of this science who has had the least intercourse with the Muses or the Graces.' In 1499 he went to England in the entourage of Lord Mountjoy and began his ascent into the courtly world. He started publishing Latin compositions and met Colet who persuaded him to continue serious theological pursuits.

In the early years of the fifteenth century he was learning Greek and trying to make a living out of translations from that language. In 1504 he found in a library at Louvain the unpublished notes on the text of the New Testament by Lorenzo Valla. This brilliant application of philological principles to the problem of translating the Greek New Testament into Latin excited him and inspired his own work in that field.

From 1506 to 1509 Erasmus visited Italy, where he came into contact with the papal court and acquired a disapproval of the military aggressiveness of Pope Julius II. This was why he later published *Julius Exclusus*, in which he imagined the pope appearing at the gates of heaven and being refused entry because he was a warmonger. His assertion of the properly spiritual role of the papacy, probably written in 1513, is an interesting case of the possibility of serious criticism of authority in the tolerant days immediately preceding the Reformation. In 1508 Erasmus was in Venice while Julius was organising the attack by the League of Cambrai, a league of European powers, on the city. Another result of his Italian trip was his fruitful contact with the printing and publishing house of Aldus at Venice, which helped to encourage the spread of his European reputation.

After Italy he returned to England for five years, where he lived for part of the time in the house of Thomas More. In 1514 he moved to Basel, a good printing and publishing centre, like Venice on a smaller scale, where he published his new edition of the Greek New Testament with a Latin commentary. He was by now a famous man and in 1516

Erasmus,
Holbein, 1523 (Louvre, Paris)

was made a councillor of the future Emperor Charles V. In 1517 Luther's Reformation began. Erasmus spent most of the rest of his life at Basel and Freiburg, where he was relatively free from the political pressures of Reformation conflict. But as a famous theologian and biblical scholar he could not entirely escape. Luther tried to involve him on the Protestant side; Erasmus rejected his advances. Pope Paul III urged him to defend Catholicism. Erasmus remained in an ambiguous position, his sympathy with Reform declining as the difference between Reformers and Catholics developed into acute political struggle.

Erasmus was central to the Renaissance in many ways. First of all as a classical scholar. No one did as much as he to raise the level of the study of Greek and Latin as the essential basis of good education in the Northern world. This was probably his most significant contribution to civilisation because it strengthened classical education both as a discipline and as a liberal introduction to literature, history and philosophy which was the foundation of all thought.

But he also had more specific ideas that were influential. One of his achievements was to direct attention to the New Testament as the chief source of religious and ethical truth. Erasmus had little sympathy with those attached either to university scholasticism or to humanist Neoplatonism. The truth was simple and was contained in the gospels. He said in the introduction of his edition of the New Testament:

If princes in the execution of their duties would manifest what I have referred to as a Vulgar doctrine, if priests would inculcate it in sermons, if schoolmasters would instill it in students rather than the erudition which they draw from the fonts of Aristotle and Averroes [both philosophers influential in medieval universities], Christendom would not be so disturbed on all sides by almost continuous war, everything would not be boiling over with such a mad desire to heap up riches by fair means or foul … and, finally, we would not differ from those who do not profess the philosophy of Christ merely in name and ceremonial.

This simple teaching carried weight when it came from the lips of the most learned classicist of his day and the most perceptive student of the text of the New Testament itself.

Erasmus wrote many works in Latin and left a huge corpus of letters composed in that language in an improved style. The *Adages* was a series of essays expounding the meaning of proverbs which Erasmus added to at various times throughout the period from 1500 to 1533. The *Adages*

developed out of the kind of reflective writing contained in fifteenth-century Italian dialogues. Their form is similar to that of modern essays and they provide a bridge between the dialogues and the essays written later by Montaigne. They are clever pronouncements on manners, morals and history, composed by a scholar who can use the classics in relation to the sensible secular experience of a detached observer of life. An example, interesting because it contains Erasmus's ideas on contemporary kingship, which he also expressed in other works, is the Adage about the proverb, 'One must be born a king or a fool.'

Erasmus begins by using the *Iliad*:

What could be more idiotic than to be up in arms like a little boy for the sake of a little girl from a foreign land and then, when he couldn't keep his sweetheart [the reference is to Agamemnon] to filch one from Achilles and put the whole army in danger? And then there is Achilles himself — how foolishly he rages when bereft of his ladylove and how childishly he goes crying to his mother. And yet he is the one whom the poet sets before us as the perfect example of an excellent prince.

History shows that princes are generally bad and the praises commonly bestowed upon them for their wealth, their eloquence and their capacity for drinking are irrelevant to the real purpose of kingship.

It was not ill-advisedly that divine Plato wrote that the only way for a state to attain happiness was for the supreme command to be given to philosophers, or else, inversely, that those who govern should themselves follow philosophy. And to follow philosophy is not just to wear a mantle and to carry a bag around, or let your hair grow… It is to despise those things which the common herd goggle at, and to think quite differently from the opinions of the majority.[1]

Drawing from Erasmus' *In Praise of Folly*,
Holbein, 1508 (British Museum, London)

Christian kings ought to follow the example of Solomon who 'wished for wisdom alone, and that wisdom by which he might rightly govern people'. Erasmus points out the absurdity of taking care in choosing the captain of a ship but handing over the infinitely more complex management of the state to a man who merely happens to have been born into the office. This hereditary principle makes it essential to pay attention to the education of the prince, to make sure that he learns to devote himself to the well-being of his subjects and avoids war. What actually happens is the opposite of this. He learns the belief that he is above the law: 'Imagine the poison of flattery, frolic and pleasure, luxurious living, wealth and magnificence, the sense of power'. Erasmus's comments were, of course, the natural reaction of educated intelligence, reinforced by bold perception and by the classical riches of a sophisticated mind.

Erasmus's most remarkable work was the extended essay *In Praise of Folly* written in 1509. This gave a fuller statement of the points he had made straightforwardly in recommending the New Testament. All-embracing philosophies were to be distrusted. 'If there be anyone among you who appears to himself to be wise, let him follow Paul's advice and become a fool with Christ, the Prince of this world so that he may be truly wise. Those who are swollen up by Aristotelian, Averroistic or Platonic philosophy are accustomed to despise the mystical allegories of Scripture; some even laugh at them and reckon them to be dreams.' But the book also depended on linking up the 'folly' of the New Testament with the ecstatic madness that Plato recommended in *Phaedrus*. The true moving force in human life is an irrational folly that persuades men and women to marry and forces heroes into patriotic exploits. But, on a superior level, folly is also equated with moral behaviour that allows calculating self-advancement to be bypassed, and ultimately with the opposite of the worldly-wisdom found in Christ and St Paul. Erasmus also admired the Greek writer Lucian whose comedy he thought made points similar to Paul's preaching; familiarity with and admiration of his satirical work is one of the pillars on which *In Praise of Folly* depends. But it was classical scholarship that encouraged a modern man's rejection of scholastic nonsense and his insistence on a realistic approach to human life.

The Latin title of *In Praise of Folly* was *Encomium Moriae*. 'Moria' is the Greek for folly and the title was in part a joke about the name of Erasmus's friend Thomas More, in whose London house it was written. More was an extraordinary combination of a highly successful lawyer, a devout Christian and a humanist, who later became Lord

Chancellor and who was martyred for his refusal to accept Henry VIII's Reformation. As a humanist he was an intimate member of Erasmus's international circle of scholarly acquaintances. The title of More's most famous book, *Utopia*, was again a joke requiring knowledge of Greek: 'ou' means not, 'topos' place – 'No Place'. The word has been adopted for a long line of ideal, imaginary states but More's was the first.

The ideal state described in *Utopia* was a reaction to the ills that More, an experienced practical man, observed in contemporary society – the devotion of kings to warlike conquest and the injustice caused by great inequalities of wealth. More leant towards pacifism and egalitarianism. But the work could not have been written without More's acquaintance with the ideal states in Plato's *Republic* and Aristotle's *Politics*. *Utopia* is dominated by its capital city, Amaurot, which makes it a kind of city-state. It is ruled by an elite of scholars who bear a resemblance to Plato's guardians, and the citizens eat at common meals. Although the society is made up of ordinary families, surprising duties are allowed to women, who stand shoulder to shoulder with their men in battle and become priests if they are widowed, a feature inspired by the equality of the sexes in the *Republic*.

The religion practised by the Utopians is essentially what we should call 'Natural Religion'. They believe on rational grounds that the soul is immortal and rewarded after death. 'Though these are indeed religious beliefs, they think that reason leads men to believe them and accept them.' They are monotheists and worship in churches that are austere buildings without images. Here again is the Christian humanist's ideal of Christianity pared down to its ethical essentials and stripped of the paraphernalia of images and ritual. Scholasticism is unknown to them and rather sharply dismissed. 'They have not discovered even one of those elaborate rules about "restrictions", "amplifications" and "suppositions", which our own schoolboys study in the Small Logicals.' They are interested, however, in the nature of the good and the relationship between virtue, pleasure and happiness. They accept pleasure, without the frills of fine clothes, precious stones and hunting. The picture is reminiscent of the Epicureanism that More would have read about in Cicero, and of the humanist conception of rational pleasures advocated by Erasmus in *In Praise of Folly*.

Utopia and *In Praise of Folly* were both works of genius which succeeded, by combining humanism with a fresh, secular appraisal of contemporary customs, in creating a novel framework of thought. These were achievements made possible by the relatively tolerant society of northern Europe before the Reformation broke. Soon that state of mind was to be destroyed and replaced by one in which politically supported conflicts of conformity created intense pressures that were to lead to More's death and Erasmus's troubled old age. However, the broadly humanist outlook, which they and their many colleagues created, survived, to be amalgamated in complex and varying fashions with the orthodoxies on both sides of the iron curtain.

THE RENAISSANCE IN FRANCE

One of the devoted admirers of Erasmus, the teacher of all sixteenth-century humanists, was François Rabelais, the author of *Gargantua and Pantagruel*.[2] He wrote a letter to Erasmus in 1532:

Father, I have said; I shall even say mother, if your indulgence permits it. You have done what we see pregnant mothers doing every day when they nourish children whom they have never seen and protect them against the rigors of the air. I, whose face and even name was unknown to you, have been guided by you in such a way, you have nourished me in such a way at the chaste breasts of your divine learning, that the little that I am and all that I am worth comes from you alone. If I did not acknowledge it to you I should be the most ungrateful of men, living and to come.

Therefore I salute you again and again, loving father, father and adornment of our country, protector of letters, invincible champion of the truth.

Rabelais must have been, to a lesser extent, a devoted admirer of More, for in his book he named the country ruled by Pantagruel 'Utopia'. Rabelais was, like Erasmus, a monk who had left the monastery, and he evinced an even more violent distaste for monasticism in his writings. He was also a lawyer and a doctor.

Gargantua and Pantagruel is the story of a family of giants and its most obvious characteristic is that it is a satire, hugely, rumbustiously and obscenely comic, of the romance legends about Arthur and other heroes, that were still popular in the sixteenth century. It has a slight kinship with Cervantes' very different satire of romance in *Don Quixote* written later in the century. The episodes are endless, fantastic, forming an eventful narrative without a plot. Rabelais was, however, a learned man with strong feelings about the intellect of his day, which he brought into the story at various points and which no doubt had as much interest for him as the comic inventions for which he is more famous. The book is, among other things, an expression of the Erasmian commonsense view of the intellectual world.

The work was written and published in parts over a long period extending to Rabelais' death in 1553. The first book, *Pantagruel*, published in 1532, begins with the birth of Pantagruel, the son of Gargantua and Badebec, in Utopia. He travels through various parts of France to study in Paris and there meets Panurge, who becomes his friend. As a result of his prodigious precocity he is made judge in the case between Kissmyarse and Suckfart. Panurge disputes by signs with a learned English visitor, Thaumast, and then has an absurd love affair with a Parisian lady. After this they leave Paris to fight against the Dipsodes, who are invading the country of the Amaurotes, and most of the rest of the book is concerned with their deeds in that conflict.

When Pantagruel goes to Paris he works in the library of the abbey of Saint-Victor and Rabelais produces a comic list of books found there. Saint-Victor had in real life a famous library and the abbey was known also, like the rest of the University of Paris, for its devotion to scholastic learning and the hostility of some of its scholars to Erasmus. Some of Rabelais' invented titles are merely amusing, like 'The Decree of the University of Paris about the Gorgeousness of Prostitutes'. But some are skits on notable Aristotelian scholars, like 'Béda on the Excellence of Tripes', Béda being a well-known opponent of the Erasmian distaste for the traditional university scholastics.

In the next chapter Pantagruel receives a letter from his father, Gargantua, about his education. This is for the most part straightforward and serious. Gargantua comments on the recent revival of ancient languages and the spread of printing. He advises his son to study Greek, as Quintilian advises, Latin, Hebrew for the scriptures, Chaldean and Arabic. He should model his Greek style on Plato, his Latin on Cicero. Finally, he should read the New Testament in Greek and the Old Testament in Hebrew. This is a statement of an Erasmian approach to education, distinct from the scholastic world that had been lampooned in the previous chapter.

The name of the learned Englishman, Thaumast, with whom Panurge has a disputation, may have been based on Thomas More, but there is nothing else clearly connected with More in these chapters. The disputation is conducted in sign language and the description of the signs used by the disputants allows for a good deal of absurdity. One of the main points about the episode, however, is that the Englishman is chiefly interested in oriental philosophy and magic. He says at the end that he came to Paris to confer 'on certain problems of magic, alchemy, the Cabbala [Jewish mysticism, which interested some humanists], geomancy, astrology, and also philosophy'. Rabelais expresses here his contempt for particular kinds of philosophising, that had attracted the Florentine Neoplatonists but were certainly not approved of either by Erasmus or by Rabelais himself, both of whom preferred the simple truth of the New Testament.

Rabelais' injection of Erasmianism into his fantastic comedy is, as far as literature goes, a very important example of the reception of humanist ideas in France. His writings were regarded with suspicion by the University of Paris but his links with great men enabled him to go on publishing them. Though he was outspoken in his criticism

Jean Calvin,
mid-sixteenth century
(Bibliothèque Publique et Universitaire, Geneva)

of traditional views, however, Rabelais was not a Protestant. His standpoint was Catholic humanism.

The most fundamental attempt to amalgamate humanism and reformed theology was carried out by another Frenchman, John Calvin, who is known as the founder of the state dominated by religious ministers that he established in Geneva in the 1540s and 1550s. Geneva was an independent city where Calvin, in effect exiled from his native France because of his Protestantism, was able to bring about the establishment of a new regime. His Church, governed by pastors instead of bishops and priests, was, in his view, to have a power similar to that claimed for the Church by the medieval papacy. It was the interpreter of the will of God with the right to enforce its decisions. Calvin's theological system involved a belief in predestination, in contrast to the medieval Church's generous allowance of the possibility of the individual man's saving his soul by good works and prayer. The authoritarian and repressive Calvinism spread from Geneva to Holland, to Scotland, and to Commonwealth England, where it is associated with the narrow bigotry of the Roundhead, with the belief that some men are condemned by God to eternal damnation and that an austere life should be imposed on others by those granted religious authority.

There was, however, another face to Calvinism. The freedom of thought that was allowed to men like Grotius and Descartes in seventeenth-century Holland made it at times the haven of libertarianism. Calvinism, in the century after Calvin's establishment at Geneva, was inextricably bound up with the social and political complexities of broad sections of northern Europe, and, like Catholicism, it had many varieties of freedom and repression.

When we move into Calvin's life we are far removed from the world of a Bruni, a Machiavelli or an Erasmus. They were observers who commented on a society that they either did not wish to change or had no hope of changing. In contrast, Calvin acquired power, his successors

Francis I on horseback,
François Clouet, 1540 (Uffizi, Florence)

widespread power, and they naturally became as corrupted by it as the rest of human society. Calvin was a Renaissance humanist, continuing where Erasmus had stopped, but the point had now been reached where Renaissance ideas both became extremely widely diffused in the political world and became attached to religious and political programmes.

Calvin's ideas about Christianity and the Church were set out in the *Institutes of Christian Religion* which was published in both Latin and French, with many changes, at various times between 1536 and 1560. In that book Calvin emerges as a humanist, as is shown by his frequent references to classical authors, his unmentioned dependence on Erasmus at some points, and his approach to a number of problems; and he is also of course mainly concerned to present the theology that results from conversion and an intense awareness of the power of God. The work is a complex combination of humanist attitudes and piety. Calvin's first work was a commentary on Seneca, inspired no doubt by admiration for Stoicism. He described Erasmus as the 'ornament of letters and the first delight'. Many of his attitudes and methods were Erasmian in origin.

Calvin regarded knowledge of Latin, Greek and Hebrew as essential for the understanding of the Bible. He explicitly followed Lorenzo Valla, Lefèvre d'Etaples, the French

217

The Gallery of Francis I,
designed by Rosso Fiorentino, 1534-7
(Château de Fontainebleau)

humanist contemporary of Machiavelli, and Erasmus in seeing the total inadequacy of the Vulgate Latin Bible. Philological study and exegesis were indispensable. His attitude to the Bible was similar to that of Erasmus: it contained truth that surpassed the pleasures enjoyed by educated readers in classical literature. 'When we read Demosthenes or Cicero, Plato or Aristotle or some others of their kind, I confess indeed that they wonderfully attract, delight and move us, even ravish our minds. But if from them we turn to the reading of Holy Scriptures, whether we will or not they so pierce us to the heart and fix themselves within us that all the power of rhetoricians, compared with them, seems no more than smoke.' The return to the New Testament – 'we must unlearn everything we have learned apart from Christ' – was a

continuation of what Erasmus had said. He also derived from humanist predecessors his dislike of scholasticism and indeed of philosophy in general. Philosophers were pursuing a useless quest and their chatter was as vain as that of old women.

Calvin repeated the humanist dislike, expressed by both Erasmus and More, for the abuses of kingship as exhibited both in ancient history and in modern times; he accepted the humanist tradition that connected the tyranny of the Roman Empire with vice, corruption and decay; and he showed a preference for republicanism in spite of his doctrine of non-resistance to monarchical authority. His political instinct was in this respect similar to his attitude to Church government, with which he was much more concerned. His enlightened political thought involved a removal of the unjustified or unauthorised hierarchy that was a result of the political manipulation of human failings. In all these ways Calvin followed the humanist line of favouring a rational and realistic humanity, illuminated by historical understanding, and rejecting the powerful vanities of royal and papal power. The abolition of priests and bishops was part of a humanist programme. At the same time Calvin differed profoundly from the pure humanists because his conversion forced him to grapple with the problem of his relation with God as his supreme task, which they in general had avoided doing. In this sense his career marked the end of humanism.

The writings of Rabelais and Calvin came after a generation of French humanism. To put them fully in perspective, one would have to take account not only of Erasmus but also of his contemporaries, the great Hellenisers Lefèvre d'Etaples and Guillaume Budé, who had been working at Paris since the 1490s. The early stages of French humanism, very much concerned with philosophy and theology, were a result of the easy transport of books carrying the humanist model from Italy.

Visual art has a different history. Although great interest

Danaë,
Primaticcio, 1534-7
(Château de Fontainebleau)

in Italian models had been shown since the beginning of the sixteenth century, and Francis I had persuaded Leonardo da Vinci to live in France from 1516 to 1519, Italian influence at that time was limited. In contrast with Dürer, who went to Italy and brought back what he found there, French classicism, which happened later, depended on copying the styles of Italians who migrated to France. It was largely Francis I's plan to rebuild and decorate his castle of Fontainebleau that led to the importation of three important artists to work there. Rosso Fiorentino and Francesco Primaticcio, both primarily painters, came in 1530 and 1532; Sebastiano Serlio, a Venetian architect, in 1541. Rosso and Primaticcio came respectively from Florence and Mantua and were descendants of Michelangelo and Raphael. These three were invited because they were already established artists, and they stayed long enough to create a new French school.

The decoration of the Francis I Gallery at Fontainebleau by Rosso is the first real piece of French classicism. The walls have a series of panels with painted classical scenes, each surrounded by elaborate ornaments of stucco, some of them finely made nude figures. The general scheme was a novelty and created a new kind of classical decoration. After Rosso's death in 1540 Primaticcio painted other rooms at Fontainebleau, including the Gallery of Ulysses, with scenes appropriate to its title. Some of Primaticcio's individual paintings have survived, including, for example, the charming study of the two torsos of *Ulysses and Penelope*, apparently seated side by side in bed. From these and from his many drawings it is clear that Primaticcio was a

219

Ulysses and Penelope,
Primaticcio, c.1563 (Toledo Museum of Art, Ohio)

marvellous exploiter of the elegant figures in delightful poses introduced in Italy by Parmigianino. Serlio took charge of building at Fontainebleau in 1541. Both before and after his arrival he was writing a series of books on architecture, influential in both France and Venice, of which it is said that they inspired 'more hack architects than he had hairs on his head'. Not much of his architecture survived but he was the main figure in the transferral to France of a classical style.

The Italian immigrants were followed by a generation of Frenchmen who adopted their methods, so that the School of Fontainebleau became a French school. The architect Philibert de l'Orme was, like Serlio, also a writer. He designed the circular chapel at Anet that carried Bramante's approach to architecture into northern Europe. But a better impression of the effects of the classical invasion, since so much early classical architecture in France has been destroyed or changed by rebuilding, can be gained from the paintings of François Clouet and the sculpture of Jean Goujon. Clouet's painting of a *Lady in her Bath*, believed to

Nymphs,
Jean Goujon, 1547
(Fontaine des Innocents, Paris)

be a mistress of Charles IX, has a Northern air in its arrangement of figures: the child's head peeping out from behind the Lady, the nurse suckling a baby, and the servant girls seen in the distance. But the dominant nude torso of the Lady is Italian in inspiration. Goujon's reliefs of nymphs from the Fontaine des Innocents at Paris show the influence of Cellini in the complicated and delicate drapery clothing the sinuous bodies. From the middle of the sixteenth century onwards the Renaissance in visual art and in literature was firmly in the hands of Frenchmen.

BRUEGEL

By the middle of the sixteenth century Antwerp had become the metropolis of Northern painting. There were said to be 300 artists in the city. Antwerp's artistic position was the result of its stature as the most important commercial city in northern Europe, the great entrepôt for trade across the sea to and from the Mediterranean, Iberia and Britain. It could also draw upon the rich resources of Flemish art that had been built up since the early fifteenth century. Though it was at this time pre-eminent, Antwerp was not the only busy centre of painting in northwest Europe. Haarlem, Leiden and Amsterdam, farther north, had also become thriving centres. The earlier tradition of Netherlandish painting was spreading out into a still more extensive and widely scattered industry supplying the markets of industrial and commercial cities as well as the nobility.

In contrast to France, where Italian ideas took root as a result of the king importing Italian artists, the Netherlandish Renaissance, apart from the by now significant effect of prints, sprang from Netherlanders going

Danaë,
Gossaert, 1527
(Alte Pinakothek, Munich)

to Italy and coming back excited by what they had seen there. The painting of the classical stories and nudes was becoming fairly common. Classical architecture provided the setting for figures drawn in imitation of Raphael. Exaggerated and elegant poses, imposed upon the complex groups of people that had always been typical of Netherlandish art, created a Northern Mannerism in which the human form was displayed for decorative scenic effect and for the expression of extreme emotion.

One classical painting from a Northerner was Jan Gossaert's *Danaë*. The story is a piece of Greek mythology; Danaë was raped by Jupiter in the form of a shower of gold

falling upon her. This Danaë sits in a circular, temple-like building, resting on classical marble columns. In the distance is a group of fantastic structures, classical and gothic. The girl herself is a nude with a blue cloak wrapped around her, seated with a look of expectation or perhaps surprise. Little emotion is displayed by this pleasing painting of a purely classical subject.

Gossaert, who was trained partly at Antwerp, made a trip to Italy in 1508 as servant to a Netherlandish nobleman, an illegitimate son of Duke Philip the Good of Burgundy. On his return he worked largely in Utrecht and elsewhere in the northern Netherlands. *Danaë* was painted a long way from the Mediterranean world that it reflects. Gossaert was, like most Northern artists, a considerable portraitist. The rest of his work varied between a rather heavy imitation of the classical – for instance in his *Neptune*

222

and Amphitrite which adapted the Dürer engraving of Adam and Eve – and a continuation of the Northern altarpiece tradition. Figures might be placed in front of an elaborate piece of classical architecture, as they are, for instance, in his *St Luke Drawing the Virgin*.

In the next generation Maerten van Heemskerck came from still farther north in the Netherlands, from Haarlem. He went to Italy, in 1532, and stayed there for four years. His drawings from that time constitute an essential part of the information that we have about the condition of buildings at Rome, both ancient and medieval. Twenty years after his Roman trip he painted a *Self-Portrait Before the Colosseum* in which a seated figure is drawing the Roman ruin while Heemskerck's head is superimposed on the scene, presumably a testimony to the significance that he attached to his experience of acquaintance with classical remains. Heemskerck's paintings included a wide range of classical subjects, of figures drawn from both classical and Renaissance art, and Italian influences. He painted, for example, a *Triumph of Bacchus*, containing a riot of celebrating nude drunkards before a circular classical temple, and a *Venus and Amor*, which transferred to the far North the reclining Mediterranean goddess.

The most striking feature of Heemskerck's art, however, was the style of his figures. In 1532 he painted a striking *St Luke Painting the Madonna*. This was a familiar subject, painted many times before, but Heemskerck's painting offers a much more down-to-earth version. The painter seems closer to a real craftsman in a workshop. The figure looking over his shoulder may be another self-portrait. The faces of St Luke and the Madonna and the Child he is copying are adaptations of the Italian type of drawing to the Netherlandish conception of a Christian scene. Their innocence or roughness, according to which is appropriate, is combined with the Italian manner of representing the face. With the work of Heemskerck the Italian Renaissance had become fully integrated in a fairly advanced way in the Netherlandish scene.

The most remarkable Netherlandish painter of the sixteenth century, however, was Pieter Bruegel who worked in Antwerp and Brussels in the 1550s and 1560s. Bruegel too visited Italy, but there are no drawings of classical remains by him. Curiously enough, the only records of his Italian journey are drawings of Alpine landscapes, mountainous terrain that presumably impressed a visitor from the flat Netherlands. Bruegel had an intense interest in the painting of panoramic scenery which he often did with tender attention to detail over a large canvas and a capacity to catch the atmosphere of a countryside at a particular season. The *Hunters in the Snow* is an evocation of the country in the depths of winter, carpeted by snow and ice, the hunters themselves trudging across the soft surface. In contrast, the *Magpie on the Gallows* evokes with equal skill and feeling a summer landscape, the bright vegetation of the foreground backed by a great valley filled by hazy heat. The countryside of northern Europe has never been better presented.

Bruegel was in some respects a traditionalist in the art of his own area. The earlier artist of whom he most obviously reminded contemporaries was Bosch. As a Netherlandish writer a generation later said, he 'made similar, weird scenes and drolleries'. As in the case of Bosch, though, there was a good deal of steel in this presentation of the weaknesses of the human race. Bruegel's *The Triumph of Death* was a comprehensive picture of the pretensions and pleasures of men hideously ravaged in a burnt-out land by the invading skeletal demons. Some have thought that Bruegel was a devotee of a heretical sect, but as others have pointed out, there is no God in his paintings. There is no doubt, however, that he could observe men with the same critical eye as his predecessors.

Bruegel's relation with the classical world is a mystery. He did some paintings in which it appeared elusively. His *Tower of Babel* is a building of fantastic hugeness which, in its

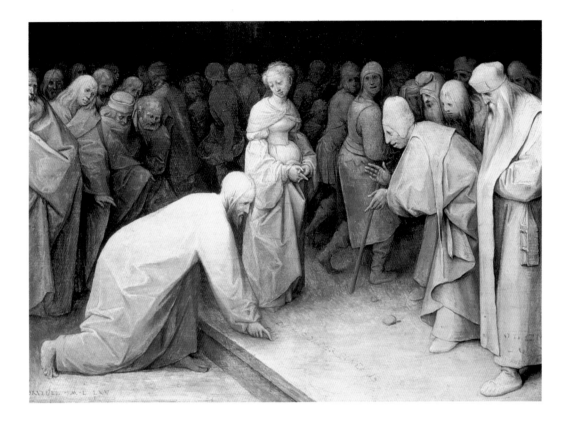

Christ and the Woman Taken in Adultery,
Bruegel, 1565
(Courtauld Institute, London)

details, recalls, and was perhaps based on, the Colosseum. But it is difficult to decide what commentary on the behaviour of the men building it – admiration of engineering skill or despair at the folly of human grandeur – the painting was intended to convey. The *Fall of Icarus* was based on a story by Ovid about Icarus falling into the sea from his attempted flight on artificial wings. Bruegel's main interest was directed towards the peasants on the hillside showing little concern for the drowning man.

It is clear, however, that Bruegel had learned from the Italians the capacity to draw human figures in more realistic postures. He showed the connection in his grisaille painting of *Christ and the Woman Taken in Adultery*, whose imposing and realistic group of figures, engaged in a spiritually

significant moment, looks forward to Rembrandt's etchings. Bruegel's great achievement was the use of this sophisticated figure-drawing for scenes of Northern life. In these paintings the class-consciousness and ethical awareness of the North was amalgamated with the elegant realism that Italy had developed to form a new manner.

This combination appeared in the *Peasant Wedding*, whose scene of rude peasant life could also be viewed as another complex and satisfying arrangement of figures in space. The wedding feast takes place in a long room, witnessed from one corner so that the board bearing the dishes as they are carried in and the long table, viewed diagonally, dominate the scene. The central figure is the bride, seated against the back wall with a self-satisfied smile

224

Procession to Calvary,
Bruegel, 1564 (Kunsthistorisches Museum, Vienna)

on her face. Around her are family, guests, musicians and erving men with a wide variety of expressive faces and postures. The figures are anchored by their heavy peasant boots but the postures of, for instance, the two men carrying in new dishes, the musicians, and the men turning round at the near end of the table, are conveyed with perfect success.

Perhaps Bruegel's most remarkable painting was the *Procession to Calvary*. Here the broad landscape, the peasant crowd, and the figures appropriate to Calvary are integrated into a scene of great beauty and desolation. The site of the cross is far away in the distance. Christ struggles under his cross with little attention from the bystanders, who are more drawn towards the lamentations of the thieves, transported in a cart. The Marys are painted on a large scale in the foreground, but the main focus of the painting is the crowd of figures in the middle-ground. They are in varying ways interested and detached, and this variety of dull crowd reactions is successfully represented in their different faces. We do not know what were Bruegel's

225

Peasant Wedding,
Bruegel, c.1566 (Kunsthistorisches Museum, Vienna)

religious opinions. This is not essentially a religious scene, but a crowd of Netherlanders, reacting to a supreme spiritual moment with human inadequacy. These are the ordinary people of Bruegel's world, made credible by the Renaissance painter's skill now practised by a Northern genius. Dürer, Altdorfer, Holbein, Erasmus, More, Rabelais, Calvin, and Bruegel all contributed to the adoption of Italian ideas in the Northern, monarchical world in the first half of the sixteenth century. By 1550 the Renaissance had been naturalised in the North. Then came the upheaval of the Wars of Religion in France and the Netherlands which dominated the international scene in the later part of the century. Out of this turbulence the new commercial empires of England and Holland emerged to provide the Renaissance's final stage. But first we must glance at the continuation of the Renaissance in Venice.

226

VENICE IN THE SIXTEENTH CENTURY

VENICE AND GENOA SURVIVED as great commercial centres through the sixteenth century. In the case of Genoa this was to a large extent the result of its association with Spain and its South American empire. But the Genoese did not produce a great school of thought and art. Venice, however, flourished as an artistic centre. It continued in its earlier guise as ruler of an essentially eastern Mediterranean commercial and landed empire, assisted by the growth of industry in the home city, and it operated as a naval power against the Turks in the Battle of Lepanto in 1572. The Mediterranean Sea with its seaborne exchange of commodities between Europe and Asia was ceasing to be the centre of world trade only at the very end of the century. Venetian painting and architecture became even more grandly spacious in this period than before, as can be seen in the huge canvases of Veronese with their groups of

Villa Rotonda, Vicenza,
Palladio, c.1565-70

Assumption,
Titian, 1516 -18
(Santa Maria dei Frari, Venice)

figures placed before classical columns.

The physical setting of Venice, as we see it today, was substantially changed by the work of the architect Andrea Palladio (1508–80) who was responsible for two of the most prominent churches on the waterfront: San Giorgio Maggiore (started 1565) and the Redentore (started 1577). San Giorgio, looking across to the Arsenal, the Doge's palace and the Marciana Library, is arguably the most dominant feature of the basin at the entrance to the Grand Canal, where the galleys from Asia arrived in the sixteenth century. Its white façade, with broad columns extending to the upper storey, the deep, triangular pediment above and the two half-pediments at the sides corresponding to interior side-aisles, was an original conception; as was its magnificently broad, open and light interior. Palladio developed his architectural style out of the buildings of antiquity and those of Bramante and Michelangelo in the earlier Roman Renaissance. In parallel with the separate architecture of the Jesuit churches, established by the Gesù at Rome whose façade, designed by Jacomo Vignola, was complete by 1577, the San Giorgio façade set up a lasting method of dealing with the difficult problem of using classical motifs – columns, pillars, round arches and pediments – for a Christian church.

Architecture does not figure extensively in this book because, unlike painting, sculpture, poetry or philosophy, it does not directly present a view of humanity. It does, however, lay down the setting in which humanity lives. No one was more important than Palladio for establishing this classical setting. This development was accomplished also in his secular buildings. In his book, *Quattro Libri di Architettura* (*Four Books of Architecture*) (1570), he provided an up-to-date guide based on Vitruvius and appealing to the learned reader, though Palladio himself had started life as a stone-mason and was expert in the more practical as well as the more sophisticated aspects of building. Palladio's reputation for secular architecture owed most, however, to his palaces

Sacred and Profane Love
Titian, c.1515
(Galleria Borghese, Rome)

built on the Venetian *terra firma* in and around Vicenza. The Palazzo Chiericati, completed about 1580, is a long narrow building facing a square with space in front of the portico and a row of massive columns. The floor above, partly open, has further columns of the same size. The practical use of the building has been to some extent sacrificed to the generous presentation of the broad classical façade. Palladio was not by any means always so prodigal with space but his most famous building, the Villa Rotonda, near Vicenza, shows a similar desire to sacrifice convenience to beauty. This is a symmetrical building, with each of the four faces having a broad classical portico. The villa is topped by a flattish cupola and it stands magnificently on a small hill. It was a building designed not for convenient living but for display. It states its classical message uncompromisingly. Palladio's work fascinated Europe more than that of any other architect. It inspired Palladianism in England and imitation in every European country for two centuries.

TITIAN

In the twenty years following the death of Giorgione, between 1510 and 1530, Titian became the most influential artist of the sixteenth century apart from Michelangelo. His exceptional range extended to painting altarpieces for churches, portraits, and classical mythology.

The huge *Assumption* that he painted in 1516–18 still dominates the church of Santa Maria dei Frari in Venice from above the high altar. It is one of the grandest early sixteenth-century attempts to paint a tall altarpiece which incorporates both celestial and temporal scenes, one above the other. It sprang in part out of the Florentine artist Fra Bartolommeo's impressive compositions using Leonardo's technique, about which Titian may have learned, and has some resemblance to Raphael's *Transfiguration*, painted in Rome a year or two later, which also has celestial figures rising above an earthly scene. The Virgin looms above the centre of the painting on a cloud inhabited by angel *putti*

229

with God appearing above her. On the ground below, the watching apostles look up with gestures of salutation and adoration. The Virgin's figure, clothed in vibrant red and captured in dramatic movement, forms the central focus of a painting that splendidly exemplifies religious grandeur. For the side of the nave of the same church Titian painted the *Pesaro Altarpiece* which shows the Pesaro family being presented to the Virgin by St Peter and St Antony of Padua. This is a less powerful painting, but has an impressiveness characteristic of Titian, achieved partly by turning the scene around, so that we see it obliquely, and partly by introducing imposing columns backing the figures.

The early portraits include the *Man with a Blue Sleeve*, *La Schiavone*, and the famous *Sacred and Profane Love*, painted

Worship of Venus,
Titian, 1519 (Prado, Madrid)

about 1515. This is now thought by some to be a marriage portrait of a bride placed in the same scene with the nude Venus, who is invisible to the heroine, and imagined as representing the joys of marriage. It may follow the same plan as the *Concert Champêtre*, usually attributed to Titian, which shows music-makers in an Arcadian landscape, accompanied by nymphs or muses of whom they are apparently unaware. Both these paintings (if they are both by the young Titian) show him as a master of the pastoral idyll, which he developed from the art of Giorgione.

Titian was one of the most erotic painters. Many female nudes were intended for private chambers of rich men, rather than being, as some have thought, paintings with a complicated symbolism recommending chastity. The erotic impact of sixteenth-century nudes, unlike those of the fourteenth century, is still clear in the twentieth century. In addition to technical improvement, the new fashion depended on increased attachment to classical themes which allowed womanhood and love a new role in painting; it also depended on the growth of aristocratic domestic luxury. From the late fifteenth century onwards the rich paid artists to gratify their taste for sexual entertainment and in the early sixteenth century this fashion became widespread. Raphael and Giulio Romano's paintings for Agostino Chigi, Pope Julius II's very rich banker, belong to the same trend as Titian's Venuses, as do Marcantonio Raimondi's less expensive prints. At the end of the century religious censorship curbed the commission of nudes. Although it was rather temporary and geographically limited, this marriage of skill and patronage had a considerable impact because it revealed potentialities of appreciation of the female form which had been unrecognised in medieval Europe and which made a permanent contribution to Western art.

Titian's repainting of part of Bellini's *Feast of the Gods* was one of the fruits of his employment by Alfonso d'Este of Ferrara. Ambitious, snobbish, self-confident and anxious

Bacchus and Ariadne,
Titian, 1520 (National Gallery, London)

for high rewards, in addition to being immensely hard-working, he accepted with willingness commissions from the Este lords of Ferrara and later from the still more elevated Habsburg family. Titian's habits of work were very different from those of Michelangelo who was roughly his contemporary. Michelangelo was often forced to accept the patronage of the great but, awkward and introspective, he may have had little interest in money for its own sake. Titian remained a craftsman and a family man, utterly devoted to the tastes of the highest bidder. Alfonso d'Este was important in his earlier career and Este patronage was responsible for the creations that turned him fruitfully in the direction of classical *poesie*.

Between 1518 and 1525 Titian painted three classical scenes for Alfonso, all with great skill and verve: the *Worship of Venus*, *Bacchus and Ariadne*, and *The Andrians*. The *Worship of Venus* shows Venus raised on a pedestal, before which a crowd of *putti*, the dominant feature of the painting, are playing and fighting like young children in a nursery school. At the right two mortals are entering the scene. The *putti* create an appearance of charming baby innocence, possessing none of the slightly sinister, manic features of Donatello's *putti*. *The Andrians* is an uninhibited scene of intoxicated abandonment. Two girls in modern dress reclining on the ground are surrounded by gods devoted to Bacchus, drinking and in various stages of undress, culminating in the beautiful nude nymph who has fallen asleep. The most impressive of these paintings is *Bacchus and Ariadne* in which the rhythm of the figures of Bacchus leaping from his chariot and Ariadne beginning to

231

The Andrians,
Titian, 1523-5 (Prado, Madrid)

flee is satisfyingly harmonious. *Bacchus and Ariadne* drew on various quotations from ancient and Renaissance art, for instance Laocoön trying to escape from the snake, and it has been suggested that its programme might have been the work of Ariosto. If it is such an assemblage from Greek and Italian antecedents, this is entirely appropriate. Rich Mediterranean landscape, the blue of Titian's skies, the convincing ingenuity of the figures, sometimes recalling classical models, the free expression of the delights of the human body and of love in the language of classical myth, created an arcadian world of sensual pleasure that had not yet been equalled and a full release of the irreligious potentialities of painting. Titian invented the Mediterranean

dream-world that was to appear again and again until the days of Picasso.

In the 1530s and 1540s, Titian's circle of grand patrons outside Venice widened to include the Gonzaga rulers of Mantua, the Habsburg Emperor Charles V, who was the most powerful man in Europe, and the Farnese Pope Paul III. This encouraged the artist to reveal himself as a Renaissance portrait-painter with a capacity both for acute attention to the individual face of the sitter and for the conception of new poses suitable for the representation of the mighty. Titian and Raphael were the only two Renaissance painters who responded to the challenge of dealing individualistically with superior people as well as

LEFT Charles V,
Titian, 1548 (Alte Pinakothek, Munich)

BELOW Pietro Aretino,
Titian, 1538 (Palazzo Pitti, Florence)

with courtesans.

The portraits of *Federico Gonzaga* and of *Francesco Maria della Rovere*, one with a resplendent blue satin coat, the other in armour, established the convention of the three-quarter length portrait. Equally impressive is the tight-lipped *Eleanora Gonzaga della Rovere*, a great and beautifully elegant lady with a business-like face. Charles V quickly recognised Titian's merit and sat for him several times. The last painting Titian did of him was the seated black-clothed portrait at Munich which portrays the emperor with great intimacy as an ageing, world-weary statesman who has seen too much of the world's politics but retains a sensitive, rather shy face. Titian also painted a memorable portrait of

the writer Pietro Aretino. Aretino was a scandalous and outspoken commentator on the Italy of his time, sometimes regarded as the first pornographic journalist. He was also a perceptive appreciator of Titian's painting, which he praised in a number of pieces, for its unique capacity to capture living reality and embody emotion in colour. He was well known to Titian and was captured in a swaggering portrayal that brought out both the open intelligence of his face and the appalling bulk of his frame, swollen by decades of good living.

The most surprising of Titian's portraits, however, were those of *Paul III*. The individual painting of *Paul III* portrayed him as a shrunken old man, lost inside the volume of his

Pope Paul III with his Grandsons,
Titian, 1545-6 (Museo di Capodimonte, Naples)

clothes. In the triple portrait of *Pope Paul III with his Grandsons Cardinal Alessandro and Ottaviano Farnese*, which is unfinished, he is still decrepit and accompanied by two young men who look as though they are carefully managing him. It is of course unlikely that Titian's deference would have receded far enough for him to paint a deliberate criticism of his subject in the style of Goya, but this case shows interestingly the extent to which realism of character had advanced in the hands of its greatest living practitioner.

Titian's work during this period also ranged from dramatic altarpieces, which showed his willingness to respond wholeheartedly to religious subjects, to nudes clearly designed to give pleasure. An example of the former

is *Ecce Homo*. At the top of a flight of steps leading to a classical building is the figure of Christ, a sadly tortured and exhausted man, mocked by his guards. The larger portion of the painting is occupied by the onlookers who are a lively gesturing crowd. The picture is distinguished in part by the free and open style of its painting and, apart from the blue sky and one red robe, the rather dark colouring, which is typical of Titian's late work. In 1538 Titian painted the *Venus of Urbino* for a member of the della Rovere family. In this very beautiful painting one remembers the calmness that the blue sky seen through the window and the servant kneeling before it add to the composition. But of course its most surprising feature was the direct staring face of the

Venus of Urbino,
Titian, 1538 (Uffizi, Florence)

woman, contrasting strongly with Giorgione's *Sleeping Venus* from which it descended. More sensuous perhaps is the *Danaë with a Cupid*, painted for a Farnese cardinal, which shows the girl at the moment at which she is raped by Jupiter, who has assumed the form of a golden shower. It is ironical that Titian should have painted it, most probably in order to further his hope of securing a papal appointment to an ecclesiastical benefice for his son.

During the last quarter-century of his life Titian continued to paint with apparently unflagging energy and in some of his works achieved a subject matter and style reflecting the experience and problems of old age, which can also be found in the late work of Donatello and Michelangelo. One aspect of his work that does not fit in with this description, however, was his mythological painting for King Philip II of Spain, who became the great patron of his last years. Philip, unlike Alfonso d'Este, had a taste for religious paintings, which was natural in the age of the Counter-Reformation when the crown of Spain was identified with the struggle to preserve Catholicism. To satisfy the other side of the King's personality, Titian painted a new series of classical *poesie* for him. Eight major classical paintings, which have survived, were sent or were intended to be sent to Philip II between the early 1550s and the early 1570s and are now distributed among various art galleries: the *Danaë*, *Venus and Adonis*, *Perseus and Andromeda*,

Diana and Actaeon,
Titian, 1536-9 (National Gallery of Scotland, Edinburgh)

Diana and Actaeon, Diana and Callisto, the *Death of Actaeon, Tarquin and Lucretia* and the *Rape of Europa.* The paintings concerned with Diana and Actaeon, loosely based on Ovid's *Metamorphoses,* were clearly a series and can easily be considered together. Diana and her nymphs were accustomed to bathe in a certain pool. One day they were surprised by Actaeon – the subject of *Diana and Actaeon.* Actaeon was turned by Diana into a stag and, as he fled, was brought down by his own hounds – the *Death of Actaeon.* When they were bathing, Diana discovered the pregnancy of her nymph Callisto, who had been seduced by Jupiter – *Diana and Callisto.*

Diana and Actaeon is one of the most appealing of all paintings because of its successful exploitation of so many opportunities: for romance, for the female nude, antiquarianism, and landscape. These paintings do not have the same abandoned charm as the *poesie* painted for Alfonso d'Este but they have a mellower and on the whole more serious romanticism, which was certainly not less appropriate for their mythological subjects. They use the darker colours, ingenious lighting and impressionistic painting of Titian's later years. The scene of *Diana and Actaeon* is a grotto by the ancient and decaying remains of a Roman building. Actaeon enters, registering dramatic surprise at the cluster of nymphs before him while Diana, attended by a black woman, hastily covers herself. The complex colouring of the stream and its natural surroundings is backed by Titian's blue sky. *Diana and Callisto* is rather less satisfactory partly because of the awkwardness of pregnancy as a subject. *Tarquin and Lucretia* also disappoints mildly because the figure-drawing of Tarquin is one of Titian's less successful efforts, and gave substance to Michelangelo's earlier complaint that he could not draw. But the alarmed face of Lucretia is wonderfully captured. *Venus and Adonis*, which shows in full the naked back of Venus as she clings to her lover to stop him leaving for the hunt, and the *Rape of Europa*, in which Europa is carried across the sea on the back of Jupiter, in the form of a bull, against a landscape of molten splendour in which the water, the rocky hills and the sky merge into one another in the richness of their colours, are both in different ways successful evocations of legend. Titian's capacity, in spite of being a non-Latinist, to enter into the spirit of classical legend created paintings that captured its stories in a world of imaginative, intensified colour and gesture.

Some of Titian's last great paintings, the *Death of Actaeon*, the *Crowning with Thorns*, and the *Pietà* in the Accademia at Venice, are puzzling because, in contrast to works painted a few years earlier, their colouring is relatively flat with rough outlines. Are they unfinished, since we know that Titian often put work aside to take it up years later, or does this change represent a new style, since the *Pietà* was finished by Palma Giovane presumably in the way he believed the master would have liked? The question is unanswerable and we can treat the *Death of Actaeon* as a foreshadowing of Titian's future style or as a canvas that Titian would have embellished. Whatever the truth about this, it is clear that Titian was becoming increasingly carried

Rape of Europa,
Titian, 1559-62 (Isabella Stewart Gardner Museum, Boston)

237

Death of Actaeon,
Titian, 1555-7 (National Gallery, London)

away by rougher and more impressionistic painting in a manner similar to Michelangelo's last sculptures and even with a later innovative work of literature, Shakespeare's *King Lear*. In each of these cases Michelangelo and Titian seemed to move beyond the perfect command of beauty that their earlier work had shown.

It is also clear that Titian retained a capacity for dramatic statements in both fields of secular mythology and religion. If he did design the *Pietà* for his own tomb, which may not be the case, he presumably intended to make a personal statement, and we should attribute significance to the prominence that he gave to two figures: that of Jerome, an old man kneeling before the emaciated body of Christ, and that of Mary Magdalen, a young woman stepping out in an attitude of proclamation to the world. Titian had painted harsh scenes of cruelty and suffering in his religious work but here he seems, in contrast to the last vision of Michelangelo, to have wished to present a balance between age and the vigour of youth.

VERONESE AND TINTORETTO

Titian's contemporaries at Venice in his later years were

238

Alexander and the Family of Darius,
Veronese, 1578
(National Gallery, London)

Veronese (1528–88) and Tintoretto (1518–94), two strikingly original painters who developed different styles. Veronese's reputation has probably declined somewhat since the enthusiasm of Ruskin's time when the large canvas of *Alexander and the Family of Darius* was brought in triumph to the National Gallery in London. That painting of the 1570s, which is exceptionally well preserved, presents some of Veronese's characteristics. The mother of Darius, defeated by Alexander, has mistaken a subordinate for him and the victor puts the kneeling family at their ease. Veronese uses generously massive classical architecture to emphasise the grand ambience, rich colouring particularly in the red costume of Alexander, and portrays the scene with a sense of gentle decorum and decency. The painting does not embody Veronese's grandiose manipulation of spatial illusion, used with precision unlike Tintoretto's, which was often the most striking feature of his larger works for the walls of churches and palaces.

The fully developed Veronese style appeared in the paintings of the mid-1550s for San Sebastiano, Venice. *The Triumph of Mordecai* on the ceiling, for example, shows to the full Veronese's interest in the dramatic use of space. The scene is observed illusionistically from a low vantage point so that we see the crowd looking over the cornice apparently at a great height. The horses appear to be stopping at the edge of a wall just above us and both men and horses are elaborately foreshortened to create the illusion of an upward view. The trick is used persistently and with great skill in many of his paintings. Another early example, less spectacular and more conventional, was the ceiling of the Sala dell' Olimpo, which was part of Veronese's grand decoration of a villa at Maser for the rich and intellectual Venetian, Daniele Barbaro, who was also interested in artistic theory. The villa itself was designed by Palladio and the whole setting is a good example of the effects of the spread of Venetian patrician wealth to the *terra firma*. Veronese filled the centre of the ceiling with a ring of zodiacal planets portrayed as human figures seated on clouds, while above them in the centre the muse Thalia presides over the harmony of the spheres. Again, the sense of a dramatically perpendicular vista is conveyed.

Veronese was capable of painting pictures of classical scenes or legend for secular consumption but he did this with less outrageous boldness and dedication than Titian.

Marriage at Cana,
Veronese, 1562-3 (Louvre, Paris)

Marriage of St Catherine,
Veronese, 1575 (Accademia, Venice)

His painting of *Mercury, Herse and Aglauros* tells the dramatic story of Mercury turning Aglauros to stone for interfering in his courting of her sister, but we are more conscious of the rich colouring and design of the setting than of the intensity of the moment. The *Rape of Europa* in the Doge's Palace at Venice portrays a country scene in which Europa appears three times, once in the foreground taking her seat on the bull, once carried down the slope, and again disappearing across the water. It has the appearance of a festival in a park, faintly reminiscent of the world of Watteau, not of the high romanticism introduced into the story by Titian.

The fullest expression of Veronese's art can be found in the vast religious and ceremonial canvases that he did for churches and for public buildings in Venice. The *Marriage at Cana* was painted between 1562 and 1563 for the refectory of San Giorgio Maggiore. It portrays the feast at a table in the open air before a balustrade beyond which stretches a vista of classical buildings. The central group around Christ is marginally below the middle of the painting. Before them are musicians, dogs and servants. The architectural setting behind teems with life – people walking about behind the balustrade and climbing around the pillars. Veronese engulfed Christ and the religious moment in a ceremonial

Venice Triumphant,
Veronese, c.1582-4
(Hall of the Great Council, Doge's Palace, Venice)

most sumptuous. In this vast imaginary classical structure, with foreshortened horses prancing above us, and Venice symbolised by a mature and handsome female figure borne aloft, the public Veronese creates splendour for the sake of splendour.

Tintoretto is a more difficult painter to understand. No one painted so many vast canvases. No one worked so hard to beautify the churches and scuole of Venice, where many of his paintings still remain on walls and ceilings. His devotion to ecclesiastical painting was different from the more varied work of Titian and Veronese. He was not incapable of portraying secular stories displaying female nudes, and indeed a number of excellent examples survive. But they were not his favourite work and formed a relatively small proportion of his repertoire. Some of his best paintings were spectacular; they exploited the perspective of distant vistas in a way that was unnecessary for the subject and seemed to be intended only to provide visual excitement. His colouring verged on the surreal as though he were driven towards a world of nightmare. In some of his later works he combined colour and perspective to produce a visionary otherworldliness of floating space and figures that did not correspond to any known physical landscape. It is easy to believe that he captivated his audience by carrying them into a religious environment of heightened sensibility. One cannot know what part was played in this feat by his own religious fervour and what part by the enthusiastic exploitation of painterly techniques, but there is no doubt that he created religious spectacles for popular consumption.

Tintoretto appears first, almost fully formed, in the late 1540s when he was clearly in command of recent

display. More attractive is the *Marriage of St Catherine*. Apart from the steps leading up to the Virgin and the two massive columns behind, presumably inspired in part by Titian's Pesaro Altarpiece, not much use has been made of architecture or height. The emphasis here is on rich colour combinations, the other feature one associates with Veronese. The setting is again highly ceremonial but we are struck chiefly by the contrast between the brilliant red and blue of the Virgin's clothes and the flowered dress of Catherine, the red hangings around the columns against the subtle colouring of the angel-filled sky. *Venice Triumphant*, painted for the ceiling of the Sala del Gran Consiglio at the end of the painter's life in 1582–4, shows Veronese at his

Susanna and the Elders,
Tintoretto, 1557
(Kunsthistorisches Museum, Vienna)

developments in the complex positioning and posturing of the human body, which we associate with Mannerism, and also of the older understanding of perspective, which, through designs for architectural vistas, had been given a new excitement in Venice. *St Mark Freeing the Slave* was a dramatic presentation of an unpleasant story of torture. In the painting St Mark swoops down from the sky to halt the torturers while the onlookers gesticulate around the prostrate figure of the mishandled victim. The *Washing of the Feet* in Madrid places the main, domestic subject in front of a lake, stretching deeply into the background, with solemn classical buildings on either side of it and a triumphal arch at the end. A few years later Tintoretto painted the *Presentation of the Virgin* for the Madonna dell' Orto which again spectacularised the subject by putting the small figure of the young Virgin at the top of an ingeniously rounded flight of steps, watched by a number of elegantly clad women. It makes an interesting contrast with the more straightforward *Presentation* that Titian had painted about fifteen years earlier.

Among the paintings of stories exploiting the female nude that Tintoretto produced in the 1550s was the very beautiful *Susanna and the Elders*. The naked, slightly plump Susanna sits on the edge of the pool with her clothes, jewels and trinkets beside her, apparently drying herself and unconscious of the old men peering round the bushes. The figures are set in a delightful garden, stretching far away, whose hedges, flowers and grass are painted with mellow hues that convey the impression of an idyllic place of calm and beauty. This lyrical direction was not the one Tintoretto was to take. A few years later came the dramatic panels for the Scuola Grande di San Marco. In the *Stealing of*

Stealing of the Body of St Mark,
Tintoretto, 1562-6
(Accademia, Venice)

the Body of St Mark the body is being furtively carried away by a group of men followed by a camel. Behind is the typical deep perspective of a square with a loggia on one side and elaborate arches at the rear. People are fleeing to shelter from the hurricane that allows the theft and the buildings are lit to a ghastly white by the lightning flashing from the dark sky. The scene is perfectly comprehensible in rational terms but it creates an impression of eerie unreality, the design of which was to be exploited for quite irrational purposes by modern surrealists.

In the later years of his life Tintoretto devoted a considerable amount of time to decorating rooms of the Scuola di San Rocco. One of the earlier works done here

was the huge *Crucifixion* of 1565. Immaculately designed, the surface pattern of the figures effectively points inward to the central position of Christ on the cross, like the spokes of the bottom half of a wheel. The more attractive side of Tintoretto's artistic personality appeared in smaller paintings at San Rocco of other scenes of episodes from the life of Christ. The *Adoration of the Shepherds* offered an original conception of the story, with the Holy Family in the loft of a barn and the shepherds appearing below with their farm animals. The *Baptism of Christ* was an adaptation as an open-air scene of the design that he had used for the *Stealing of the Body of St Mark*. The crowds in the distance are ranged along the bank of the river in which the baptism is taking place, creating a vista similar to the square in the St Mark painting. The *Last Supper* again adopts the oblique, deeply receding view that Tintoretto often favoured, so that the long table at which the supper is taking place is seen from one end with passers-by and a dog. These paintings showed Tintoretto's capacity for realistic depictions of country life with episodes from the farm or the meadows, paradoxically, a stronger feature in the painting of sea-girt Venice than of Tuscany. Among the late paintings at San Rocco were the *Flight into Egypt,* in which Mary and Joseph are passing through a landscape dominated by Tintoretto's command of romantic colour in broadly sketched trees, and the terrifying *Massacre of the Innocents* with its mass of struggling and writhing bodies.

Tintoretto's paintings in the *scuole* could make a fitting end to the story of Italian Renaissance art. These paintings were religious art for the people, designed to appeal to the ordinary piety of popular confraternities in the city, as had been the painting of small altarpieces in Florence and Siena out of which the art of Giotto and Duccio grew three centuries earlier. Although humanists and princes with their different tastes were influential, the religion of the people of a city was the bedrock of Italian art throughout the Renaissance period. Tintoretto, who commanded all the resources of figure and space that had been built up at Florence and Rome, was directing his work to people's religious instincts in a society to which centuries had added wealth and artistic sophistication.

BASSANO

The contemporary of Tintoretto and of the older Titian, Jacopo Bassano (*c.*1517–92) is known as a painter of scenes in which an engaging attention is paid to landscape and animals. He pleases us because his treatment of the natural world seems to look forward to one with which we are more familiar in the nineteenth century. This is not an inappropriate reaction because Jacopo did in fact withdraw from Venice to paint in Bassano, the home town from which

his name is taken, where the hills and the flocks were closer to hand. He did not compete in either the great international world of Titian or the city-confraternity world of Tintoretto, but established a family business that continued to sell and popularise his landscape scenes after his death. But the view of him that has been propagated neglects the earlier stages of his career, in which he responded to the international Mannerist competition that was also affecting Titian and Tintoretto, and this experience influenced his later work.

Samson Killing the Philistines, an early work by Bassano, shows a Mannerist interest in portraying a mass of struggling figures, using techniques of foreshortening that absorbed other artists at the time. The master who probably

Flight into Egypt,
Tintoretto, 1583-7 (Scuola di San Rocco, Venice)

Departure of Abraham for Canaan,
Bassano, c.1576 (Gemäldegalerie, Berlin)

contributed most to this development at Venice was Pordenone, a Venetian painter who had also worked in central Italy and therefore combined the styles of several schools. The influence of the Lombard Mannerist Parmigianino also seems present in the elegant Madonnas to be found in some of his paintings. Bassano retained a sure capacity for dealing with the convolutions of the human form, often kneeling or bending forward in difficult poses. A later and rather grand painting, *San Rocco Blessing the Sufferers from Plague*, contains in the lower half a number of acutely observed figures. This Mannerist interest, however, was superseded by a novel treatment of colour and an interest in the natural, non-architectural world which may seem to have more importance in his paintings.

Like the other Venetians, Bassano was a great colourist. He paid more attention to preliminary drawing than Titian or Tintoretto and this was no doubt connected with the clear characters of his human figures. But it was in colour that he excelled and his use of it was different from that of his two greater contemporaries. Bassano did not attempt to startle by the intemperate brilliance of his treatment of light. His aim, perhaps in response to the more modest desires of the provincial patrons for whom he worked, was a more realistic and straightforward colouring that used the light of dusk but did not glorify it. Although his paintings commonly have a somewhat sombre, summer-evening appearance, they also seem to approach the tonal precision of the nineteenth century.

246

Bassano began fairly early to introduce pastoral elements into his paintings. In the *Departure of Abraham*, whilst there are a number of human figures, a substantial proportion of the scene is occupied by mules and sheep and by an indistinct vista stretching into the distance. This was typical of his country scenes. The result was that many of his paintings have a quiet bucolic atmosphere, produced by the combination of human and natural life, with an interest in the latter that was relatively uncommon in sixteenth-century Italy. At the end of his life Bassano was producing *genre* paintings in which the landscape-animal-farmyard element predominated and for which there was presumably a market.

The contrast between Bassano and another notable painter of the mid- to late sixteenth century at Venice, Paris Bordone (1500–71), emphasises the results that could follow from different patronage and experience after a similar training. Bordone worked for a time at Fontainebleau, Augsburg and Milan. He was orientated towards a rich and to some extent international clientele that encouraged him towards fashionable mythologies peopled with women, and towards half-clothed courtesans, in a manner similar to the work of Titian without being as imaginative. His famous painting of the *Delivery of the Ring to the Doge*, an early work of 1534, displays his talent for architectural backgrounds creating a sumptuous setting. In the *Jupiter and Io*, of about 1558, he shows capacity for mythological love scenes with very deliberate realistic eroticism. Bordone had other talents as well, but his work as a whole creates the impression that the wish to serve sophisticated tastes, one of the main forces behind aesthetic originality in the sixteenth century, was not necessarily helpful in producing original work unless it was combined, as in Raphael and Titian, with talent of the very highest order. Bassano, working in relative obscurity at home, made more remarkable advances.

Although he was not a spectacular painter, Bassano

Jupiter and Io,
Paris Bordone, 1558 (Kunstmuseum, Göteborg)

undoubtedly passed through a phase of confrontation with the Mannerist style and was thoroughly competent in employing it. If this had not been the case he would not have been able to deal with figured landscape so successfully. In *Susanna and the Elders* at Nîmes one sees him, unusually, producing a combination of the alluring nude figure and the pastoral landscape in much the same way as Tintoretto had done and with much the same success. But in the end it was his discovery and presentation of the natural, non-human world with an accuracy mellowed by romantic feelings which made him stand out as a link between the Renaissance and the romanticism that was to come.

THE RENAISSANCE IN 1600

IN 1600 MOST OF EUROPE WAS dominated by the three great ruling families of Habsburg, Bourbon and Tudor. The Spanish Habsburgs (Philip II died in 1598 to be succeeded by Philip III) governed Spain, Portugal, much of Italy, the southern Netherlands, and the vast empire in South America which made them the richest monarchy. The German Habsburg Rudolph II was Holy Roman Emperor. His power was concentrated in the old Habsburg lands of Austria, Bohemia and Hungary with some authority in Germany. The Bourbon Henry IV of Navarre was crowned King of France in 1594, ending the long series of wars of religion that had divided the country for decades. Elizabeth Tudor still ruled England and Ireland. Monarchy had never been stronger. The pockets of city-dominated Europe in northern Italy, the Rhineland and the Netherlands were struggling to survive in a continent overawed by Habsburg might. They were much less independent and confident than they had been in 1500.

This Europe was sharply divided by the confrontation between Catholic and Protestant. The major wars of the later part of the sixteenth century – the repeated conflict in France and the long revolt of the Netherlands against Spain – were wars of religion in which Catholic had been pitted against Calvinist, as well as political struggles for power. The great atrocity of the Massacre of St Bartholomew in 1572 was a massacre of Huguenots by Catholics, and the defeat of the Armada in 1588 was seen as a victory by Protestant England over Catholic Spain. These central political events of the late sixteenth century revolved around religion as well as conflicts over land. Catholic recusants were persecuted in Protestant England and Englishmen expected to be tortured in Spain. The English statesman Lord Burleigh no doubt expressed the views of many of his compatriots when he advised against travel in Italy, 'for they shall learn nothing there but pride, blasphemy and atheism'.

Nevertheless intellectual intercourse between Catholic and Protestant Europe was considerable. Sir Philip Sidney could travel profitably in Italy and import Renaissance ideas into England. Dr John Dee, the Elizabethan polymath, could transfer himself to the court of the Catholic emperor at Prague. Ideas and books flowed to and fro. By the late sixteenth century the Renaissance had become a European phenomenon: the books of Ariosto and Castiglione were known in every part of Europe; the paintings of Raphael and Titian were admired everywhere in the North; even Renaissance architecture, the least transportable part of the Italian imagination, was beginning to move towards acceptance in England, a backward area in the visual arts, in the work of Inigo Jones at the beginning of the next century.

The general diffusion of assumptions derived from Italy means that it is impossible to write about the Renaissance in this period as a history of isolated lines of development such as existed in the fifteenth century. The whole of Europe was affected by the Renaissance. All that can be done is to indicate a few outstanding instances of the promotion and development of Renaissance conceptions by great artists and writers. We shall look first at the Catholic world.

One of the most notable books of the late sixteenth century, Cervantes' *Don Quixote*, was written by a man whose life was for long periods bound up with the fortunes of the Spanish Habsburg dynasty. Cervantes, fighting as a Spanish soldier, was wounded in the naval battle of Lepanto against the Turks in 1571. He was captured by Moors from Algiers on the way home and spent five years as a prisoner, later becoming a tax-collector helping with preparations for the despatch of the Armada against England. His drifting inconsequential life, almost as inconsequential as that of Don Quixote himself, was punctuated by substantial periods of writing, which produced the great story published in two parts in 1604 and 1615.

Don Quixote could not have been written if Cervantes had not been deeply influenced by Ariosto whose *Orlando Furioso* he read, with many other Italian works of literature, when he was a young man. Like *Orlando Furioso*, though written in prose, *Don Quixote* is a romance story, a long series of episodes of love and adventure, strung together without an obvious structure. It continues the custom of telling romance stories, which in Spain descended from the Middle Ages, and is a parody of that romance tradition. Don Quixote, an elderly gentleman, read the story of Amadis of Gaul and became so obsessed by it that he decided to turn his own life into a parade of knight errantry and courtly love, with absurd consequences that held the romance tradition up to ridicule. Ariosto's *Orlando Furioso* (*Mad Orlando*) took its

Cervantes,
J. de Jáuregui (Academia de la Lengua, Madrid)

title from the temporary madness of Orlando that was an important episode in the poem. Don Quixote, though he was capable of decisive actions, was deranged by his comic belief that he could turn himself into a knight.

But, like Ariosto, Cervantes was concerned neither with simply retelling romance stories nor with simply parodying them. He was creating a different world of adventure, comedy, irony, social observation and authorial comment intertwined in an inextricable manner. Cervantes' world was very different from that of Ariosto and medieval romance in that it contained characters drawn from his own experience of low life during a long career as an executive in southern Spain. There are innkeepers, thieves, prostitutes and peasants. The chief low character is his 'squire' Sancho Panza: 'All this while Don Quixote was plying a labourer, a neighbour of his and an honest man – if a poor man may be called honest – but without much salt in his brain-pan. In the end, he talked to him so much, persuaded him so hard and gave him such promises that the poor yokel made up his mind to go out with him and serve him as squire. Don Quixote told him amongst other things, that he ought to feel well disposed to come with him, for some time or another an adventure might occur that would win him in the twinkling of an eye some isle, of which he would make him governor. These promises and others like them made Sancho Panza – for this was the labourer's name – leave his wife and children and take service as his neighbour's squire. Sancho said ... that he was also thinking of bringing a very fine ass he had, for he was not too good at much travelling on foot. At the mention of the ass Don Quixote hesitated a little, racking his brains to remember whether any knight errant ever had a squire mounted on ass-back; but no case came to his memory.'[1]

When Quixote eventually meets the woman whom he accepts as his lady, Dulcinea del Toboso, she is a 'country girl, and not a very handsome one at that, being round faced and flat-nosed' and she flees as a country girl might. 'She prodded her hackney with the point of a stick she carried, and set off at a trot across the field. But when the she-ass felt the point of the stick, which pained her more than usual, she began to plunge so wildly that my lady Dulcinea came off upon the ground. When Don Quixote saw this accident he rushed to pick her up, and Sancho to adjust and strap on the pack saddle, which had slipped under the ass's belly. But when the saddle was adjusted and Don Quixote was about to lift his enchanted mistress in his arms and place her on her ass, the lady picked herself up from the ground and spared him the trouble. For, stepping back a little, she took a short run, and resting both her hands on the ass's rump, swung her body into the saddle, lighter than a hawk, and sat astride like a man.'

Towards the end of the book Quixote is completely taken in again by another woman at an inn who sings outside his window pretending to have fallen in love with him. She ends the episode by throwing a sackful of cats with bells tied to their tails into his room and Quixote, in spite of stabbing with his sword at the 'crew of sorcerers', is severely scratched on the face. The atmosphere of comedy is constant and it is impossible to disentangle any serious didactic or realistic purpose in Cervantes' writing, although it is both realistic in its portrayal of ordinary people and ironic in its portrayal of the high-mindedness of Quixote and in Sancho's hope of elevation to a governorship. Don Quixote is sometimes considered the first great novel but,

though its picaresque quality exerted much influence, it was not really like the novels of Richardson, Fielding or Sterne in the eighteenth century.

At one point in *Don Quixote* Cervantes introduced an essay on literary criticism, put into the mouth of the Canon of Toledo who had tried to write 'a book of chivalry' which had a shape 'with a whole body for a plot, with all its limbs complete, so that the middle corresponds to the beginning and the end to the beginning and the middle', but had given up the attempt because it would not have won public approval. This perhaps reflected the disputes among critics in Italy provoked by Ariosto's *Orlando Furioso*. The most famous contender was Torquato Tasso, author of the *Gerusalemme Liberata*, which attempted to be a modern epic, conforming more to classical standards of composition. However, the aim of combining romance with morality and literary form did not lead to a valuable new literary genre. Story-tellers had to begin again in the eighteenth century with tales of common life. Neither Ariosto nor Cervantes did that. What they produced was suitable for sixteenth-century taste, romance infused with the new sensibility created by the Renaissance and, in Cervantes' case, with the social awareness that invaded high art in his lifetime.

A similar transitional character is to be found in the *Essays* of Cervantes' older contemporary, the Frenchman Michel de Montaigne. Montaigne was a learned gentleman, with substantial means, who lived near Bordeaux throughout the period of the French Wars of Religion: his essays were written between the 1570s and the 1590s. Although this was a troubled period, the essays convey an atmosphere of calm reflection on life, of a man writing in a library, as indeed he did. 'When at home, I turn a little more often to my library, from which I can easily overlook my whole household. There I am above the gateway, and see below me my garden, my farmyard, my courtyard, and most parts of my house. There I turn the pages now of one book, now of another.'[2] Montaigne was a classical scholar,

250

extremely well read in Greek and Latin literature, and a devotee of Plato, Cicero, Seneca and Plutarch. He quoted from them continually, either using them as inspiration for his reflections or as embellishments on his own observations of life.

His reader also learns about the man himself: 'The companionship of beautiful and virtuous women is also pleasing to me "for we too have eyes learned in such matters" [Cicero]. If the mind derives less enjoyment from such company than from that of men, the bodily senses, besides having a greater share in it, also succeed in raising it to a level almost as high, although, in my opinion, it still falls a little short. But this is a relationship in which men have to remain slightly on their guard, especially those, like myself, over whom the body exercises great sway. I scalded myself in my youth, and suffered all the torments that poets say come upon those who abandon themselves to it without sense or discipline.' But his purpose was not primarily autobiographical. It was philosophical, in the tradition of Erasmus's *Adages* or of Italian writers of dialogues, from Petrarch to Castiglione.

Montaigne was a Christian who adhered to the Catholic faith and set forth his beliefs about the relationship between religion and philosophy in his *Apology for Raymond Sebond*, which became the longest of the *Essays*. Philosophy could not teach men the truth. 'Have I not seen this divine saying in Plato that nature is but an enigmatic poetry? As one

Michel de Montaigne,
late sixteenth century (Musée de Chantilly)

might say a shadowed and dark painting, exercising our conjectures with an infinite variety of false lights. "All things lie hidden, wrapped in a darkness so thick that no human mind is sharp enough to pierce the heavens or to sound the earth" [Cicero]. And certainly philosophy is only a sophisticated poetry.' In the rest of the *Essays*, however, he was principally concerned with moral, philosophical and social questions. Here he is, for example, discussing virtue: 'I imagine virtue to be both something else and something nobler than the propensity towards goodness that is born in us. The well-disposed and naturally well-controlled mind follows the same course as the virtuous, and presents the same appearance in its actions. But virtue sounds like some greater and more active thing than merely to let oneself be led by a happy disposition quietly and peaceably along the path of reason. One who out of natural mildness and good-nature overlooks injuries received performs a very fine and praiseworthy action; but another who, though provoked and stung to anger by an insult, takes up the weapons of reason against his furious desire for revenge, and after a hard battle finally masters it, is undoubtedly doing a great deal more. The first man is behaving well, the second virtuously.'

Believing in the inadequacy of reason to achieve a demonstration of the truths of Christianity but also in the value of rational discourse within its own sphere, Montaigne was in the same position, as far as belief was

Cardsharps,
Caravaggio, 1594 (Kimbell Art Museum, Forth Worth, Texas)

concerned, as the earlier humanists who had discussed human behaviour with the medium of the dialogue, in which two or more characters put forward discordant views. His opinions were often paradoxical and took account of conflicting attitudes. But he did not write dialogues; his essays were highly personal reflections in which he often quoted his own experience and admitted the reader to the intimacy of his own life. At the same time his authorities were nearly all classical.

The comedy of village life in Spain portrayed by Cervantes in *Don Quixote* and the unromantic observation of common faces and postures in the paintings of Caravaggio in Italy, also about 1600, display a similar sense of common humanity. Caravaggio was not incapable of humour. His painting of the *Cardsharps* shows three men, two playing cards, one of whom has hidden a card in his belt behind his

back, while the third conveys the information to him from behind the other, innocent, player. The group is a skilful presentation of a simple youth, an alert young twister and an older scoundrel, which was no doubt based on observation in a tavern. Most of Caravaggio's important paintings, however, were of religious subjects, in which the common people, who often inhabited them, added to the human seriousness of the stories, in contrast with the idealised religious figures common in the Mannerist painting of the previous half-century.

Caravaggio was a man of violent and perhaps distorted temperament. The apparently still-living head of Goliath, held up sadly by David in his late *David with the Head of Goliath* was thought by some to be a self-portrait depicting his own powerful and despairing personality. He arrived in Rome in 1592/3 and stayed there, working for

ABOVE St Matthew and the Angel,
Caravaggio, 1602-3 (San Luigi dei Francesi, Rome)

ecclesiastical patrons until 1606 when an accusation of murder led to his flight. The remaining four years of his life were spent in Naples, Sicily and Malta. His employment by Roman cardinals, the Knights of St John at Malta, and patrons of chapels elsewhere in southern Italy placed him at the heart of Counter-Reformation Europe, and his paintings exhibited the intensity of feeling about biblical subjects appropriate to that environment. But he was not inclined to adopt the flowing emotionalism of later Mannerist religious painters. He cultivated instead a direct and plain observation of the figures in the scene. Emotion was supplied by an extreme use of chiaroscuro — most of his paintings were dark with important sections emphasised by bright light — and by dramatic patterns that focused attention on the faces and movements.

In 1602 Caravaggio did a painting for a chapel in Rome

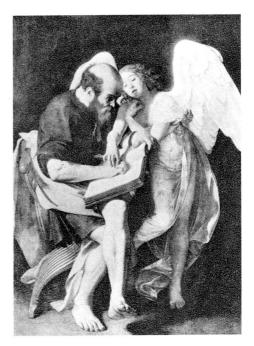

St Matthew and the Angel,
Caravaggio, 1602
(destroyed, formerly Kaiser Friedrich Museum, Berlin)

ABOVE Supper at Emmaus,
Caravaggio, 1598-1600
(National Gallery, London)

of St Matthew being instructed by an angel. It showed a
poor old man, trying to read a book with the help of an
angel who looks like a charmingly helpful child. It was too
realistic. The ecclesiastical authorities made him replace it
with a more dignified and ethereal painting. His paintings
continued, however, to show people in homely settings.

Caravaggio was not an expert in perspective but he was
supremely skilled in portraying details of human physique.
His skills were well demonstrated in two Roman paintings
of about 1600. In the *Supper at Emmaus* Christ is seated at
table between two disciples with the innkeeper standing
behind. Christ is a full-faced beardless young man, one of
Caravaggio's androgynous figures. The same detailed
realism is present in the food on the table. The centre of the

RIGHT Madonna and Child with St Anne,
Caravaggio, 1605-8
(Galleria Borghese, Rome)

Conversion of St Paul,
Caravaggio, 1600-1 (Santa Maria del Popolo, Rome)

scene is lit with a brightness without a source that gives an intensity to the meeting. In the *Conversion of St Paul* most of the painting is taken up by the rather brightly lit, and again highly realistic, side of the horse, from which Paul has fallen. The furrowed brow of a servant holding the animal looks over his mane. Below them is the prostrate body of Paul on the ground, his arms raised in exaltation. The effect of the light on the partly white side of the horse and falling

on the saint's receptive figure conveys the message of conversion in response to divine illumination in a setting that is nevertheless prosaic.

A later (1605–6) and still more visually dramatic painting was the *Madonna and Child with St Anne*. The Madonna holds the Child carefully upright, his left foot placed on hers, which is crushing the head of a snake, symbolising their victory over sin. The tall figure of St Anne

Judgment of Paris,
Rubens, c.1600 (National Gallery, London)

256

stands to one side, looking down on the scene. She is dark, but the mother and child are brilliantly lit. The most striking part of the painting is the pattern formed by the striding legs of the child below the maternal face of the Virgin. The use of light on these forms adds a memorably magical effect to a rather simple scene. Caravaggio was thus able to bring a new effectiveness to the religious painting that was central to the culture of Catholic Europe. He achieved this through the simplicity of his people, thoroughly integrated into the human content of the story, and through the drama of brilliant lighting falling on the faces and limbs essential to the story. If he was the most influential painter of seventeenth-century Italy, this was due to his ability to give an added seriousness to movements of religious significance, far removed from the mere decoration and empty elevation towards which Italian painting had often tended in the late sixteenth century.

The man who summed up the achievements of Italian art up to 1600 was, however, a Netherlander, Peter Paul Rubens. He was steeped in the work of the Italians of the sixteenth century and, because of his long stay in Italy, and eventually, as a collector of Italian paintings, was well placed to develop a connoisseur's taste. His good classical education enabled him to read Latin easily and during time spent in Italy he acquired the habit of writing his letters in Italian. Rubens completed his training as a painter in Antwerp in 1598. The *Judgment of Paris* painted about 1600 showed the extent of his assimilation of Renaissance taste to which he had already added his own recognisable personal style. The arrangement of the three goddesses, Juno, Venus receiving the reward, and Minerva before the seated Paris, with Mercury behind him, was derived from an early sixteenth-century print by Marcantonio Raimondi, an associate of Raphael. Rubens' stamp can be seen in the full figures of the nude women, and the characteristically dramatic combination of reds with blue and vivid green with which the nudes were set against the landscape. This

was a clear demonstration that Rubens had, before he left Antwerp, acquired and enhanced a Renaissance manner, in which both the Italian and the Flemish traditions were incorporated.

In 1600, at the age of twenty-three, he went south to Venice where he was attracted into the service of Vincenzo Gonzaga, Duke of Mantua. The Gonzaga had been great patrons since the fifteenth century, when Mantegna had worked for them. They were also deeply involved in the diplomatic games between the princes of Italy, France and Spain. Rubens was drawn into the Italian art world and also into the diplomacy of the Catholic powers. His horizons were extended in both fields to make him into a man of the world in the fullest sense, both the art world and the political world, a position that he retained for the rest of his life. During his service for the Gonzaga family, which lasted until 1608, he visited Florence, Genoa and the Habsburg court at Madrid and, most significantly, spent two long periods at Rome. The Italian period gave him the opportunity for close acquaintance with the work of Michelangelo and Raphael and his contemporary Caravaggio at Rome, and also with the Venetians, Titian and Tintoretto. The importance he gave to these artists was shown by the large number of drawings of their paintings that he made.

Rubens' profound knowledge of the classical tradition is evident from some of the paintings completed during his stay in Italy. *Aeneas Preparing to lead the Trojans into Exile* was probably painted for the Gonzaga dukes of Mantua, Virgil, who told the story to Aeneas, being a Mantuan. This unusual painted scene, based on a close reading of the second book of the *Aeneid*, shows the Trojans as a group of refugees waiting between the burning Troy on the left and the coast on the right. To the left Aeneas is leading away his father Anchises. The painting is dominated by the central figures of the brilliantly lit standing mother and child. The rich dark colours and the daring approach to sketching

Aeneas Preparing to lead the Trojans into Exile,
Rubens, c.1602 (Musée Nationale de Fontainebleau)

figures show the influence of Titian.

Hero and Leander was a bold attempt to illustrate a classical legend. The story was that Leander was drowned while swimming across the Hellespont to meet his lover Hero, who threw herself in despair from her tower into the sea. Rubens painted the dead Leander, floating face-upward on the surface of the sea, attended by a group of swimming Nereids, while Hero falls from her tower on the right of the picture. The painting presents effectively the figures caught up in the turbulent swell of the waves, in a great moving semi-circle of water, a wonderful combination of romantic legend and realistic seascape.

The *Fall of Phaethon* was a still more dramatic subject taken from classical legend. Phaethon, the son of the sun-god Apollo, drove his father's chariot across the sky, accompanied by the Hours, the ancient Greek goddesses of the seasons. When he lost control of the chariot, Apollo intervened by throwing a thunderbolt that destroyed him. Rubens' painting showed the moment when the thunderbolt struck, with Phaethon falling head-first and behind him the tumbled mass of his horses, the chariot and the Hours as female nudes. The scene is taking place in the darkness of the night, lit diagonally by the thunderbolt's beam of light. The horses and nudes are a confused mêlée, and the model to which the painting was most obviously related was Leonardo's fragment of the *Battle of Anghiari*, the prototype of later Renaissance scenes of cavalry encounter, of which Rubens had made a copy. But Rubens went beyond Leonardo's conception, presenting the movement of animals and humans in space without a floor to stabilise the action, so that he could evoke a totally fantastic mythical scene.

Rubens developed far beyond his work of the first decade of the seventeenth century, with a profuse output of religious and historical scenes, landscapes, and portraits. His production of paintings led him to be seen as the most monumental painter of his age and to be associated particularly with his great celebrations of Marie de' Medici, the Queen of Henry IV of France, and of James I of England, and with the altarpieces he painted for churches in Antwerp, that led him to be regarded as the quintessential painter of the Catholic Counter-Reformation. He was a well-balanced, enthusiastic servant of the society which enriched him, apparently undisturbed by the theological

Hero and Leander,
Rubens, c.1605
(Yale University Art Gallery, New Haven)

Fall of Phaethon,
Rubens, c.1605 (Private Collection)

disputes that divided Europe into persecuting camps. He was not incapable of psychological subtlety, as shown, for example, by his *Samson and Delilah*, painted in 1609, soon after his return to Antwerp. Apart from the depiction of physical power in Samson's torso and arm and the careful arrangement of light to fall effectively on the two bodies, the sad and loving expression of Delilah's face, as she witnesses the destruction of her lover through her wiles, vividly captures an imagined psychological moment. In general, however, Rubens' delight in beauty and grandeur is the main impression that we carry away from his works. At the same time, the early classical scenes, painted by a master of Italian art who was also an educated classicist, by an artist who was fully in command of the techniques developed by both his Italian and his Flemish predecessors, exhibited the summation of the style which had been developed in the Renaissance and which had spread to Europe as a whole. Rubens' devotion to nobility and indifference to the plight of the lower classes, except as a traditional mark of Flemish nationalism, distinguished him from some movements in literature and art in the early seventeenth century; but his characteristic style made him the natural symbol of the last stage of the traditional Renaissance ethos.

ENGLAND AND THE NETHERLANDS

While these artists, at work in the Catholic and Mediterranean world, continued to develop the approaches invented in Italy a century or more before, new movements with greater originality were beginning in the North. Their power was derived, as we explained in chapter 7, from the commercial energy of London and Amsterdam that enabled a fresh range of ideas to come into existence. The impact of Renaissance ideas had by this time become universal, multifarious, a part of common European thought and the inhabitants of London and Amsterdam were profoundly indebted to Italy and the classical traditions which the Italians had passed on to them. Out of these traditions, however, they developed novel perceptions that the Italians themselves would have been incapable of envisaging. This final stage of the Renaissance is the subject with which this book will end. A general picture of the Northern imagination in the early seventeenth century cannot be provided but we shall attempt to indicate very briefly how the work of its two greatest geniuses, Shakespeare and

Judas Returning the Thirty Pieces of Silver,
Rembrandt, 1629
(Private Collection; on loan to National Gallery, London)

Rembrandt, depended on and carried forward the existing Renaissance traditions. In both cases it must be remembered that they were practitioners who were the supreme members of a numerous profession. Shakespeare cannot be understood without the intensely competitive London theatre-world that included Marlowe and Jonson, nor Rembrandt without the world of Dutch painters. Neither of them could have worked as they did without the environment of the expanding city.

Shakespeare's plays are rightly more valued for their successful integration of character and plot than for the display of a single character, and the capacity to present that total structure was his most important gift. But it was in the delineation of the individual character that his intellectual innovation most obviously appeared and his conception of character therefore has a particular historical importance.

Shakespeare studied the classics in the tradition established by Erasmus, read the plays of Plautus and Seneca and perhaps had some knowledge of Euripides. He was familiar, at least in translation, with Ovid's *Metamorphoses* and Plutarch's *Lives* and knew the work of Montaigne in Florio's English version. He was therefore fairly well rooted in the Italian Renaissance background. This information was used to write plays that would capture the attention of a London audience. A five-act play lasting three hours can hold only a simplified story, a rapid interaction of characters. Shakespeare's success was to fuse the presentation of a gripping plot with the development of an original subtlety of character so that his heroes and heroines achieved a new fine delineation of personality.

A fairly simple example is provided by *Coriolanus*. The life of Coriolanus, a highly successful general who despised the common people of Rome and was eventually destroyed by their enmity and his subsequent friendship with Rome's enemies, was written by Plutarch in an account that Shakespeare followed quite closely; but he developed certain aspects in his skilful adaptation of the story. It has been thought that his perception of the haughty general's attitude to the rabble was further inspired by King James I's conflict with his parliaments or by the reactions of the gentry to the Midland peasants' discontent in the famine of 1608. Whether that was the case or not, he did present a clear picture of people anxious for bread who were despised by a potential ruler.

Bid them wash their faces
And keep their teeth clean.

Shakespeare also elaborated on the relationship between Coriolanus and his mother, Volumnia, which was less prominent in Plutarch. Volumnia was immensely proud of her son and urged him to gain power but eventually she was forced to beg him not to hand over Rome to its enemies.

Her successful plea signed the downfall of her son. His relationship to her is that of a man driven to bravery and cruelty in order to fulfil his mother's frustrated desire for expression. Thus Coriolanus becomes a character-study of a man's relationship to a particular kind of mother, a psychological study left to the audience to interpret. Coriolanus is both a politician in a political situation and a son and husband in a family situation. This was a new conception of the character of the politician. The politician and the son interact, the interaction leading both to his success and finally to his failure. The complexities of character are implicit rather than explicit.

A more complicated case of character development is that of Cleopatra. *Antony and Cleopatra*, written in 1608, was also, though less exclusively, based on Plutarch and it is sometimes very close to its model, notably in Enobarbus' great description of Cleopatra: 'The barge she sat in like a burnished throne...' But in Cleopatra, although she was an oriental queen, Shakespeare was clearly giving his audience an English noblewoman, with all the complexity of mood and expression of a powerful and demanding woman in love. Cleopatra is in love with Antony but when he is present she plays with him, wanting to know exactly how much he loves her and jeering at him as a servant of Caesar. When he is absent she longs for flattering reports of him but when he returns she cannot sympathise with him over the death of his wife. She is tortured by Antony's new marriage to Octavia, strikes the messenger who brings news of her and wants to criticise her. She interferes in Antony's battle plans, apologises and then insists on performing the menial, wifely service of helping him strap on his armour. Until his death she is an obsessively attractive and infuriating lover. Then, at that moment of doom, she rises to a new power, revealing her true realisation of Antony's greatness and her utter devotion to him, and refuses to become a showpiece in Caesar's triumph, preferring to die. If this was the greatest tragedy for 2000 years, Cleopatra was the most complex and brilliantly conceived female character that the Western world had yet seen. This was a somewhat different case from the character of Coriolanus. Cleopatra is a character who, after her lover's death, displays a grandeur of which she had not been capable before. She grows in stature, changing during the play.

But Shakespeare had already in 1599 conceived a still more complex male character in *Hamlet*. In this case Shakespeare's relation to his sources was more complicated because he was using, not a classical text, but an ancient Danish story that had been adapted by a modern dramatist, perhaps Thomas Kyd, in a play which has been lost. Shakespeare presented the story in the modern setting of a Renaissance court in which Hamlet speaks the language of a contemporary young aristocrat, familiar with the stage and with classical allusions: 'Hyperion to a satyr', 'Like Niobe, all tears', etc. So lifelike is Hamlet's witty, deliberately precious and rhetorical language that it is difficult to avoid the feeling that Shakespeare must have been influenced by knowing an English gentleman who talked in this manner. The style in which, for example, he greets the absurdly posing Osric – 'Dost know this waterfly?' – sounds like reportage.

The various aspects of Hamlet's character, which have occasioned infinite disagreement, are shown through his relationship and attitude to his dead father; to the uncle who has murdered and succeeded him; to his mother, who has now married his uncle; and to Ophelia, the woman he loves. As a result of his father's death and his mother's betrayal of him, hastening with the murderer 'to incestuous sheets', Hamlet finds the whole world darkened:

How weary, stale, flat and unprofitable
Seem to me all the uses of this world!

The heavens have become 'a foul and pestilent congregation

of vapours'. The 'To be or not to be' speech expresses his weariness with life and willingness to end it. His only positive obsessions are hatred of his uncle, whom he desires to kill in the most damaging way possible, physically and spiritually, and disgust for his whore-like mother. Ophelia, whom he loved, he can now only address with crude jokes because his mother's behaviour has made him distrustful of all women and because he thinks his uncle and mother, with the help of Ophelia's father, Polonius, are scheming to trap him, using her as a foil.

This much is clear. There have been numerous scholarly disputes about Hamlet's character, and audiences are left in uncertainty about several issues: the extent to which his father's ghost is really an expression of his own psyche; the reasons for his long failure to act against his uncle; the precise nature of his feigned madness. Shakespeare created in Hamlet a character who expresses a complex uncertainty about himself and is open to interpretation. In combination with the wonderfully rich and subtle language found in his utterances, this has made Hamlet easily the most famous character of the modern European age. Hamlet's concern about his own inability to act foreshadows the modern obsession with the subconscious. Whatever one thinks about Hamlet's place in European history as a whole, Shakespeare in creating him quite clearly made a massive innovative leap. He lifted the portrayal of character onto a new level of increased sophistication. *Hamlet* has been the most admired of Shakespeare's plays since 1599, though recently yielding to *King Lear*, and the reason has been that Hamlet's character reveals a conception of the human personality of an altogether new complexity. He was invented at a time when the English language was emerging into its fullest richness and produced by the possibilities open to genius in the late Renaissance which had stimulated literary interest in individual personality.

Rembrandt, like Shakespeare, had attended the Latin school at Leiden and perhaps for a short time the university, had burst into the throng of naked nymphs and Diana's maidens reveal the pregnancy of the unfortunate Callisto. Rembrandt's *Danaë*, revealed naked in bed, is turning to receive a bright illumination, rather than Jupiter in the form of a shower of gold pieces, as, for instance, in Titian's *Danaë*, and above her head hovers the blind and bound Cupid signifying chaste love. This *Danaë*, unlike some earlier Italian versions, is a homely lover pleasantly awaiting her mate in a Dutch bedroom. Rembrandt has adapted the classical scene to one of a more domestic kind, drawn from his own experience; and perhaps this is true of his treatment of all his classical subjects.

These stories show the connection with the Renaissance past. So do other more obvious imitations, notably the *Self-Portrait*, which presents the sitter leaning on a sill in imitation of similar postures in paintings by Raphael and Titian. Rembrandt's own collection of paintings included works by Raphael and Carracci. So the Italian Renaissance background was familiar to him and an important source of inspiration. But, as in the case of Shakespeare, his most important works showed that he had transformed the lessons of the Renaissance almost beyond recognition.

Apart from the portraits and self-portraits, Rembrandt's most notable subjects were biblical. In a comment written in 1530 Constantin Huygens, the secretary of the Stadtholder, praised the early painting of *Judas Returning the Thirty Pieces of Silver*: 'Rembrandt ... obsessed by the effort to translate into paint what he sees in his mind's eye, prefers smaller formats [than Jan Lievens, another Leiden painter], in which he nevertheless achieves effects that you will not find in the largest works by others. The painting of the repentant Judas returning to the high priest the pieces of silver, the price of our innocent Lord, illustrates the point I wish to make concerning all his works. It can withstand comparison with anything ever made in Italy, or for that matter with everything beautiful and admirable that has been preserved since the earliest antiquity. That single

Rape of Ganymede,
Rembrandt, 1635 (Gemäldegalerie, Dresden)

before being apprenticed as a painter. He must have had an introduction to the Erasmian Renaissance similar to that of Shakespeare and could therefore make a direct approach to classical myths. His classical paintings were not very numerous but they were remarkable and difficult to interpret. The *Rape of Ganymede* (1635), for example, is puzzling because the child, carried up by Jupiter in the form of an eagle, is crying in an ugly fashion and urinating. Nevertheless it is thought that the painting was probably not intended as a departure from the subject's traditional meaning: the reunification of the human soul with God. *Diana Bathing with her Nymphs with the Stories of Actaeon and Callisto* was unusual in fitting the two famous Diana stories into the same scene. Acteon is turned into a stag because he

Danaë,
Rembrandt, 1636
(Hermitage, St Petersburg)

gesture of the desperate Judas – that single gesture, I say, of a raging, whining Judas grovelling for mercy he no longer hopes for or dares to show the smallest sign of expecting, his frightful visage, hair torn out of his head, his rent garment, his arms twisted, the hands clenched bloodlessly tight, fallen to his knees in a heedless outburst – that body, wholly contorted in pathetic despair, I place against all the tasteful art of all time past ... I tell you that no one, not Protogenes, not Apelles and not Parrhasios, ever conceived ... that which ... a youth, a born and bred Dutchman, a miller, a smooth-faced boy, has done: joining in the figure of one man so many divers particulars and expressing so many

universals. Truly, my friend Rembrandt, all honour to you. To have brought Ilium – even all of Asia Minor – to Italy was a lesser feat than for a Dutchman – and one who had hardly left his home town – to have captured for the Netherlands the trophy of artistic excellence from Greece and Italy.'[3]

This is one of Rembrandt's dark interiors with heavy, richly clothed figures looming in the half-light. The success

265

Self-Portrait at the age of 34,
Rembrandt, 1640
(National Gallery, London)

pathos.

The interest in the individual face is shown by the self-portraits scattered through Rembrandt's *oeuvre*. The earliest one now thought to be original is in Amsterdam, probably painted in 1628. Here he is a young man with dark curly hair spreading well over his forehead and down his neck. A heavy contrast of light and shade obscures much of the face but the nose and mouth are painted with great delicacy. The autograph in Liverpool of 1630 to 1631 shows the face better and reveals the staring tenderness and vulnerability that were to appear in many more paintings throughout his life.

Some of the portraits are of theatrical poses but many are pictures of common humanity. Rembrandt's biblical scenes are often extremely dramatic, conveying excitement, horror, pathos. But it is the grasp of the ordinary, unpretentious person, without exhibitionism, which constitutes Rembrandt's essential breakthrough and which distinguishes him from the Italian tradition even as modified by Caravaggio. As in the case of Shakespeare, this plain realism apparently arose from the Northern city which, although more aristocratic and prince-dominated than the Italian republic, seems to have encouraged less exhibitionism among its ordinary citizens than in the Italian setting. The new manner in art was an adaptation of the Italian search for the individual, taken over with equal enthusiasm but applied in a new context.

Among Rembrandt's earlier biblical paintings, the oil sketch of *Christ before Pilate and the People* (1634) illustrates his characteristic realism well. An emperor's head above a column to one side looks down at the contrasting group of squabbling humanity. The fullest treatment is given to the marvellously alert face and hand of Pilate trying to restrain the eagerness of a fairly villainous group of priests. It is a scene from a meeting of the town council. A still better example is the sketch of *St John the Baptist Preaching* of about the same date. Here the ordinariness and at the same time

of the representation of Judas, kneeling in abject and grovelling repentance, may well be a result of the practice of acting scenes in a painter's studio in order to enhance the artist's capacity to render the emotional force of his subject. It was also no doubt connected with Rembrandt's frequent drawing of his own face, often with distorted features, as if in preparation for a dramatic painting. This more penetrating investigation of the physical expressions of the individual psyche was the feature that most clearly distinguished Rembrandt's work; he painted faces and scenes with a determination to reach the heart of their

St John the Baptist Preaching,
Rembrandt, c.1634-5 (State Museums, Berlin-Dahlem)

the passion in John's intelligent face is convincing as the central focus of the scene. He is surrounded by a complex crowd of engaged, bored and hostile listeners, an accurate reproduction of the crowd everyone has seen attracted by the religious enthusiast who has the courage to preach in the city street. The variety of faces is superb.

The complexity of the character of Hamlet, 'reading in the book of himself', as Mallarmé put it, and of Rembrandt's introspective self-portraits, is the ultimate legacy of the Renaissance and points to our twentieth-century world. We are now at some distance from the figures created by Donatello and Van Eyck but in the same tradition of mingled city individualism and respect for antiquity. Through a long struggle of historical recovery and artistic inspiration the European mind has been reborn.

267

Notes

Chapter 1

1 C. M. Cipolla, *European Culture and Overseas Expansion* (Harmondsworth, 1970), pp.20-1.
2 M. Margaret Newett, *Canon Pietro Casola's Pilgrimage to Jerusalem In the Year 1494* (Manchester, 1907), pp.140-1.

Chapter 5

1 This and other quotations from *Orlando Furioso* are taken from the translation by Guido Waldman (Oxford and New York, 1983), pp.566, 282-3.
2 Quotations from Castiglione's *The Book of the Courtier* are taken from the translation by George Bull (Harmondsworth, 1967). Here pp.42-3.
3 Ibid, p.265.

Chapter 6

1 Machiavelli, *The Prince*, trans. Quentin Skinner and Russel Price (Cambridge, 1988).
2 Machiavelli, *Discourses*, trans. Leslie J. Walker (London, 1950), p.275.
3 *Leonardo on Painting*, ed. Martin Kemp and Margaret Walker (New Haven and London, 1989), p.42.
4 Ibid, p.131.

Chapter 8

1 Margaret Mann Phillips, *Erasmus on his Times: a shortened version of the 'Adages' of Erasmus* (Cambridge, 1967), pp.36-8. *In Praise of Folly* may be read in the translation of Betty Radice and A. H. T. Levi (London, 1971).
2 *Gargantua and Pantagruel*, trans. J. M. Cohen (London, 1955).

Chapter 10

1 *Don Quixote*, trans. J. M. Cohen.
2 Michel de Montaigne, *Essays*, trans. J. M. Cohen (Harmondsworth, 1958).
3 Gary Schwartz, *Rembrandt: his life, his paintings* (Harmondsworth, 1985), p.74.

Further Reading

Chapter 1

The best account of the role of the city in European history is probably found in Fernand Braudel's *Civilization and Capitalism 15th-18th Century*, trans. S. Reynolds, 3 vols: i, *The Structures of Everyday Life*, 1981; ii, *The Wheels of Commerce*, 1982; iii, *The Perspective of the World*, 1984. Useful insights in C. M. Cipolla's *European Culture and Overseas Expansion*, *The Economic History of World Population*, 1962, and *The Fontana Economic History of Europe*, i, *The Middle Ages*, 1972, edited by him. There is an original survey of the economic background of the Renaissance by Richard Goldthwaite, *Wealth and the Demand for Art in Italy 1300-1600*, 1993. Much valuable information in *The Cambridge Economic History of Europe*, ii, 2nd edn, 1987, iii, 1963. On particular cities see R. de Roover, *The Rise and Decline of the Medici Bank 1397-1494*, 1963; H. van der Wee, *The Growth of the Antwerp Market and the European Economy, fourteenth-sixteenth centuries*, 1963. An interesting general survey of the Renaissance is John Hale's *The Civilization of Europe in the Renaissance*, 1993.

Chapter 2

For this and other periods there is a helpful general survey of Italian art by Frederick Hartt, *History of Italian Renaissance Art*, 4th edn, 1994, and a useful reference book edited by J. R. Hale, *A Concise Encyclopaedia of the Italian Renaissance*, 1981. General survey of the subject of this chapter by George Holmes, *The Florentine Enlightenment 1400-1450*, 1992. A valuable book for this and chapter 4 by Michael Baxandall, *Painting and Experience in Fifteenth-Century Italy*, 1972. A famous study of humanism by Hans Baron, *The Crisis of the Early Italian Renaissance*, 1955, and a more general book on humanism by Eugenio Garin, *Italian Humanism: Philosophy and Civic Life in the Renaissance*, trans. Peter Munz, 1965.

On Donatello see B. A. Bennett and D. G. Wilkins, *Donatello*, 1984, and John Pope-Hennessy, *Donatello Sculptor*, 1993; on Brunelleschi, E. Battisti, *Brunelleschi*, 1981; on Masaccio, Paul Joannides, *Masaccio and Masolino: A Complete Catalogue*, 1993; on Uccello, John Pope-Hennessy, *The Complete Work of Paulo Uccello*, 2nd edn, 1969. Alberti, *On Painting*, is translated by Cecil Grayson, introduction by Martin Kemp, 1991. For architecture see Rudolf Wittkower, *Architectural Principles in the Age of Humanism*, 3rd edn, 1962.

Chapter 3

For Northern art in general see James Snyder, *Northern Renaissance Art: Painting, Sculpture and the Graphic Arts from 1350 to 1575*, 1985. On the subject of this chapter the best account remains by Erwin Panofsky, *Early Netherlandish Painting*, 1953. See also M. J. Friedlaender, *Early Netherlandish Painting*, 1967, and Margaret Whinney, *Early Flemish Painting*, 1968. On Van Eyck Elisabeth Dhanens, *Hubert and Jan Van Eyck*, 1985, and Carol J. Purtle, *The Marian Paintings of Jan Van Eyck*, 1982. On Rogier van der Weyden, Martin Davies, *Rogier van der Weyden*, 1972. On Hieronymus Bosch, Ludwig von Baldass, *Hieronymus Bosch*, 1960. On Grünewald, Andrée Hayum, *The Isenheim Altarpiece: God's Medicine and the Painter's Vision*, 1989.

Chapter 4

By far the best general study, unfortunately untranslated in French, is by André Chastel, *Art et Humanisme : Florence au temps du Laurent le Magnifique*, 1959. The best general account of Lorenzo in English is C. M. Ady, *Lorenzo de' Medici and Renaissance Italy*, 1955. Excellent essay on the relation of Botticelli with ideas by Charles Dempsey, *The Portrayal of Love*, 1992. On Ficino see Michael J. B. Allen, *The Platonism of Marsilio Ficino*, 1984, and also N. A. Robb, *Neoplatonism of the Italian Renaissance*, 1935. On Botticelli see Herbert P. Horne, *Botticelli Painter of Florence*, 1908, reissued 1980, and Ronald Lightbown, *Sandro Botticelli*, 1978; on Filippo Lippi, Jeffrey Ruda, *Fra Filippo Lippi: Life and Work with a Complete Catalogue*, 1993; on Piero di Cosimo, Sharon Fermor, *Piero di Cosimo: Fiction, Invention and Fantasia*, 1993. There are valuable studies of particular chapels by F. Hartt, G. Corti and C. Kennedy, *The Chapel of the Cardinal of Portugal*, 1964, and Eve Borsook and J. Offerhaus, *Francesco Sassetti and Ghirlandaio at Santa Trinita, Florence*, 1981.

Chapter 5

On the Venetian background here and in chapter 9 see F. C. Lane, *Venice: A Maritime Republic*, 1973, and *Venice: A Documentary History 1450-1630*, eds David Chambers and Brian Pullan with Jennifer Fletcher, 1992. The structure of other parts of northern Italy can be observed in Denys Hay and John Law's *Italy in the Age of the Renaissance 1380-1530*, 1989. On Venetian art in general see Norbert Huse and Wolfgang Walters, *The Art of Renaissance*

Venice: Architecture, Sculpture and Painting, 1460-1590, 1990. For Mantegna there is R. Lightbown, *Mantegna*, 1986; for Bellini, Giles Robertson, *Giovanni Bellini*, 1968, and Rona Goffen, *Giovanni Bellini*, 1989; for Giorgione Terisio Pignatti, *Giorgione*, 1971, and Salvatore Settis, *Giorgione's Tempest: interpreting the hidden subject*, trans. Ellen Bianchini, 1991.

Ariosto's *Orlando Furioso* is translated by Guido Waldman, 1983; Castiglione's *Book of the Courtier* by George Bull, 1967. See also J. R. Woodhouse, *Baldesar Castiglione*, 1978, and C. P. Brand, *Ludovico Ariosto: A preface to the 'Orlando Furioso'*, 1974.

CHAPTER 6
Machiavelli can be approached through Quentin Skinner, *Machiavelli*, 1981, and Sebastian de Grazia, *Machiavelli in Hell*, 1989. *The Prince* is translated by Quentin Skinner and Russell Price, 1988, and *The Discourses* by L. J. Walker, 1950. Guicciardini is related to him by Felix Gilbert, *Machiavelli and Guicciardini: Politics and History in Sixteenth-Century Florence*, 1984.

There is a valuable general survey of painting by S. J. P. Freedberg, *Painting in Italy 1500-1600*, 2nd edn, 1983. There are books on Leonardo by Martin Kemp, *Leonardo da Vinci: The Marvellous Works of Nature and Man*, 1981; Carlo Pedretti, *Leonardo A Study in Chronology and Style*, 1973, and Kenneth Clark, *Leonardo da Vinci*, new edn 1967. *Translations of writings by Leonardo* by Martin Kemp, ed., *Leonardo on Painting*, 1989. Michelangelo can be approached with H. Hibbard, *Michelangelo*, 2nd edn, 1985, and Michael Hirst, *Michelangelo and his Drawings*, New Haven, 1988. *The Life of Michelangelo* by Condivi is translated by George Bull, *Michelangelo Life, Letters and Poetry*, 1987; his poetry by James M. Saslow, *The Poetry of Michelangelo*, 1991. On Raphael see R. Jones and N. Penny, *Raphael*, 1983, and J. Shearman, *Raphael's Cartoons in the Collection of Her Majesty* and *Queen and the Tapestries for the Sistine Chapel*, 1972.

There are important comments on the art of this period by Edgar Wind, *Pagan Mysteries in the Renaissance*, 2nd edn, 1967, and J. Shearman, *Only Connect . . . Art and the Spectator in the Italian Renaissance*, 1994. Study of Mannerism can begin with John Shearman, *Mannerism*, 1967. On Vasari there is now Patricia Lee Rubin, *Giorgio Vasari Art and History*, 1995. *The Lives of the Painters, Sculptors and Architects* was translated by A. B. Hines, 1900 and there are selections from it published as *Lives of*

the Artists, by George Bull, 1987, and *The Lives of the Artists*, by J. C. Bondanella and P. Bondanella, 1991.

CHAPTER 7
The political and social background of the sixteenth century may be approached through the volumes of the *Fontana History of Europe*: J. R. Hale, *Renaissance Europe 1480-1520*; G. R. Elton, *Reformation Europe 1517-1559*, 1963, and J. H. Elliott, *Europe Divided 1559-1598*, 1968. Important studies of commerce and cities are in the volumes by Fernand Braudel recommended for chapter 1, and his *The Mediterranean and the Mediterranean World in the Age of Philip II*, trans. S. Reynolds, 1972.

On Antwerp see Herman van der Wee, *The Growth of the Antwerp market and the European economy, fourteenth-sixteenth centuries*, 1963. London and its commerce are examined by A. L. Beier and Roger Finlay, eds, *London 1500-1700: The Making of the Metropolis*, 1986; F. J. Fisher, *London and the English Economy, 1500-1700*, ed. P. J. Corfield and N. B. Harte, 1990; and Robert Brebner, *Merchants and Revolution: Commercial Change, Political Conflict, and London's Overseas Traders, 1550-1700*, 1993. The growth of Dutch commerce is the subject of Jonathan I. Israel, *Dutch Primacy in World Trade 1585-1740*, 1989.

CHAPTER 8
For Dürer see E. Panofsky, *The Life and Art of Albrecht Dürer*, 1943; for Altdorfer, Christopher S. Wood, *Albrecht Altdorfer and the Origins of Landscape*, 1993; for Holbein, John Rowlands, *Holbein: the Paintings of Hans Holbein the Younger*, 1985.

Erasmus may be approached with J. Huizinga, *Erasmus of Rotterdam*, 1952; M. A. Screech, *Ecstasy and the Praise of Folly*, 1980; W. Kaiser, *Praisers of Folly*, 1964, and M. M. Phillips, *The Adages of Erasmus: a Study with Translations*, 1964. *The Praise of Folly* is translated by B. Radice, 1971.

On Rabelais see M. A. Screech, *Rabelais*, 1979, and the translation of *The Histories of Garganta and Pantagruel*, by J. M. Cohen, 1955. On Calvin there are books by W. J. Bouwsma, *John Calvin a Sixteenth-Century Portrait*, 1988 and F. Wendel, *Calvin the Origins and Development of his Religious Thought*, trans. P. Mairet, 1965.

The visual impact of the Italian Renaissance in France can be followed in Anthony Blunt, *Art and Architecture in France 1500 to 1700*, 1953. On Bruegel there is Walter S. Gibson, *Bruegel*, 1977.

CHAPTER 9
For Palladio and Venetian architecture there is the survey by Deborah Howard, *The Architectural History of Venice*, 1980, and more specifically on Palladio, J. S. Ackerman, *Palladio*, 1966, and B. Boucher, *Andrea Palladio the Architect in his Time*, 1994.

There is a general account of Venetian painting by Peter Humfrey, *Painting in Renaissance Venice*, 1994; also Johannes Wilde, *Venetian Art from Bellini to Titian*, 1974, and David Rosand, *Painting in Cinquecento Venice: Titian, Veronese, Tintoretto*, 1982.

On Titian see the introduction by C. Hope, *Titian*, 1980, and the full catalogue by H. E. Wethey, *The Paintings of Titian*, 1969-75. See also E. Panofsky, *Problems in Titian, Mostly Iconographic*, 1969. On Veronese, W. R. Rearick, *The Art of Paolo Veronese 1528-1588*, 1988.

CHAPTER 10
There are studies of Cervantes by P. E. Russell, *Cervantes*, 1985, and Edwin Williamson, *The Half-Way House of Fiction: Don Quixote and Arthurian Romance*, Oxford, 1984. *Don Quixote* is translated by J. M. Cohen, 1950. Montaigne is examined by Richard Sayce, *The Essays of Montaigne: a critical exploration*, 1972. The essays can be read in the 1603 translation of John Florio or the recent translation by M. A. Screech, *Michel de Montaigne, The Complete Essays*, 1991.

For Caravaggio see Howard Hibbard, *Caravaggio*, 1983, and for Rubens, Christopher White, *Peter Paul Rubens*, 1987, and Michael Jaffè, *Rubens and Italy*, 1977.

For Shakespeare it is impossible to pick out an introduction from the vast literature, but, as a guide, it may be helpful to mention *Shakespeare: a Bibliographical Guide*, ed. Stanley Wells, 1990. Individual works are best studied either in the volumes of the *Arden Shakespeare* or in those of the as yet incomplete Oxford Shakespeare.

Rembrandt can be approached with the brief study of Christopher White, *Rembrandt*, 1984, or the fuller account by Gary Schwartz, *Rembrandt: His Life, His Paintings*, 1985. An interesting recent study is by Svetlana Alpees, *Rembrandt's Enterprise the Studio and the Market*, 1988.

INDEX